Feminism, Modernity and Harmony in Islam

Asghar Ali Engineer and His Writings

Editor
Akhtarul Wasey

SHIPRA

The book is a reproduction of the journal *Islam and the Modern Age*, Vol. XLI, Nos. 3-4, (2010).

Rs. 880; US$ 44

ISBN: 978-81-7541-750-2

First Published in India in 2014

Feminism, Modernity and Harmony in Islam: Asghar Ali Engineer and His Writings

Published by:
SHIPRA PUBLICATIONS
H.O.: LG 18-19, Pankaj Central Market, Patparganj,
I.P. Ext., Delhi-110092, Tel: 91-11-2223 5152, 2223 6152
Br.Off.: 4617/18, Ansari Road, Darya Ganj,
New Delhi-110002, Tel: 9650028065, 9810522367
E-mail: info@shiprapublications.com
www.shiprapublications.com

Dedicated to

Vice Chancellor Professor Talat Ahmed

A Teacher, Researcher, Scholar, Administrator

Preface

It is a time when the entire socio-religious sphere of Muslims around the world is under constant attack from the invariably raging quarters of Orientalists to the entire range of media to the intellectual community of different ideological pursuits.

It is not only the political and social underpinning of Muslims at large has become vulnerable to a variety of assaults of varying degrees and nature, but it is coupled with the scathing attack on the religion of Islam, its canonical foundation, theology, identity, cultural and political domain, historicity, historiography, let alone its ideology and religiosity itself.

It is an era when Islam is being defined through the narrow dialectical and binary prism, where it cannot be identified in its precise Islamic bound. No study of Islamic religion would suffice unless it is explained and classified against the larger image which is very passionately termed as Islamicism or Islamism.

A host of voices are claiming to represent the real and true spiritual face of Islam and each claims to interpret the religion in its literal sense and each is carving a place for itself as a spokesperson of Islam.

This newly found fascination with Islamic text and subsequent interpretations has deflected the attention from the traditional custodians and authorities on Islam whom we very religiously call Ulema, who have reigned over the religious-cultural domain of Islam for centuries. The twentieth century witnessed the rise of a series of scholars, who not only contested the conventional methodology of introspecting and navigating the Quranic text but also challenged centuries-old authorities on Islam who had monopolised the intellectual domain of Islam and its interpretation.

One name that surfaces very prominently among those scholars of 20th century whose intellectual pursuit was devoted to doing away with the traditional division of knowledge and monopolisation of reading of

Quran and its interpretations, is of Dr. Asghar Ali Engineer (1939-2013). What gives me immense pleasure is not to introduce Dr. Ali, because he needs no introduction, but the real source of delight is to write a few words here about this towering personality who studied, wrote, contested and trampled the traditional religious intellectual domain, fought, struggled, underwent humiliation and victimisation in order to accomplish his lifelong objective of projecting a true and real image of Islam before the world.

He was a born intellectual activist with a missionary zeal to contest the rotten religious thoughts with his rooted secularist ideology. He was an eminent scholar, who expanded and stretched the narrow domain of Islamic teaching encompassing all aspects of not only human being, but the entire humanity. He was an Islamicist, Arabicist, and Islamic Sociologist, where he can be placed at par with Mr. Ali Shariati of Iran, who equally focussed on the sociology and epistemology of Islamic knowledge and its interpretation.

His thoughts were really meant for its global application in the modern globalised world. One can construe from his life mission that his religious ethos was rooted in the constant interpretation of Quran teaching. One can reduce his religious thought in a single dictum that survival of eternality lies in changeability alone, which was missed by the previous generations of our Ulemas. He was an honest intellectual with a critical mind, who seldom spared an opportunity to condemn the radical and fanatic interpretation of Quran or its theology. He was a strong advocate of tolerant Islam and his Islamic approach was always laden with pragmatism.

The issues of gender equality, human rights and domestic violence may be a novel experience for the Muslim world, but it was the central intellectual agenda for Dr. Ali, who highlighted these issues very prominently as a scholar and activist. He never hesitated in raising the issue of women freedom and equality in the light of Quran and its true rational interpretation.

The present volume offers a highly readable assessment of the present day crisis within Islam and its outside image. In one of the sections of the volume, he focuses on Islam and its relation with present-day feminism where he lays down the Islamic teaching about the prevention of domestic violence and strongly argues as to how Islam would suffice to create an equal and free society.

This highly intellectual volume offers fresh insights into the social issue of Muslim community and it also provides a remedy for the present malice. This volume will shape a new discourse in the years to come and lead to a new understanding of Islam in purely Islamic perspectives. This will add to the existing pool of literature on the relevant theme and would also discard many of the conventional wisdom regarding Islam and women.

The accessible style of the author and its persuasive methodology would make this volume a significant part of entry for anyone wishing to understand Islamic religious tradition and its relevance for the modern-day society in the social and political context.

Akhtarul Wasey, Padma Shri

Contents

Introduction

Of all the living Islamic scholars and intellectuals in India who have also made themselves prominent as social and civil-society activists and concerned citizens, Asghar Ali Engineer enjoyed a special place in many ways. His varied interests and concerns and his versatility of action make a rare combination that very few have been able to achieve and sustain. The most striking feature of his scholarly vision and intellectual activism is characterized by the way he achieved the synthesis in his mind, heart and actions of his commitment to Islam and his unwavering faith in Indian democracy and secularism. It is this towering achievement that made him a role-model for thousands of Muslim youth who feel themselves and behave as much Indians as they are Muslims, without the slightest conflict between the two.

Asghar Ali Engineer is a name that evokes many, often mutually contradictory, responses. For many, who believe in the essential truth and relevance to modern times of the eternal teachings of Islam and want this divine guidance to function as a liberating and civilizing force, see him as a champion of Islamic values and a crusader of Islamic universalism. But for many others, who want to keep the religious establishment intact and the domination of a certain religious class undisturbed call him a modernist and revisionist, determined to undermine the religion itself. But beyond this conflict of perceptions, there is yet another group that admires Engineer for the scholarship and academic excellence he achieved over the years because of his sharp intellect, sincerity and hard work. He was also widely recognized as an unwavering promoter and crusader of secularism. His undaunted work, during communal riots, of collecting and publicizing facts and promoting peace and sanity firmly established him as a committed and interventionist public intellectual who cared for the well-being and welfare of the people and society. But his defining identity is that of a reformer who boldly raised his voice and mobilized public opinion against the religious establishment of his own Bohra community, which, according to him, imposes certain unacceptable practices on its adherents which are un-Islamic. He suffered a lot of persecution for his non-conformist views and actions, still he remained steadfast on the path that he believed to be the path of righteousness.

Asghar Ali Engineer was born on 10 March 1939 at Salumbar, a small town near Udaipur, Rajasthan, to religiously devout parents. He was brought up in a very orthodox religious atmosphere. His father was a deeply religious man but still he had a very tolerant and liberal soul. He never said anything against other religions. He was very friendly with a Brahmin priest and used to have religious dialogue with him. Both the friends respected each other's religion. This ambience of coexistence left a deep imprint on the growing Asghar's mind and acted as a catalyst for the development of his liberal views based on tolerance and coexistence.

Engineer's father was an 'amil' who delivered religious sermons. He dutifully attended his sermons which laid the foundation of his knowledge of Islamic creed and history, that later became a basis of his development as an Islamic scholar. His father also gave him first lessons in the Arabic language, tafsir, hadith and fiqh.

It is very interesting that Engineer had his early schooling through Urdu medium. His Urdu teacher at Government High School, Dewas, who was known as Shama Saheb, inculcated in his young impressionable mind the values of seeking knowledge, social service and fearlessness. According to Engineer, 'Shama Saheb was also a source of strength to me. He was a firmly believing Muslim but was far from being narrow-minded, much less communal. He inspired us to be good Muslims but never to be orthodox' (*A Living Faith* (autobiography, Asghar Ali Engineer). It shows that the seeds of religious tolerance and coexistence were sown in Engineer's psyche very early in life. He has narrated in his autobiography a very revealing incident that must made a deep impact on his impressionable mind. The incident related to a very interesting encounter he happened to have with a postman, when he was in the 8th standard at Dewas. Engineer says: 'one day, the postman met me on the road and began to talk to me. He said in a very philosophical way that all paths, though they differ each other, lead to God and that all paths are true. I protested and said that that could never be. For example, idol worship can never be a true path and it can never lead one to God: Islam believes only in one God and everything contrary to it is false. I remember the postman smiling at me and saying that if one has *shraddha* (faith) in idols that can also lead to God. I, however, stuck to my point and the postman left it at that. But whenever he met me, he smiled in a charming way' (p. 11). Naturally, at the stage of mental development of his age, he could not understand what the postman wanted to say. Perplexed, he asked his teacher Shama Saheb to explain its meaning to which he told him to wait till he was grown up.

After the matriculation result was declared, Engineer's father, following the mandatory practice in the Bohra community, took him to Mumbai for *Qadambosi* (kissing the feet) of the high priest. It turned out to be a horrifying experience for him which became a turning point in his life. Believing that Islam does not allow to perform *Sajda* before any human being, he refused to do so. Noticing his disinclination, a marshal who stood by caught his neck and forced him to perform *sajda* of the Syedna, and said, '*Shaitan* (devil), you are refusing to bow down before our *maula* (spiritual master)'. The young Engineer was enraged at such a behaviour but had to comply because of his father and also because 'I would have been lynched then and there, had I been persistent in my refusal' (p. 14). On their way back, Engineer told his father not to ask him to go there again, otherwise he feared he would refuse. To these words tears began to roll down his father's cheeks and he said 'My son, you do not know why I brought you here. It was not out of my pleasure but of compulsion. You have seen the kind of culture which prevails here. That is why I want you to become a doctor or an engineer and liberate me from this stifling atmosphere' (p. 15). This incident proved to be the catalyst that prompted Engineer to become a crusader for reforms in his community, a job he continues to perform, in spite of facing grave threats to his life.

Engineer informs us that he had very orthodox religious views till he was studying in intermediate. But two influences brought about a change in his outlook. One was Niyaz Fatehpuri's book *Man o Yazdan* which, according to him, 'left a deep impact on my mind and I began to review my traditional views about religion. A new intellectual vision had opened before me. However, my commitment to Islam remained unshaken' (p. 19). Another influence was Marxism to which he got introduced by a left-oriented student. He gave him *Das Capital* and some other works of Marx and Engels on religion. These books profoundly impacted his mind and, 'Thus, although, I remained a believer, I too was converted to Marxism. In my opinion it is not necessary to be an atheist to be a Marxist' (p. 21).

After completing his B.Sc. (Civil Engineering), Engineer came to settle in Mumbai. Soon he got a job in the Bombay Municipal Corporation. It was a job that involved a lot of corruption at different levels, and it was a great challenge for an upright employee to remain clean.

Engineer, however, had strong commitment to principles and successfully waded through these dirty waters of corruption. During this service, he also joined a union and struggled against injustice. In 1983, after completing twenty years of service, he took voluntary retirement and got devoted full-time to the causes most dear to him, the Bohra reform movement and communal harmony.

It was time now for Engineer to perform what he was destined to. He had already started writing in English and Urdu and contributed articles to leading newspapers and journals of that time. He was now an interventionist intellectual in his own right. Together with writing, his crusade against communal violence and for the promotion of inter-religious peace and harmony was in full swing.

Engineer's involvement in the Bohra reform movement has been the defining feature of his life as an activist. His first encounter with the Bohra religious establishment came in 1973 with his open support to the stir launched by some Bohras against the priesthood in Udaipur. His support was in the form of an article that appeared in *The Times of India* (Mumbai). It was taken as an act of sacrilege and rebellion and Engineer was forced to apologize for it by his relatives and friends, but true to his spirit, he refused to oblige as he believed he had done nothing wrong. All his relatives turned against him and none of his family ever met him thereafter. His mother, who lived with him, was forced to live separately and severe all links with him. As he continued with his reformist activities, a series of murderous attempts were made on his life, which he was fortunate enough to survive.

Engineer faced all these attempts on his life and efforts to stifle his voice steadfastly and without harbouring any hatred and rancour against those who were doing and instigating these acts of repression and coercion. With firm faith in God he remained steadfast on his way to propagate and promote the Islamic message of peace, equality, justice and coexistence. He immersed himself completely in the study of Islam and other religions, in order to strengthen the process of dialogue with them. He devoted all his life and time to make the world understand that the core Islamic values are in no way in conflict with modern democracy and secularism. He asserted very forcefully that it was Islam that announced in categorical terms that 'there is no coercion or compulsion in religion', which laid the foundations for the emergence of a pluralist society in Madina. He extensively wrote on the issues relating to the interaction of Islam and Muslims with the modern world realities. His views on *jihad* bring out its essential meaning of its being a concerted struggle for truth and justice. Based on Hadith, he also defines *jihad* as telling the truth on the face of a tyrant ruler. He firmly believed that Islam does not permit wanton violence, and violence is permissible in *jihad* only in exceptional circumstances for self-defence, and for that too it should be avoided as far as possible. Engineer also wrote with conviction and clarity on gender equality and justice in Islam and stressed that Islam does not discriminate against women as unequals, but actually accords them all the rights and privileges that men enjoy. As already mentioned, communal peace and harmony were closest to his heart. He not only wrote extensively on the subject but also was actively involved in studying the causes of communal violence and providing relief to the victims.

Taking inspiration from a couplet of Allama Iqbal, he was a staunch believer in the way Iqbal interprets the terms '*momin*' and '*kafir*', and says that 'A real Kafir is one who lives for himself and for comforts of his own life making serious compromises with fundamental values of life, such as truth, justice, compassion, human dignity and inflicts suffering on others for his own comforts and lust for power. He is a worldly person. The real *momin* is not only one who formally accepts Islam but one whose life is a continuous struggle for truth; he refuses to compromise with falsehood and is an embodiment of compassion, always engaged in relieving the sufferings of others' (p. 338).

Engineer believed that 'no religion is possible without freedom of conscience, fearlessness and commitment to truth', and also that 'religion should not divide but unite humanity. Human solidarity is the common denominator across religions. The feeling of superiority over other religious traditions is arrogance rather than the religious spirit' (p. 340). He concludes his autobiography with the following words which define the mission he had been engaged in all his life:

> I believe that all religions are a source of rich values. These values coupled with reason, which is a precious gift from God, can help us transform our earth into a real paradise of peace. Thus, what we need is a real synthesis of faith and reason to achieve our goal. Faith, reason, love and non-violence are our real saviours. These should be the guiding stars of our life and humanize our progress and development. (p. 345)

This special issue is being dedicated to the scholarship and activism that Dr. Asghar Ali Engineer has been committed to all his life, and his struggle for the promotion of the Islamic values and strengthening the forces of peace, tolerance and coexistence as also of democracy and secularism. By devoting this issue to an Islamic scholar enjoying respect among enlightened intellectual circles at home as well as abroad, we are only re-dedicating ourselves to the values that the *Islam and the Modern Age* has always stood for and been committed to. We believe that the contents of this issue would go a long way in serving the cause of bringing the message of Islam closer to those who want to know more about Islam and also clearing the misgivings with regard to Islam that cloud many minds.

Editor

Writings on Asghar Ali Engineer

1
Asghar Ali Engineer: My Teacher, My Friend

*Irfan Engineer**

There are two types of parents, one are those who know what is best for their children. They envision their future careers and life. All that the child is required to do is to live the life as desired by his/her parent's. However, everything may not go as smoothly as desired by parent's. There is resistance, assertion and even revolt in the story as children have their own experiences, their own agency, their own desires and dislikes and some may even have their own career plans. It may be extremely difficult, if not impossible to find children completely submissive to their parents who happily mould themselves in the image of their parents (moot question again will be, which parent? For mother and father may have different personalities, visions and desires). The counter response of the parent's is also varied in case children have different aspirations. Some parents give in, learn and understand their children and revise their desires and expectations from their child even though holding on to their original plans to the extend possible. There is minimum violence used in this case. Other parents may use every means possible for them to enforce their expectations and desires on their child, which can include physical violence to threat of disinheritance. The second category of parents have love towards their children as their only plan. They may bring up their children with certain values. Parents are the first school for their children where they learn meanings of various things around them, learn their language and improve their communication skills. Parents educate their children about various choices and leave the child to exercise his/her own choices. Parents play a supportive role in helping the child achieve what she has chosen to achieve, comfort her and encourage them her in case of failures. There is no occasion for using physical or other kinds of violence as the child

---

* Irfan Engineer, Dr. Asghar Ali Engineer's son.

is not forced to do anything that may find resistance in him/her. Of course the two categories are not 'either/or' situations. In reality we find parents combine both categories in various measures.

My father Dr. Asghar Ali Engineer was a parent falls in the second category. I have very fond memories of my father in my childhood. He imparted values and gave meaning to my life. He educated me about various approaches to life and left me to chose my approach and path. He was my role model. I may have been a difficult child but he handled me with ease and plenty of love. I learnt many things from him through dialogue with him since my childhood. But my regret is that there are many things that I could have learnt which I didn't and even wonder if only he had picked up a stick. I would have learnt those things—like Urdu, Persian and Arabic languages and through these languages, rich Islamic History. Whatever I learnt from him, I did so by agreeing with him during our dialogue sessions. But I learnt much more by often disagreeing with him during these dialogue sessions and then learning through experiences that my father was after all right. Even now we disagree on many things and I learnt more by an honest disagreement at the first instance and then reflection over a period of time on the disagreement.

As a child, I do not remember of ever being forced by my father to do school homework. He would occasionally inquire whether I had finished my homework and whether I needed any help and that was the end of it. But Dad (as I would call my father) would persuade me to learn Urdu alphabets when my attention would be drawn towards going out for playing with other children. Dad was incapable of forcing and so eventually I 'succeeded' in not learning Urdu. I learnt my Urdu while in Government Law College. There was *Bazm-e-Urdu* as extra-curricular activity which taught Urdu. Dad would also often tell me stories of Russian revolution and about Marxism. Again I had little interest in them. I would listen for sometime and then run away. When my father told me Lenin had started living underground, as a child I literally pictured Lenin digging tunnels or opening manholes and living 'underground' and always wandered, why police did not enter these tunnels or the manholes to arrest Lenin. Our geography teacher in school Mrs. Shaikh was staunch anti-communist and would often talk against communism in our class castigating Russian system. According to her, communism means shortages and king queues and everyone required to wear blue uniforms. As I was exposed to conflicting views, I decided to ask my father about what my teacher told me at school. Without any ill feelings towards my teacher, he asked me to search my own answers and posed certain questions to help me. He pitted long queues against lack of purchasing power of people (and we were surrounded by slums to easily understand that). As we were buying meat he explained to me that if all had purchasing power, there would be a long queue here too. This generated interest in me and I started looking for books that could help me reach a conclusion. Though I rebelled when Dad wanted me to study Marxism, eventually through his patience, love and non-imposing approach, I did develop interest in Marxism on my own.

Once I announced to Dad when I was in eight standard that if I ever joined a medical college and fell in love with someone and we married. I wouldn't allow my wife to practice medicine. It was unusual for a 13 year old child to be able to talk so freely with his father about such matters. 'Why?' Dad asked. 'Because who would look alter my children?', I replied. Then there was a disarming counter question from Dad. 'What if your wife thought the same that she wouldn't allow her husband to practice as there should be someone to look after her children?' I didn't have any answer to that but the question posed made me think on the issue of gender justice. Dad would asked me to read *The Times of India* daily and write the story that I read in my own language or write an essay on any topic I desired. He would then correct the essay and discuss with me. I would write essays with great interest and wait for Dad to correct them and discuss what I had written. It was like creating something and then I had as a reader my great father to appreciate. He would not only correct my grammar and spellings, but also discuss the ideas that I had. I remember waiting for Dad eagerly whenever I had written an essay so that he would appreciate and discuss the same. This inculcated the habit to read and write. Whatever little skills I have developed to write, I would thank Dad for it. Dad's question regarding my wife too wanting me not to practice medicine had made me think and this process was helped further by my regular reading of *The Times of India*. Every Sunday there would be a page on gender issue and that made me more gender sensitive than my other friends. My sister Seema was a more favoured child for Dad and I was always slightly resentful of my sister for that though I loved my sister.

After I appeared for my SSC examination in May 1978, Dad took me to the meeting of 'Committee for the Protection of Democratic Rights' to introduce me to human rights activists so that I get broader outlook towards life and become socially sensitive. He often discussed Islam with me and its liberating values. However, at the same time he shielded me from all attempts to force rituals on me by other family members. He wanted me to practice religion after understanding the same and follow religion of my choice, or even reject religion. I became an atheist in my early school days and remember converting a friend and fellow school mate to atheism. Dad took my atheism with a smile. I remember arguing with him regarding my atheism Dad explained to me that if at all I stood for any higher values that I would want to submit myself to with all sincerity and honesty. God is those values. My search for truth should be my religion, he advised. I remained an atheist and Dad was happy that I had reached my own conclusion. Those arguments with Dad made me search for my own answers to the problems and dilemmas that I faced in life and my search often made me differ with Dad and bitterly argue our own respective positions. However, during those arguments, he never ridiculed me nor showed any disrespect to the views of an insolent inexperienced child that I was. Those arguments made me more confident about my views, and I learnt to fearlessly express my views. Soon I found myself expressing views that were contrary to my Dad from public platforms just after he had addressed from the platform. I remember doing so on during All World Dawoodi Bohra Conference in Pune and then in Ahmedabad on the issue of participation of youth in the Bohra reformist movement. The delegates attending the conference were amused by an adolescent publicly differing with such a tall leader and it was not something very common for them. However, when the delegates of the conference expressed their amusement. Dad came to my rescue and told them that I had every right to differ with him and that on the contrary he was proud of me.

In the year 1984, there were riots in Bhiwandi and Mumbai. I accompanied Dad for fact finding mission. I closely observed how he elicited information from the victims, politicians and other socially engaged people. That was my first experience of fact finding. Dad later sent me to Jogeshwari with a questionnaire to do fact finding of the riots in Majaswadi, Jogeshwari and I did so. He appreciated my fact finding which later became part of the fact finding report of the Bombay-Bhiwandi Riot. The essay writing skills stood me in good stead. I along with other students of St. Xavier College visited Bhiwandi again to sensitize the students about communal riots and help in relief work. This we did along with Anna Kurien and other organisations in Mumbai. My social engagements increased and Dad was worried whether I would pay enough attention to my studies. I eventually passed my law and started working full time among tribals in Gujarat and without any financial support or resources. That was the time when Dad also had sacrificed his job to dedicate himself to the work of social reform movement among Bohras in particular and for communal harmony in general, With my growing inclination towards activism I started spending more time among the tribals and would meet Dad only occasionally from 1989 to 1993. During this time, I reflected on my ideological differences with Dad and found myself gradually agreeing with him. However, this truth I learnt through my own experiences and truth, non-violence, socially engaged religion meant a lot to me. They were not mere words, these words had lot of meanings and that I learnt thanks to my friend, philosopher and guide and his patience. Had these words or for that matter any values or rituals been imposed on me, I would have merely rote memorized these words without understanding the profound meaning they now have for me. My friends in school were jealous that I had Dad who was more a friend to me rather than a parental authority. Knowledge and wisdom do not come through the 'teacher's' stick that forces one to memorize. They come only through pursuit of an honest seeker and with teacher sharing his/her experiences, showing the path and the pitfalls and leaving the seeker to choose his/her own journey and reaching own conclusion. I never feared my father and never experienced him to be a coercive authority. I have learnt to respect him as an authority in his subject, his wisdom and scholarly knowledge, and more than all that, as a very humble human being amenable and accessible to one and all. I have internalized his vision and mission for a peaceful and just society. May God give me and him, both, strength to tread this path and contribute our might towards this mission.

2
Asghar Ali Engineer: A True Embodiment of Secular Spirit

*Fazlur Rahman**

Dr. Asghar Ali Engineer, an Islamic scholar of global repute, a renowned exegesist, a vocal voice, a social reformer, an interventionist intellectual, a political commentator, a visionary, a thinker, an activist, a prolific and progressive writer, an advocate of a culture of peace, non-violence and communal harmony and what not ...

It has always been a steady task to pen down something about a person like Engineer who embodies a mission and carries the diminishing light of Indian secularism and has pledged to keep it inflamed till the last breath of his life. Today, I feel honoured to present a brief sketch of the life of Dr. Engineer and be the part of this volume devoted to the service Dr. Engineer has rendered to the nation and the world. He is the man who throughout his life struggled and is still struggling against all kinds of odds to preserve and protect the core values of Indian culture and civilization. He has been more critical against his own conservationist mates rather than the people belonging to other religions or sect.

Though it is very difficult to present a comprehensive picture of his life, his work, his mission, his suffering and pain because of his mission but I will try to cover some salient feature of his life and will highlight what it meant to be Dr. Engineer for this nation and how intensely, constantly and patiently he engaged himself to promote the values of secularism, multiculturalism, religious tolerance which are close to his hear.

He was born in a family of Bohra Ulema (a Shiite sect) on 10 March 1939 in the state of Rajasthan where his father was posted. Since his childhood he was made to imbibe the religious values. When he opened

---

* Dr. Fazlur Rahman, Research Fellow, Indian Council of World Affairs, New Delhi.

his eyes, he found nothing but an ambience full of religious knowledge and debate and discussion. From an early age he has been a witness to an environment where Brahmin priests used to enter into religious and metaphysical debate with his father and other scholarly members of his family which shaped the intellectual orientation of this legendry Islamic scholar. His surrounding environment was so tolerant and receptive of other religions that he (in his own words) was asked strictly not to condemn idol worship but just to refrain from worship them.

He was a voracious reader from his childhood and his literary taste ranges from Urdu, Arabic, Persian, English literature to poetry, religious writings of medieval scholars and modern religious commentators. His academic interests were not confined to exegesis or Hadith but he was equally fond of other kinds of writings like literary criticism, satire and other kinds of writings ranges from the subcontinent. This reading habit shaped his empirical mind and experimental attitude. His vast canvas of knowledge never prevented him from landing in all kinds of ideological debates with his student-friends ranging from Marxism to socialism to Islamism and several other perspectives of erstwhile global politics.

According to him, a poem (*Khizr-e-Rah*) by Iqbal induced him to learn Persian further and this poem had greatly influence him. He also learnt the philosophy of Islamic socialism from the concept *Self* of Iqbal. He is also influenced by the Sufi poetry of Dard, Asghar Sahib is also fond of Urdu literature and he is greatly influenced by Niyaz Fatahpuri's writings and his contestation with the traditional beliefs about religion. These were the people who left their imprint on his mind. Writings of Hosrat Mohani and Ubaidullah Sindhi were quite instrumental in shaping the religious views of Mr. Engineer.

He had a good friend in Jan Nisar Akhtar and Sahir Ludhyanvi and was highly impressed with their style of poetry. This shows the versatile nature of Dr. Engineer's personality that combines many streams of thoughts.

He received his initial education in various cities because his father, during his service period, was transferred from one place to another at short intervals. He had not yet entered his teenage that the partition of the subcontinent came which was another trauma for this growing genius. He himself was a victim of this trauma when he decided not to join AMU fearing that it would hamper his job prospect in future.

The erstwhile environment gave an opportunity to him, if not to comprehend, to observe the socio-political dynamics of India society which in later phase would help him in shaping his own school of liberal religious thoughts.

Asghar's was a rebellious mind from the very beginning and he never accepted anything that does appeal to his rational and inquisitive mind and he conveyed this in a very categorical term to his father by refusing the ritual of *Qadambosi* (a ritual of kissing of feet) when his father took him to Bombay to Syedna Sahib after he passed his matriculation. Under pressure from his father, he did so but asked his father not to ask him to do this in future. The scene at the spot was a horrible experience for him and according to him; this became a turning point in his life and acted as a catalyst for his fight against the un-Islamic and exploitative practices of the priestly class. This was a revolt of a young mind and it speaks volumes about his rebellious attitude against religious innovation and orthodoxy which is today increasingly seen in our society. This episode laid the foundation of his reform movement amidst Bohra community.

When his individual effort yielded no fruits, he decided to form a board and he opted for other means to awaken the people against the high-headedness of the high priest. This was the period of complete activism with single motto of reforming his community. In this phase he was making every effort to muster support for his cause from the intelligentsia in which sometimes he succeeded and sometimes failed. He never accepted defeat and continued his effort. His major achievement was the formation of Tarkunde-Nathwarni commission for which he suffered a lot of condemnations from the Muslim community.

Before this incident, he always mixed with his own classmates from Bohra community and was part of several Bohra political activities and served as a member of several of the political groups like Bohra Students Union. But this incident alienated him and was almost outcast for his co-religionists.

His real struggle began with himself and an orthodox surrounding when he came from to Bombay in 1963 and joined the Bombay Municipal Corporation. Here, he came into contact with the real subaltern masses where he was offered bribes every day for one work or the other. He was exposed to a different reality of Indian society. This bitter experience and reality was a different of trauma for him and each and every experience was sowing in him the seeds of reform. This was the phase of resistance against himself for Dr. Engineer and agitation against the existing system.

Here he was fighting against official corruption and on the streets he was involved in a battle against religious corruption. While he was serving the Railways, he came across a number of incidents which shocked him and allured him to take up the social cause and this phase of his life was full of activism. Meanwhile, he had started writing political and literary columns both in English and Urdu in several National Daily and reputed Journals, apart from being a full-time activist for the Bohra Reform movement which he joined in 1973.

It was Jabalpur Riots of 1961 and Bhivandi Riots of 1970 which shook his conscience considerably and he launched a public campaign against the menace of communalism and this is the real mission which he is still living for. He is fighting this intellectually, politically, socially, and physically and raising his voice for the elimination of the communal and sectarian divide of the country. Following the riots of 1961, he started holding weekly meeting of like-minded people to discuss the blue print to fight this menace.

Dr. Asghar Ali Engineer began the religious reform within his own community and expressed his grave concern over the growing orthodoxy and innovation in the Bohra sect. He started his open fight against Bohra priest syndicate who had established a monopoly on all the social rituals of the Bohra community and it was difficult for to liberate the tutelage of the priests. He left no stone unturned to bring internal reform in the religious character of Bohra Priest ranging from writing to staging protests, to meeting several delegations to mobilizing public opinions against this religious authoritarianism and absolutism. He himself suffered a lot when his mother was ordered to leave her son and shift to some other place for the so-called heretic acts of Asghar but he did not budge and continued to fight.

Several committees were set up both by the state and central governments to look into the issues. Several top national leaders like J. P. Narayen, Justice Tarkunde, Justice Nathanvi along with others were involved to resolve the confrontation between the Priests and the oppressed Bohras and this was, if not the whole, a partial victory for the efforts of Asghar when an organized Board was formed to look into the entire issues.

After some respite from the issue of Bohra reform and enabling himself to open some avenues Tor negotiations with Bohra clergy, he turned his attention towards the communalism, particularly after the Bhivandi Riots of 1970 that had saddened him the most.

It was the phase when India was facing a different sort of political crisis as war of 1971 was looming large over the Indian horizon and internal political struggle was in full swing among different political parties. But for Engineer, nothing was more important than to fight and suppressing the communal ideology disrupting the cultural fabric of the country. He raised his voice against the communalism both of the Hindus and Muslims, and clubbed both Hindu and Muslim communal organizations together.

This was the period when he travelled throughout the country, meeting all political leaders and religious leaders with an intention to mobilizing national opinion against rising communal incidents in India. Now, it had become his mission to contain and uproot this menace. He diversified his activities at different levels and began with organizing a weekly programme with the motto of raising consciousness about social harmony. He involved himself in Indo-Pak friendship mission and came into contact with all those writers and artists like Ali Sardar Jafri, Jan Nisar Akhtar, K.A. Abbas, R.S. Bedi, Akhtarul Iman, Balraj Sahni Kaifi Azmi and several others who were fighting the communalism in their own way. Mr. Engineer was very instrumental in forming Anti-Communal Youth Front in 1969 just after the Ahmadabad riots in the same year.

He had all the courage and audacity to go against the line of majority Muslim leadership and he faced all sorts of condemnation. He argued that the battle would further deepen the Hindu-Muslim divide and this must be taken as a constitutional matter. He wrote several political pieces in numerous journals and dailies highlighting the gravity of the issue and warning about the repercussions of the movement. Many Muslim leaders accused him of being an RSS agent but he did not heed and continued to speak out his conscience.

He organized several workshops in different parts of the country to discuss the intricacies of communalism in India and for that he received praise from several quarters of the government. In those workshops, he used to invite high-level police officers to discuss and teach the police forces and civil society groups about the issue. He was very instrumental in forming several organizations and for a fight to the communalism.

He himself took up the investigation of Bombay riots of 1993 when he visited different localities and met people and came up with a comprehensive report. This was an eye opener for other civil-right activists who joined him gradually in great numbers. It was 1970s and 1980s when Engineer devoted most of his writings to highlighting the issue of communalism and he wrote both in Urdu and English to awaken the masses. He did not merely highlight the Hindu part of communalism but was equally against the minority communalism and in his biography, he mentions that 'once Sayyed Shahbauddin asked Asghar Sahib, what the cause of communalism is? He lashed back saying that you are the real cause.

Engineer is equally concerned with the new form of religious fundamentalism and global jihadist terrorism. He is constantly writing and speaking at various public forums that terrorism has nothing to do with the religion of Islam and presenting a true picture of Islam and sayings of Prophet. He has never shied away from condemning the acts committed in the name of Islam but meanwhile he speaks against the forces that instigate the innocents to take the weapons and according to him, it must be redressed.

One can thus say that the story of Asghar Ali Engineer revolves around his fight against orthodoxy and conservatism. His present mission can be divided into three parts. First he began his fight within his own Bohra community that speaks volumes about his sincerity that contains a message that conservatism or orthodoxy needs to be fought even if it is in one's own sect and community.

His battle against Bohra priest was followed by his struggle against communalism when he interacted with the larger world and got exposed to the socio-urban political life of India and had his firsthand experience with this menace of communal divide. The last part of his mission took him abroad where he met people from different religions, cultures, sects and communities and involved himself in the process of culture interactions. He addressed many major known think tanks around the world and the mainstay of his intellectual foundation has always remained the religious freedom and the cultural tolerance.

For the promotion of his religious vision and cultural harmony, he has been rewarded 'Right Livelihood Reward', one of the highest civilian award by the Swedish Government. This award is presented exactly in manner of the Nobel Prize the Nobel is given by the King of Sweden while this Award is given by the Speaker of Swedish Parliament.

He has visited UK, Switzerland, Italy, France, Germany, Australia, Russia, Malta and Holland and in each of these countries, he has addressed the intellectuals and for his intellectual depth, he command high respect amongst the academia of Europe and the award by the Swedish Parliament is testimony to that. He has been frequent visitor to all the Arab and Central Asian countries to impart his own vision of religious philosophy and intellectual wisdom.

He has a lot of friends and also equal or more number of enemies. Many people appreciate his contribution to the promotion of religious harmony while others condemn him for his liberal religious attitude. He was attacked in Egypt by some religious fanatics.

He says that the what saddens the most him as a peace activist is that those who believe in communal harmony do not work consistently and perhaps this is the reason that his commitment to the mission of combating communalism does not stop at writing articles and columns but it goes further. In 1995 he started holding police workshop in Bombay and his main motto was to change the attitude of the policemen and later he moved beyond Bombay and held these workshops in all major cities and achieved great success. Once he had said that one should try to become Sir Sayyed and not Jinnah.

His individual mission was never confined to his fighting against the absolutism and authoritarianism of Bohra Priesthood or against communalism but he very fearlessly raises his voices on the critical Muslim issues too like Shah Bano and Babri Masjid. He had the courage to argue with erstwhile clergies and had no fear in telling them that Supreme Court decision was in accordance with the spirit of Koran in Shah Bano's case.

Likewise, he never hesitates in maintaining his own individual opinion on several issues like Babri mosque and even today holds the same view that let the battle be fought by Hindu secular forces and involvement of Muslim will communalize the matter. He has been a champion of democracy and freedom and this was this democratic ethos which induced him to oppose the Emergency.

His entire life bears full witness to his commitment to his principles, human values, true ideology, and honesty that he adheres to for working this world more beautiful. He has been a messenger of peace, love, affection, tolerance, cultural plurality, religious diversity and has always promoted the intellectual dialogue among different religious groups. The mission of his life has been to highlight the democratic and moral values enshrined in Islam.

3
A Scholar, A Teacher and A True Guide

*Qutub Jahan Kidwai**

During my university days I did a fair reading of Dr. Asghar Ali Engineer's work on Shah Bano issue. I profoundly recall during a presentation of my seminar paper on 'Shah Bano case and rights of Muslim woman', thanks to my teacher of sociology who suggested some good books to refer to prepare my paper, was highly appreciated by the panel. I still remember the Sociology department in my University. SNDT Women's University, was holding a workshop and had invited Anna Hazare. They wanted to invite someone championing the women's rights as well and I requested them to invite Dr. Asghar Ali Engineer. My professors too were great admirers of Dr. Engineer's articles but unfortunately we could not get his availability.

In 2002 I came across a vacancy for Researcher's post at the Center for Society and Secularism and I went for an interview. To my pleasant surprise I could see the scholar whom as a student I and my friends craved to listen. Both as a scholar and as a human being I found him extremely humble and he didn't mind when I opened the plethora of questions and was very kindly be responded. I was praying that I should be appointed for the post and should get a chance to work under him. I was blessed. My first research was on Uniform Civil Code and Muslim Personal Law in India with the perspective of gender rights. Being a Muslim and a woman there were several unexplainable thoughts as far as religion of Islam and the status of Muslim woman was concerned. Islam and its history, when taught to me by Dr. Engineer, were sheer revelations for me. Like any layman in the community, what was inculcated during my upbringing in the family or in the private tutor madrasa was true and the only right information for me. During university days, we did engage in gender studies and at length discussed the rights and plight of women in different

* Ms Qutub Jahan Kidwai, Women's Rights activist and former Managing Director, Centre for Study of Society and Secularism, Mumbai.

communities but somewhere religion was portrayed as a culprit for all forms of suppression of the fairer sex.

The research topic compelled me to read, discuss and debate Islamic perspectives of gender equality. This idea was alien to me. How can rights and religion be complimentary to each other? Dr. Engineer would smile to my queries and would teach me the whole concept of religion, culture and society. He said there are four aspects of religion. These are, first the thought system which should encourage reasoning, questioning and change. The second aspect is value system which remains permanent and transcending. The third is Institutional system where one learns these values and behaviour. Finally the fourth aspect is rituals and this is not liable to change. Religion needs to be understood in the light of the socio-cultural ethos. One cannot compare advanced and developed society with underdeveloped one. Every society evolves and consequently norms and behaviour change. Religion has certain values which should be an integral part of life. Inner spiritual development is necessary along with the material gains. Dr. Engineer says 'Material gain is like a mirage. The more you run for water the more you become thirsty.'

He says that Islam is the only religion which upholds rights of women. This is how he logically narrates that any act in conformity with moral consciousness is a religious act. This too has got subjective elements. Koran gives equal dignity and equal freedom of conscience to women. On the authority of the Koran it is a proven fact that man and woman are equal. However feudalization of Islam destroyed the Koranic values of equality and many degrading practices against women given precedence over Koran. While explaining the *Shariah*, Dr. Engineer said that while formulating *Shariah*, Koranic values were ignored and social needs were given importance. Islam was revealed among the Arab tribals. There was no state and source of law. It was entirely based on oral tradition. Only 17 people were literates when Islam emerged. Among the tribes was *mala'a,* senate which was based on oral tradition. Since the Koran was the first law giver and hence the obsession with Koran for formulating law. He said there were more than 250 verses which gave laws. The Arabs to establish a state like Romans and Greeks they needed a source and the source was Koran. Obsession began as law became more important and the intention of the *Shariah* was to introduce value-based law. But values became subsidiary and law became primary.

Dr. Engineer further elaborates that values are of two types.

One, Fundamental values and second, Instrumental values. While explaining the methodology of understanding Koran he highlights that these two values are of great importance to understand, Islamic legal science. According to him, Fundamental values can never change.

Instrumental values act as tools or help implementing fundamental values. Instrumental values are contextual and change from time to time. These can be rejected if found inapplicable or reformed or changed. This reasoning also proves that Shariah can be changed according to societal needs, taking into consideration various dynamics of human society. When dealing with any existing Islamic law, whether it is in conformity with Koran or not, we need to examine the Instrumental values in the light of Fundamental values and constantly device new Instruments. Most of the Shariah laws are instruments. If these Instruments are injuring Fundamental values then they should be changed and reformulated.

On methodology of understanding Koran, Dr. Engineer says that the verses in Koran can be divided into two categories, i.e. Normative verses and Contextual verses. While formulating Shariah one of the important sources after Koran is Hadith, the traditions of Prophet Mohammad PBUH. Both in Koran and Hadith we need to understand the context. Hadiths are also based on the context. If the context misfits the present social needs then it cannot be applicable. He explains that *Shariah* has two objectives, i.e. *maqaasid* (objectives) and *masaalih* (problem). In *maqaasid* if the law does not fulfill the object or *maqsad* then it has to be changed. In *masaalih* if that problem doesn't exist then no such law is needed. In *Shariah* or *law, maqsad* is important than *masaalih*. Interestingly having their own significance both are interdependent and independent. And he says that *Shariah* should be such that it fulfills both the *maqsad* and *masaalih*. Since Hadiths forms the major part of Islamic jurisprudence, Dr. Engineer has simplified the whole science of Hadith by identifying its criteria for its acceptability. He says that five things are, important to learn to judge any Hadith. First is to examine the chain of narrators, who narrated have a particular hadith. Secondly character of the narrator which one can read from *ilm-ul Rijaal* (History of narrators). The third criterion to judge hadith is whether the chain of narrators reaches Prophet PBUH or not. Whether the narrator saw or met the Prophet PBUH or not. If it is *A had Hadiths* that means single narration.

Books like Sahih Bukhari and Tabqaat Ibn Saad, a commentary on Bukhari give comprehensive details of such hadiths. The fourth criterion is when a particular Hadith emerged, i.e. in which period this hadith appeared. This will also give an understanding of the narrators and their context. And a final criterion according to Dr. Engineer is *Dirayat*, i.e. reasoning which is of utmost importance. Why Dirayat is important is because of several factors which resulted in fabrication of hadiths. Tribal and regional prejudices and rivalries, incited some people to forge traditions to be produced as evidence of their superiority over others? Then personal ambition or earning goodwill of the reigning Caliph was another stimulant which prompted some to be included among the scholars of *hadith* through forgery. Controversies and differences among jurists *(fuqaha')* prompted some scholars to fabricate traditions to be invoked in support of their own legal positions. Dirayat is a must so that acceptable Traditions can be separated from unacceptable ones.

According to him Koran wants to give full dignity to the women and grant gender equality. There is equality in obligations and rights. He discusses at lengths the rights of woman in Islam, rights in marriage, divorce, maintenance, property, etc. To my astonishment, he narrates several incidents in the history of Islam where women tremendously contributed and their contributions were no less in significant. Did women really participate in socio-economic and political front? I hesitatingly raised my doubts on Islam wanting women to be like *Umm-ul-momineen* (mother of ummah, the Prophet's PBUH wives). The role of Umm-ul-Momineen to me was that of the one who lives a life of total obedience to men and in Purdah or Hijab. My querry led to a discussion on a very crucial issue in the world of Islamic feminism and this issue by and large has its impact on the lives of all the Muslim women. Dr. Engineer asked me to open the chapter in the Koran and read out the verses on Hijab. Chapter 33 is *Surah Al-Ahzab*. Verses 53 and 59 says that tell your wives, daughters and women of believers to wear *jilbaab* so that they are not misunderstood or harassed as slave girls. Or wearing *jilbaab* would be a mark of distinction of pious woman. Chapter 24 namely *An-Nur,* verses 30 and 31 first command men to lower their gaze and safeguard their private parts and then the command is addressed women. Tribal culture was getting transformed into urban culture. Nomadic culture was changing into a sedentary one. Here one needs to understand the sociology of Koran. The revealing outcome of our discussion is that all the verses in Koran for men are duty based and surprisingly for the women are right based. Islam began with right based discourse. There is no verse in Koran which is duty based for woman. Even as if a mother does not wish to breastfeed her baby her husband should provide a wet-nurse. However in reality the practice is topsy-turvy and to get duties internalized by women the socially constructed gender role is legitimized by religious sanction. There fore *purdah* in reality has become duty-based defined by our patriarchal society and it is not a Koranic recommendation.

He says that Koranic contextual injunctions are the product of societal reference and verses on values do not require any social situation. One should understand the circumstances and not accept it as an absolute. In most of the verses commanding to guard one's chastity are 'addressed to both men and women. Both have to dress in modest and dignified way. Also one has to understand the background of the verses, like the influence of the society and its cultural practices. Holy Koran has provided the space to rethink and reason. What he says about reasoning is very important but it is a double edged sword. It can be used to justify the traditions and also can be used to critically evaluate these traditions. Reasoning can be done when one has the basic premises. In our case Koran is the premise to build our reason. First understand this premise to develop reason and evaluate our traditions.

Dr. Engineer throws light on how to understand the holy Koran. There are four ways to understand Koranic verses Normative, Contextual, Obligatory and Recommendatory. Normative verses provide us with principles and values. These verses are transcending in nature. They are Applicable in all ages. The values like justice, compassion, benevolence and wisdom are the pillars of the Koran. Our reasoning should be based on these premises, these values which are central to Koran and Islam. The second are contextual verses. These verses were revealed as a result of social, cultural and political circumstances and are applicable to that particular context. Their relevance diminishes if the context does not exist any more. It is important to take into account the occasion of revelation which is known as *asbaab-un-nuzul*. The third category of verses is Obligatory verses. In these verses one is addressed to follow particular injunctions compulsorily. It is an absolute command and this too is transcending in nature. Like the five *Ahkamaat* in Islam all the *ibaadaat* Kalma, namaaz, fasting, haj and zakat are obligatory. The fourth category of verses comes under Recommendatory verses. It means certain practices or traditions are recommended. What is the purpose behind particular injunctions. You are asked to follow a rule for more specific purpose and hence they are not applicable to all the times and cannot be made compulsory as obligatory verses. Wherever there is a social matter discussed one has to use reasoning and find out the purpose. For example on the women's issues or the issues concerning other weaker sections of the society we need to rethink and make necessary changes. Shariah is based on contextual verses and contextual hadiths and one needs to take into account the changing times and world, and frame a law accordingly. Over all Koranic values and natural justice these are important criteria for practicing right teaching of Islam. No blind following or blindly rejecting of the traditions but one needs to think analytically. Unbiased and open mind is the biggest *ni 'amat* for the human being. Dr. Engineer said. What a wisdom he carries in this line. He further said that a Muslim needs to be duty bound to spread knowledge and thinking without any expectation. Sense of mission is very crucial and only our conviction can bring that.

It is the need of the hour to frame a new Shariah law incorporating only normative verses given in the Koran. Customs and traditions got inserted in Shariah law namely *'Aadal.* Present Shariah law is full of Arab *'Adaat* which do not have any resemblance to the non-Arab *'Adaat.* We can judge these traditions by setting criteria of values given in Koran. Hadith is not a unanimous text and therefore there is, ambiguity and dispute. Sometimes it negates Koranic values. Dr. Engineer says that it is every Muslim's duty to understand Koran. A knowledgeable Muslim is the one who is close to Allah than anyone else. With *Imaan, I'lm* is also necessary and one needs to understand the right interpretation. He said like physical health, spiritual health is equally necessary. Holy Koran emphasizes on reflection and observation and then decide.

Islam's contribution is that it evolved in a society which was in transition. This society was in need of norms and values which the prophet provided. Pre-Koranic discourse was completely duty-based of women but Koran completely changed it to a rights-based discourse. Koran is actually a liberator of women. The concept gender is shaped by the society. I raised my doubts that religion is part of culture and hence somewhere religion dominates individual or society's behaviour. To this Dr. Engineer replied that religious practice have been shaped by the social ethos. It is not religion which defines social or cultural behaviour or role. Hence the origin of gender role is actually patriarchal or feudal ethos of a certain society. The whole gender role of Muslim women in India is constructed by Indian feudal culture. If one conforms to the assigned gender role or any role of both men and women it becomes a part of collective consciousness. While those who are non-conformist will always challenge the status-quo. Non-conformism brings progress and dynamism.

While discussing the issues of Islamic feminism Dr. Engineer clarifies that there are qualitative differences in western feminism and Islamic feminism like bodily rights, sexual rights, etc., which went to extreme in course of time. Islamic feminist movement started very recently in 1980s challenging old concepts within the framework of Islam. The feminist movement started in Egypt, Morocco, Tunisia and Algeria. These were French colonies so there was awareness in these countries. Islamic feminists discovered that Koran has proclaimed gender equality in every sense. Dr. Engineer elaborates by saying that Koran has different levels, one is the given practice in the society which was reformed and included and the other is what we call values which will remain permanent. Koran proclaims gender equality and through various verses supports these claims. Verse 71 of Surah 9, *At-Taubah,* says that, both believing men and women are protectors of each other. Both men and women are given responsibilities to spread good words and contained wrong deeds. Both require enforcing what is good and fighting what is evil. This verse declares equality of sexes in all aspects in the society whether social, cultural, political and economic.

The most interesting part during my study course with my teacher was to develop an understanding of the Koranic discourse and to analyze the social behaviour to extract whether it is culturally assigned Islamic role for a women or it is sheer socio-cultural ethos which is given religious sanctity. Dr. Engineer gave a very enlightened course here. He said Holy Koran provides knowledge to both commoners and intellectuals. The basic understanding requires here is that the verses in Koran be categorized into *Mohakamaat* and *Mutashabihaat*. *Mohakamaal* verse gives direct command and it is imperative whereas *Mutashabihaat* verses lead one to explore new understanding. While explaining the philosophical aspect of learning Shariah, he said that any phenomenon in society is related to Superstructure. He means to say any act, behaviour or role is the structure built on a base. And the base of this Superstructure is the structure of society i.e. patriarchal ethos and traditions. So to understand any super structure it is equally important to know its base. He further explained that to connect the two mechanically will be unfair. Superstructure and base both are autonomous. Therefore while dealing with Islamic law or Shariah one need to penetrate into the history of Islam when Shariah emerged. And it emerged in a feudal society. Feudal system is based on patriarchy. It was considered as divine and manufactured Hadiths to support it. In my previous paragraphs I shared my enriching experience of what it means to be the student of Dr. Asghar Ali Engineer. I would also like to share about him at personal level. There is no doubt about his intellectual credibility but his magnanimity is seen in his approach to life and his inter-personal relationship. It occurs to me that during my study period under him he never discouraged me to ask questions. In fact he would love to answer any querries without any hitch. He is a great figure of wisdom not just in his thoughts but in actions as well. The hardwork and dedication is tremendous and when it comes to commitment to a cause he would never bow down what may come. I recall a peace and conflict resolution workshop in Kashmir and some mischievous elements intended to sabotage the workshop. Few speakers invited for the camp were biased and started accusing Dr. Engineer and labelling him 'Indian Dog'. The students in the hall shouted the slogans 'Azadi lekar rahenge' 'Go back Indian Agents.' I was fearing some attack, lot of commotion and deafening slogans from the audience I could hear but Dr. Engineer bravely made his way to the dais and holding the mike he said 'I accept that I am an Indian Dog but listen to us and allow us to answer your querries. We want youth to play role in the peace making and we don't want you to play in the hands of vested interests'. I admire his courage and the way he addressed the unruly crowd. Security personnels wanted him to leave the venue but he refused and said 'I will never allow the young blood in Kahsmir being used by vested interests', I also pleaded to him that we halt the programme and continue next day. I still remember his word, he said 'Our Prophet PBUH has faced more atrocities and opposition than this but he never ran away and these challenges will come on our path and we have to stand these challenges with truth and commitment.'

Since I was working with the Center I had a privilege of accompanying him to many such camps and workshops. I found him firm on his principles for the cause of communal harmony when any communal elements tried to counter his views with their provocative questions. I have observed his audacity, being a part of such camps more often that he never ever tried to escape or skip the questions from the RSS people present in the camp. Mostly the speakers cleverly escape such encounters with communal elements but Dr. Engineer would step down from the dais and come into the audience to clarify their views. He always preached Gandhian principles whether the session is on Islamic issues, history of communalism in India, Secularism in India or the peace process in Indian Sub continent. In humour I would tell him that, 'Sir there are three Gandhis in India'. He would curiously ask 'what do you mean?' I used to reply 'There is one Mahatma Gandhi, another Frontier Gandhi and the third one is you who is *'Behadd Gandhi'*. Very humbly he used to give a huge smile.

Dr. Engineer lives with complete devotion to communal harmony and Muslim woman's right. He would never indulge in activities or behaviour which would harm any other individual or sentiments irrespective of any religion, caste or creed. He never uses harsh words even for his opponents Since he is leading a Reformist movement in his Bohra community he suffered for decades for being not a silent watcher of such on exploitative system. He was attacked numerous times and in one of these attacks he almost lost his eyesight but fortunately his well wishers helped him to go for a surgery in Russia and he gained his eyesight. My point here is even after being mistreated and maligned by his opponents he never used his pen to demean them. He only made people aware of an exploitative set up where there is gross violation of human rights and Islamic values by their *Dai*. Dr. Engineer's character reminds me of our great Sufis who never bear any grievances and never retaliate against their enemies. They preached and practiced '*ishq*' (Love) and '*sabr*' (Patience) and simple living. I always asked him from where you imbibe so much of patience and never react. He always advices to control one's anger. He says anger leads to irresponsible behaviour which will harm one's own self.

There were several occasions in the official matters where he was advised that a small bribe can make our work done but he denied offering bribe even if we have to wait for several years. Since I was looking after the administration and programmes, he did not allow nor did he misuse even a rupee of the donors. He often foreoes his honorarium. During tours for camps and workshops he never make any fuss about his lodging and boarding and readily agrees to sleep even on the floor to take his afternoon nap. He would never complain even if the accommodation or the venue is not up to the standard. All he wants is the quality of trainees who are attending our camps. The number and the sincerity of the participants make him happy and contented.

I would like to narrate one more experience where I salute his hardcore activism and dedication for the Muslim woman's cause. In March, 2010 Institute of Islamic studies as usual was holding its three-day national level training camp. There were participants from most of the states in India. Few days before the camp Dr. Engineer was critically ill and was hospitalized. I was away in Pakistan and when I heard about his ill health while the camp was going on, immediately I rushed to Mumbai and arrived at the venue where the programme was being held. Later in the evening I went to see him in the hospital. I found him very restless and seeing me he kept on insisting that 'I want to take my sessions." I assured him that the camp is going well and we have other speakers too. He was grumbling on hospital staff saying they love to keep patients even if there is no need. He told me that if he is unable to deliver lectures on the topics which provide a strong base for the Muslim women to assert their Koranic rights then he will not be at peace. These women have come from far-off places and it is our duty to train them giving complete information. To this I replied that we all need you and the treatment is important so that you continue to remain active and deliver as many lectures as you could. He said that even you were not supporting me. I was praying for his health but was truly sad to see him craving to be among the participants. He staunchly adheres to the principles he has derived from the Koran to support the weaker section, specially the women in Muslim community. And here he was in a critical condition and still wanted to work. I succumbed to his immense dedication and commitment and promised him that I would arrange his lecture on phone. Next day he gave a call from the hospital and spoke at length for one and a half hour, replying to the queries of the participants. We all were amazed and speechless. He feels himself so deeply and inwardly connected to gender equity in Islam that he always wishes that the Muslim community should produce woman theologians who will counter the misogynist groups.

Not to forget his sensitivity towards the sufferings and apathetic attitude of the government often kept him restless and he condemned defiantly the unjust and divisive policies and governance. His voice is minority's voice. Whatever there is riot or blast incident would be first to condemn and write extensively to expose the elements and question the authorities. He has widely exposed all the vested interests in the society which work for the communal divide, through his writings. At the international level, he maintained that Islam and Muslims are peace lover and vehemently condemns the American policies and failure of the Arab world.

His life is an inspiration for a generation which lacks great saintly personalities or community leaders who think and act with wisdom. He would teach me on the issues even while we are travelling in a vehicle, discussing Islamic feminism. Sometimes for hours on the beach he takes my class, while buying his daily dose of *paan* he would take a session standing under the tree near the *paan* shop. There are numerous memories which I will be sharing in another article about which I feel I am truly fortunate to have a teacher and a guide like Dr. Asghar Ali Engineer. He has a very precious and well-known collection of books and literature in Islam. He attaches great importance to these collections. His work is characterized by knowledge, moderation and tolerance having insight of the issues. He was born in a priestly family so had the atmosphere deeply imbued with the religious activities of his Bohra community. His father was a wise and tolerant man and he owes his present expertise to his father. In his early age he came under the influence of Marxism and read several scholastic works and progressive works in the Urdu literature. However he found the answer to all his queries in the Holy Koran and with his deep conviction he is promoting and projecting the true image of Islam and Muslims. I witnessed several high profile people and experts of various subjects like Islamic jurisprudence and religious studies who condemned his work earlier, are now confessing to be reformed after reading him and paying highest tribute to his scholarly work. Some people term him as a real son of India, a true Muslim and a man of wisdom. He advocates Islam in a true sense whether it is human rights, socialism, economic justice, environmental awareness or spiritualism.

In all, I would say a true living figure with tremendous humility without the slightest tinge of pride or vanity. It will not be wrong to call him 'Dervish'. A soul equipped with serenity is dignified, balanced, confident and assuring in his behaviour and if these values are personified becomes my teacher Dr. Asghar Ali Engineer.

Writings by Asghar Ali Engineer

4
Constructing the Civilizational Pillars of Islam

It is well-known that Muslims believe in five pillars of Islam, i.e. (1) Tawhid (Unity of Allah), (2) Prayer, (3) fasting, (4) Hajj (pilgrimage) and (5) Zakat (alms or tithe). There is complete unity among Muslims on these pillars of Islam though some sects like Isma'ilis add two more pillars in addition to these five. But five are accepted by all. It would be seen all these pillars mentioned here are theological and form part of what is called in sharia 'ibadat (i.e. relating to acts of theological piety).

These pillars have inspired Muslims for centuries and they have practiced them regularly. They may have differed in details but never in principles behind them. They will continue to remain both in principle and practice as 'ibadat have their own meaning and significance and spiritual content. And one aspect of religion is deeply spiritual and being related to higher being through 'ibadat and other spiritual acts. Religion cannot be complete without that.

However, there are other this worldly aspects to which religion does provide guidance for proper and meaningful life. These, as against 'ibadat or other worldly aspects, we can call civilizational aspects. Islam is not a religion of renunciation. It wants its followers to take this worldly life seriously and relate it to other worldly life. It is balance between the two. Even the Sufis who, in some cases practiced sort of renunciation, were aware of this and hence most of them used to marry and raise family.

Thus we need pillars which can guide us for successful worldly life in the light of Koranic teachings and Prophet's Sunna. It would enable Muslims to connect more purposefully with this worldly life and its continuity in the other. Of course for centuries Muslims have related only to those five theological pillars indicated above. The life then was simpler and more localized. Today, in the globalised world, life is far more complex and worldly success is measured only in terms of growth of income. It is far more competitive in very complex ways than before.

In such a situation it can be very useful, if we establish, like theological, five civilizational pillars dealing with this worldly life. I suggest they can be called five civilizational pillars of Islam corresponding to five theological pillars. The theological pillars dealing with 'ibadat have enriched spiritual life for centuries, these civilizational pillars would help enrich our civilizational life and make Islam a religion which has and could contribute immensely to modern human civilization.

The Islamic values are well-known so it is not that we are going to suffest something entirely new. However, in view of contemporary world and breath taking developments it is going through, we want to seriously reflect on Koranic teachings and extract few values to enable Muslims to contribute richly to modern civilization and its bounties to be available to entire humanity.

Thanks to media controlled by powerful interests, Islam has come under great drabbing and is being seen as terrorist menace to the world and Muslims as perpetrators of such barbaric acts. In view of highly complex situation and extremists on loose and attacks taking place everyday, the perception that Islam is a religion of violence gets repeatedly reinforced. The clever media does not report what western powers that be, have been doing. West is projected as peaceful, democratic and champion of freedom.

Islam, in contrast, emerges as denier of freedom, undemocratic, feudal and suppressor of human and particularly, women's rights. The average reader cannot be blamed if he/she equates Islam with most anti-diluvian religion with all these attributes. Also, those ulama who condemn terrorist attacks or suicide bombing do not get highlighted and are cursorily mentioned. There is no serious debate about these issues in the media. The terrorist attacks, on the other hand, attract banner headlines as number of people are killed and maimed.

Muslims have not made any serious attempt to establish media of their own. One can name only al-Jazeera which also has controlling share of Qatar Government and is subject to political pressure. The Muslim world needs a powerful media which can become an authentic spokesperson for the Muslim world initiating various debates about real spirit of Islam. It should be both print as well as electronic.

Also, we need new breed of Ulama who do not depend too much on traditional sources but equipped with modern expert knowledge exercise their own minds reflecting on teachings of Koran and very carefully sifted sources of Sunna. Various traditions (ahadith) and other sources like commentaries on Koran written by earlier generations have become main sources for understanding Islam.

We need new unencumbered approach to the Koran and authentic Sunna. The traditional Ulama are in no way ready to work for fresh approach. Also year after year new Ulama come out of traditional madrasas which rely upon all these traditional sources. We need Madrasas which equip 'ulama with modern social sciences and develop skills for political understanding, socio-economic problems and complex problems of globalised polity. Thus they will be able to free themselves from their traditional encumbered approach which keeps them in blind alley of tradition. The very spirit of Koran is thus missed.

Construction of these five civilizational pillars with detailed reasoning behind these constructions can go a long way in this direction. Islam cannot be liberated from traditional clutches without these modern skills which our 'ulama totally lack. When House of Wisdom established by Abbasids transferred Greek philosophical sources into Arabic and they became popular among Muslim intellectuals, not only philosophers like Ibn Sina, Ibn Rushd and others integrated them with Islamic sources but Ulama too enthusiastically participated in the process and developed, Ilam al-Kalam (dialectics) and debated several issues.

Rejection of knowledge, however, different from Islamic knowledge, does not help and is like burying ones head in sand when sandstorm invades. Knowledge is light be it pure white or of rainbow colours. Coming out from ignorance, as Koran puts it, is emerging from darkness to light. The word 'ilm, without any qualification, is, the key word in Koran. It was 'ilm which liberated Arabs from all that was dark from darkness of evil as well as darkness of ignorance.

It is interesting to note, as Dr. Iqbal also has very aptly observed, Koran adopts inductive as against Greek philosophy's deductive approach. Greek deductive approach leads only from known to known, not to unknown knowledge. Induction, on the other hand, is based on extensive observation of external nature and leads to new knowledge. The whole foundation of modern science, as France Beckon observed, is inductive approach. Today our extensive knowledge about the universe is based on astronomical observations.

The Muslim scientists of the Abbasid and later ages developed mathematics and astronomy to new heights and learnt from whatever sources they could learn from be it Indian or Greek or any other. It is knowledge unbounded which brings about great revolution. Europe, as long as it was bound by Church traditions and encyclicals, remained in darkness and could not progress. But once it broke those chains and liberated itself new knowledge liberated it and Europe, as is well known, benefited from the Arabs whom, H.G. Wells, a noted historian, describes as foster fathers of modern knowledge.

We have to learn much from our history to develop all potential sources of our knowledge and liberate Islam and Muslims from all irrelevant controversies about traditions, and adopt fresh direct approach reflecting deeply on Koran and extracting new sources of knowledge through its divine pronouncement. Otherwise the traditions needless and controversies will continue to drag us backward as it has been happening for few centuries now.

II

Now let us try to construct, in the light of Koran and direct reflections on its teachings the five pillars of civilization. Let us, to begin with, understand what civilization is. Civilization is both material as well as spiritual product of social, cultural and economic interactions among human beings which are fundamentally creative. It can include every thing from intellectual, spiritual to material creations.

It takes centuries of endeavours for a civilization to come into existence. Each civilization may have its own unique character. It may be different from other but certainly not hostile to other. Civilization is nothing if not creative. Thus the civilizations which Islam gave birth to, has its own characteristics and has its own grandeur and glory. Islamic civilizations grandeur has often been reflected in its grand architecture and concepts of social values.

The First Pillar

No civilization can achieve its glory without certain key values without which humanity cannot flourish. These values, as if, form its pillars and give it pulse of life. These values have been enshrined in the Koran and are greatest gift to humanity. The first theological pillar, as we saw it, is faith in unity of Godhood. This correspondingly can be transformed civilizationally as unity of humankind. Thus first civilizational pillar of Islam would be unity of entire humanity irrespective of their beliefs, language, ethnic, or tribal origin or race.

This is clearly stated in the Koran. Thus, if we accept this as the first civilizational pillar of Islam, Islam can play a vital role in bringing universal unity and building beautiful bridges across religious tradition. This pillar also reflects unity and integrity of creation. Allah has created diversity (5:48) not for any discrimination but for testing whether we can live in peace and excel each other in good deeds. Thus the whole creative spirit of the Koran leads to unity of entire humanity (unity should not mean abolishing identities, identities are important for human beings for a sense of belonging). Hence the importance of this first civilizational pillar of Islam.

The Second Pillar

Now we come to second civilizational pillar is 'justice' (called 'adl' by Koran). 'Adi implies balance between extremes, a kind of middle path which leads to better harmony and co-existence. Koran considers justice as very fundamental to establish a good society with stability and peace. All acts of violence we witness in history as well as in modern and contemporary society is due to unjust behaviour of the powerful individual or nations or coercion exercised by certain classes, groups or communities.

The Prophet of Islam, passionately loved justice even before he became messenger of Allah. He had formed, before his prophethood an organization known in Islamic history as *Hilf al-Fudul*, i.e. organization of the meritorious which was meant to ensure justice and this organization was brought into existence by the Prophet when a Yemani merchant complained that his dues are not being paid by certain powerful individuals. The Prophet is reported to have said that 'I would prefer justice over 100 red camels (which is considered as most precious variety of camels).

It is very unfortunate that over a period of time when powerful dynastic empires came into existence justice went into oblivion and repression and coercion became the norm. Even today in the Islamic world justice goes by default and those who do not agree with the rulers or ruling classes face severe repression. During early period of Umayyad rule there were many companions of the Prophet like Abudhar Ghifari, Said bin Musayyab and many others who refuse to submit to rulers if they were unjust or indulged in coercion. Koran strongly condemns zulm (injustice, coercion, unjust use of force) and these companions upheld the Koranic ideals.

However, when there were no more such individuals and companions and zulm became common at the hands of rulers, the Koranic ideal of justice in practice was lost forever. Now, in the modern world, when dynastic rule is on decline and human dignity and rights are order of the day, Muslims should re-establish the Koranic ideal of justice and make it second civilizational pillar of Islam. It will be a great contribution and will enrich Islamic civilization. Justice is a very comprehensive term which will apply justice to poor and needy, gender justice, justice for religious, ethnic, racial and linguistic minorities and in early khilfat period there are shining examples of such justice.

The Third Pillar

The third pillar for an enlightened universal civilization is peace. Peace is no less fundamental to Islam than justice. In fact justice and peace are integral to each other. Some may debate whether peace follows justice or peace first and justice later. It may depend at times depend on the concrete situation. But one thing remains certain justice and peace are integral to each other.

Even if at times peace is given priority, it cannot be stabilized without justice. However, it should also be borne in mind that Islam does not in any sense sloganise either justice or peace. It wants to create concrete conditions so that justice may be realized and peace can be stabilized. Koran, first of all, ensures that all human beings are treated with equal dignity and should be accorded equal rights.

The relevant pronouncements of the Koran are in verses 17:70 and 49:13. These pronouncements were unthinkable in those days. Thus unless we transcend beyond tribal, racial and ethnic bonds to create a concept of universal human dignity, we cannot create peace and stability in this world. And if this universal dignity is accepted and rights accorded to all irrespective of any primordial identity one cannot have peace in the world.

However, Muslims in history did not adhere to these ideal civilizational values of Islam and were often divided along these lines. That is the logic of power, not of civilization. If one examines the modern scene all the violence has been taking place for lack of practice of these civilizational values. Each race, each linguistic group, reach religious group wants to dominate over others and violate their rights and dignity With Impunity And Do Not Hesitate To Attack Other People Or Nations.

Terrorist violence, most dreaded and highly condemnable instrument of revenge, is also reaction to such rape of others rights and launching attacks on others. Powerful countries violate, without any hesitation, their own constitutional ideals to realize ambitions of their ruling classes. After all our progress to modernity or post-modernity, we have failed to honour others rights and dignity and in certain cases invited wrath of those people.

The terrorists in the Islamic world neither represent Islam nor Muslims in any sense of the word. They represent their own rage, anger and feeling of revenge, the evils strictly condemned by Koran. A believer, if he at all is serious about his faith (iman) must fight against these evils and cultivate virtues of forgiveness, taqwa (restrained, responsible and value-based behaviour).

Only such behaviour can lead to justice and peace and it is Muslims who should become harbinger of peace in the modern world, if at all they care for seriousness of their faith. The five theological pillars of Islam which are spiritual in nature also demand the quality behaviour—promoting ma'ruf (what is civilizationally acceptable) and resisting munkar (what is civilizationally destructive).

The Fourth Pillar—Freedom of Conscience

The fourth pillar of Islam would be freedom of conscience. Koran has very succinctly stated this in four words 'There is no compulsion in religion' (2:256). Its brevity is also emphasis of it intensity. No one can practice ones faith without genuine freedom of faith. Nothing can be practiced, in all sincerity, without such genuine freedom. It is right to freely choose which makes one responsible too. Freedom and responsibility are two sides of the same coin.

Unfortunately like other teachings of the Koran, concept of freedom was also totally lost in feudal age. The authorities denied freedom and began to impose their own interpretations coercively and duty (fard) became more fundamental than free choice. One cannot expect monarchs and sultans to allow free choice to their subjects. Now time has come in democratic culture to realize the Koranic concept of freedom of choice.

As deen (religion) is very fundamental and if freedom is given in matter of religion, freedom is a must in lesser worldly things, much more in matters of political governance. Unfortunately it is feudal set up even today in most of the Muslim countries which deny freedom to their own people and gives out impression as if it is Islam which is responsible for denial of freedom.

The rulers may have their own compulsions but it is duty of Muslim intellectuals to come forward and create a culture of freedom not only in Islamic world but also in world in general. Freedom is even keel of any civilization. Even artists cannot create without freedom of choice. Islam had made seeking knowledge compulsory for believers and knowledge cannot have any meaning without concept of freedom. Knowledge and freedom go together. Today knowledge is exploding on global scale and freedom is pillar of strength for quality knowledge.

The Fifth Pillar

The fifth pillar is compassion. Compassion is the one of the greatest attributes of Allah. 'He is Compassionate and Merciful. The Prophet has been described in the Koran as 'mercy of the worlds (rahmat al-

'alamin). Compassion creates inalienable relationship between men and women. It is relation both of suffering and sharing. Modern humans need it all the more.

Globalization stands today on achieving success and material gain. More wealth you gain more successful and respectful you become. It is ruthless competition. No civilization can worth its while if it is based on such criteria of success. It inevitably leads to domination not of individual over other individual but of one nation over the other. It is only sharing and caring and innate spiritual qualities which make human being worthy of herself/himself and compassion is nothing but sharing and caring together and putting ones innate spiritual qualities at the service of all. Compassion has become rarest of rare quality in the modern world and lack of compassion destabilizes any civilization. One of the instruments devised by Koran for realizing this is 'zakat' which is included in five theological pillars. Thus compassion corresponds to this theological pillar of Islam. However, I must say compassion cannot be limited to sharing of wealth but it is intimate relationship of suffering and joy in every respect.

Thus the five civilizational pillars of Islam are equality, justice, peace, freedom of conscience and compassion. These pillars will make Islam the greatest civilizational force in the world.

5

Islam as Religion and Islam as History

It is often alleged that Islam is religion of violence and jihad and is believed to have spread through sword. It is then compared with other religions like Christianity, Buddhism and Hinduism. Such argument is hardly flawless. One basic flaw in such argument is that history of Islam is compared with religious teachings of Christianity. Buddhism etc. and not with religious teachings of Islam. Such comparison between religious teachings on one hand, and, history of another religion (Islam) is unfair comparison. Religious teachings should be compared with religious teachings and religion in history should be compared with religion in history.

History of almost all religions is far from conforming to the teachings of that religion. Religion belongs to basically spiritual and moral sphere and history is product of interplay of several factors — human ambitions, personal interests, wars involving followers of one and followers of another religion and so on. Wars are often fought for reasons different from spreading of religion. The two should not be mixed. Religion can never be spread through might of sword. It is a sheer myth. Religion can spread through conversion of hearts and minds. Religion has its appeal to conscience. One can convert if a religion appeals to ones conscience or if one sees in it an opportunity to promote ones own interest by converting to that religion. But there are very few instances of conversion by inducing fear. Such forcible conversions cannot last long.

Also, be it Islam or Buddhism or Christianity, there are great similarities in their moral and spiritual teachings though there may be significant differences in rituals, concepts, theological statements and laws. Both similarities and differences should be properly understood. However, moral and spiritual truths cannot differ in any significant manner. It is on this ground that the Koran pronounces doctrine of *wahdat-e-Deen* (unity of religions) which has been developed with great clarity by Indian theologians like Shah Waliullah and Maulana Abul Kalam Azad.

We, in this paper, propose to examine causes of differences between Islamic teachings and Islamic history so that we can dispel many myths about Islam and Islamic history. Misunderstandings about Islam cannot be removed by merely quoting certain Koranic verses which represent ideals of Islam; much less one can do so by glorifying history of Islam. One also has to examine objectively and dispassionately history of Islam in the light of complex factors which mould the history.

Islamic Teachings

Islam is one of the great religions of the world which appeared in Arabia and transformed it from a backward tribal society into a great moral society of highest standards. The Arab society before Islam was immersed into superstitions, divided into often mutually antagonistic tribes causing bloodshed and fratricidal warfare, without any moral code and higher spiritual practices. Certain tribes were dominating the socio-economic fabric of society and unscrupulously exploiting weaker sections of society. The poor, the needy and women were reduced to a helpless lot. There was no political authority to enforce any moral and legal obligations. Certain oral traditions held sway as very few people could read and write. Even cadence of Arab poetry was never reduced in writing. They possessed no scripture to provide moral guidance to them.

It was in this vacuum that Islam appeared as a source of moral and spiritual guidance, which was welcomed by weaker sections of Arab society, on one hand, and by those sections of society who were unsatisfied by superstitious practices totally lacking spiritual and moral power. Islam greatly attracted all these sections of society. However, it was vehemently opposed by powerful vested interests who feared loss of their leadership to the Prophet of Islam and sensed great danger to accumulation of their wealth.

The early Koranic verses in Mecca greatly emphasized social and economic justice and powerfully attacked accumulation of wealth and all exploitative practices. Right from Meccan to Medinese period justice (*'adl* and *gist*) remained central to Islamic teachings, Koran also exhorted people of Mecca to be sensitive to sufferings of weaker sections of society. Allah is repeatedly described as *Rahim* and *Rahman* (i.e. Merciful and Compassionate—attributes not much appreciated by the powerful and rich of Mecca.

The rich of Mecca had hardly any objection to concept of one God; they would have gladly accepted it had the Koran not attacked accumulation of wealth and neglect of poor and needy. The Koranic verses of Meccan period attacked, in a way the whole social system in

Mecca and wanted it replaced by a just and sensitive system catering to all the needy and poor, besides widows and orphans. This was not simply acceptable to the Meccan tribal leaders who, besides their tribal supremacy, preferred ostentatious living and exploiting the weaker sections to increase their wealth.

Islam advocated equality and dignity of all human beings attacking any sense of superiority of one tribe over the other and of Arabs over non-Arabs. This was nothing sort of revolution and the ruling tribe of Quraysh to which the Prophet (PBUH) himself belonged, was not prepared to accept at any rate. The Quraysh of Mecca and its ruling strata were determined to maintain its supremacy. It could contemplate no compromise with such revolutionary teachings of Islam and tried to smash this movement in its infancy.

They persecuted followers of the Prophet and even attempted to assassinate him through well-planned conspiracy but failed. The Prophet (PBUH) succeeded in escaping to Madina. He was welcomed with open arms to this city as the Prophet of Islam had successfully acted as peace-maker between the feuding tribes of Aus and Khazraj. Islam firmly stands for justice and peace. One of Allah's names is Salam (peace) and even paradise (*jannah*) is described in the Koran as a place of peace and security. We see wars in history of Islam, not in teachings of Islam (Koran). I am making this point after careful study of the Koran. There are certain pronouncements inducing Muslims to fight *kuffar* of Mecca but it is purely in defence, not at all as aggressors. They are exhorted to fight only when attacked and not to be aggressors. In fact, Koran wants Muslims to be harbingers of justice and peace.

The Koran emphasizes justice to the extent of practicing it even when it goes against one self, ones parents and one's own tribe or community. Peace is possible only when justice is practiced with such rigour. A *mu'min,* a true believer in Islam, has to rigorously believe in these values. In fact a *'mu'min* was nothing but a new human person, a perfect human being (Sufis term it as *insane-e-kaamil).* And a *mu'min* as described by the Koran, has to dedicate himself to truth and patience, justice and peace, a dedicated actor to transform this society into a society free of all evils specially from injustices and oppression and exploitation.

Only such a society can be described as a truly Islamic society. Also, justice is a very comprehensive term in Koran. It is by no means limited to Muslims; all who live in Islamic society, Muslims or not, should avail of it and oppression and exploitation will not be permitted even for a kafir. Koranic verses are very clear on this. Often some verses are taken out of the context to prove otherwise.

There will be no compulsion of any kind for anyone to follow this or that religion. There would be complete freedom of conscience and even a non-Muslim poor and needy will be entitled to all the benefits, even from zakat and *bait al-mal* (state treasury) if it happens to be an Islamic country.

A *mu'min* can never be unjust and oppressor and he is always active and vibrantly working for promoting justice and peace. He/she will courageously speak truth in the face of a tyrant ruler and this has been described by the Prophet (PBUH) as real and most meritorious jihad. If one becomes truthful and constantly struggles for justice, there will hardly be any need for war with sword. War with sword is needed only to fulfil ones greed and Koran attacks greedy behaviour.

A *mu'min* will always stand for weaker sections (described by the Koran as *mustad' ifin)* and fight for them against arrogant and powerful rulers (described as *mustakbirin)*. Prophet Ibrahim fought against Nimrod, a great oppressor and arrogant ruler and hence Koran accepts him as *Hanif*—one who stands for truth and even throws himself into fire lit by Nimrod for the sake of truthfulness.

Moses fought for liberation of Israelis from the oppression and tyrannies of Pharaoh and fought against Pharaoh's arrogance (*istikbar*) and Allah rewarded Moses and punished Pharaoh. Arrogance of power and using ones power for oppressing others is greatest *kufr* and is strongly denounced by the Koran. One can be real *mu'min* if one practices this morality and if one simply accepts Islam without rigorously assimilating this morality one can be Muslim but not *mu'min,* Koran points out.

One can make this world worth living in peace and tranquillity of spirit only when one is equipped with this morality. Only such a *mu'min* can transform this world into a just world free of all conflicts and bloodshed.

Islam in History

It is well known that ideals and religious teachings make history not. The historical dynamics is very complex process and at best is partly determined by religious teachings and ideals. The main factors determining history are motives of historical actors, their interests, culture and social vision, besides religious ideals. Also, no society rises to ethical and moral standards prescribed by religion but drags those standards to its own level.

For example, neither Buddhism could raise society to the level of teachings of Buddha, nor could Christianity to those of Christ. Various interests soon hijack religious establishment to serve their own interests. Islam met similar fate. The Arabs too dragged Islam to their own level instead of Arabs rising to the level of Islam. In fact many pre-Islarnic Arab practices came back and even became party of Shari'a in the guise of *'adaat,* and during Umayyad period there was systematic revival of *Jahiliyya* culture.

The *Jahiliyya* poetry, *Jahiliyya* music and *Jahiliyya* social customs and traditions reasserted themselves and gradually became part of Islamic culture. Many of these practices could be frowned upon by any pious Muslim. However, with the conquests and resultant wealth and luxury swept aside pure ideals. The Koran had stressed need-based living (2:219) and the Prophet of Islam had provided an exemplary model of it. However, with some exceptions many of his companions started living in style and collected huge amounts of wealth.

Wearing of silk and gold was prohibited for men to usher in simple living but after flow of wealth from conquered countries Arabs began to wear costly brocaded attire and gold and silver ornaments. It was for this reason that honest companions like Abu Dharr strongly criticized fellow companions for violating Islamic norms and recited the Koranic verse 9:34 which talks of painful tidings for those hoarding gold and silver and not spending them in the way of Allah. Since Abu Dharr wanted to see strict Islamic norms enforced he came to be disliked by most of Prophet's companions who had taken to easy life and he ended up in the desert where he died and his wife had no means even to provide him with shroud and was buried in his clothes.

Also once Arabs emerged as conquerors the whole dynamics of Arab society changed. Islam then spread to non-Arab areas and now was testing time for the Islamic ideal of equality of all people irrespective of tribal affiliations, nationality, race and colour or language. However, this was not to be in practice. The Arab racial arrogance began to assert soon and non-Arabs came to be discriminated.

Whatever religious ideal, the conquerors always behave as conquerors. Islam being religion of justice and equality, attracted large number of people belonging to weaker sections of society and they primarily embraced Islam in the hope of justice and equality. These weaker sections had suffered intensely at the hands of their earlier masters and came to hate them. They helped Arabs to conquer those territories as they saw Arabs as their liberators which initially indeed they were.

However, it did not take long for the Arabs to behave as other conquerors and began to discriminate against non-Arabs. Arabs had always considered themselves as superior to the Ajam, i.e. non-Arab people. The Prophet (PBUH) was well aware of this and hence he exhorted Arabs repeatedly to shed their sense of superiority and treat all people equally and the Koran also had asserted that all are equal in dignity (17:70) and that all are created equal and their tribal or national differences were only for being recognised (4: 13).

But soon this ideal was lost and Arabs began to display their arrogance of being conquering race and non-Arabs began *mawalis* (plural of *mawla)* clients, not enjoying equality with the masters. Kufa in Iraq as emerged as a military camp and Arabs and non-Arabs, mainly *mawalis* began to live in separate quarters. Umayyad rule was primarily an Arab rule and it deviated farthest from all Islamic ideals. As already pointed out it was during the Umayyad period that the pre-Islamic (*Jahilliya*) culture was revived and Islamic ideals were slowly discarded.

The Umayyads ruled by sheer force of weapons and even did not hesitate to martyr Imam Husain and his 71 relatives and friends who stood by him demanding revival of Islamic ideals and Islamic way of rule. Husain (A.S.) was martyred in Karbala, near Kufa in Iraq which had emerged as the great centre of military power. The Umayyad seat of power was in Damascus but Iraq was an important military centre.

Now all Islamic ideals were violated with impunity—there was no justice, no equality and no compassion. There was nothing but oppression and exploitation. Kufa emerged as centre of various rebellions as it was centre of non-Arab clients. About 60 per cent of its population was non-Arab. Mukhtar, who rebelled against Umayyads and made Kufa the centre of his power, was mainly supported by non-Arab Muslims.

Again it was Hajjaj, the governor of Kufa on behalf of Umayyads, who went down as most ruthless ruler and who slaughtered more than hundred thousand men and put equal numbers in jail. He was most hated by the people and was a terror. What a contrast to the Prophet (PBUH) who did not shed a drop of blood when he entered Mecca after conquering it and pardoned all his enemies.

The Umayyad rule turned out to be most tyrannical as it had usurped power and Umayyads were motivated by their selfish interests and revived Arab culture to assert their superiority. Thus our hypothesis that religion as an ideal is distinctly different from its history whose dynamics is drawn from self-interests of the historical actors. Of course the Islamic discourse continued but actions never conformed to the ideals of the faith.

The Abbasid period which followed the Umayyad period was no different in its dynamics. Its founder came to be known as *saffah* (i.e. one who sheds too much blood) because he carried out slaughter of Umayyad rulers and wiped out its entire dynasty. Even infants were not spared and graves were dug up wherein Umayyads were buried. Only one member of the Umayyads Abdur Rehman could escape somehow who founded his rule in Spain.

Since the Umayyads had ruled over non-Arabs ruthlessly the Abbasid revolution was supported mostly by non-Arab people of Iran and Iranians took their own revenge by slaughtering Arabs settled in part of Iran. Historians have recorded that the Iranian wives killed their Arab husbands. So much intense was hatred of Iranians against Arabs.

However, the Abbasids were hardly any different from the Umayyads. Though they captured power by projecting themselves as children of uncle of the Prophet, they turned out to be no less tyrant and great persecutors of members of household of the Prophet (*ahl al-bayt*). They saw members of household of the prophet as competitors for power and spread net of spies to trace them and kill them. After all power has its own dynamics.

However, it must be said that the Abbasid period turned out to be a period of enlightenment as the Abbasid rulers took great interest in transferring Greek knowledge and philosophy and Indian knowledge and philosophy into Arabic. This was main contrast between the Umayyads and Abbasids. Umayyads power base was entirely Arab and Umayyad rulers were interested only in reviving the pre-Islamic Arab culture and took no interest in non-Arab knowledge.

The Abbasid power base was mainly non-Arab and mainly Persian who had long tradition of learning and culture and hence they helped Abbasid rulers to find house of wisdom (*Dar al-Hikmah*) wherein great treasures of Greek and Indian knowledge and philosophy were translated and disseminated. Also, it was mainly during the Abbasid period that various schools of sharia law came to be compiled.

It was for these achievements that the noted British historian Toynbee described Abbasid state as the universal state of Islam. But that apart, the Abbasid rule was no less tyrannical and ruthless in crushing their political opponents. It faced several rebellions especially the Zanj rebellion which last for over nine years and shook the Abbasid empire. The Zanj were African slaves and mostly worked in salt mines. When exploitation became intolerable they revolted. Similarly the Qaramita revolt took place during this period and Qaramita revolt was more of a peasant revolt communistic in ideal.

Thus these various events in history have nothing to do with Islam and teachings of Islam. Islam is a religion of justice, peace, equality, compassion and freedom of conscience. But these ideals are not reflected in its history as ideals of any religion. Thus teachings of one religion should be compared with teachings of another religion and history of one religion should be compared with history of another religion. But often history of Islam is compared with teachings of Christianity or Buddhism or Hinduism, which is unfair.

6
Islam and Doctrines of Peace and Non-Violence

The various Jehadi movements in Islamic world give an impression as if Islam makes it obligatory on its followers to wage war and solve all problems through war and as if Islam spurns peace and believes peace will only mean hegemony of non-Islamic forces. The media all over the world has almost equated Islam with violence. Also those scholars or journalists who are anti-Islam or have vary superficial understanding of it quote some verses from the Koran to substantiate their point. Firstly, we have to note that media, interested more in sensational and negative reporting headlines news about violent movements and statements of some Muslim leaders, though handful, who advocate jihad.

These jihadi leaders themselves have limited understanding of Islam or have powerful vested interest in taking up arms or making some people fight—in the name of Islam—to promote their interests and legitimise their actions through Koran and hadith. Their statements are taken as true representatives of Islamic position on matters relating to jihad. The media now has coined a term 'jihadi Islam' which is being used repeatedly. The media ignores those who refute such representation of Islam. It is also highly regrettable that some militants use the term 'jihad' even for territorial disputes like Kashmir. Many militant groups in Kashmir claim to be waging jihad. They often kill innocent people in and outside Kashmir for their political benefits without batting an eyelid and pass it off as 'jihad'. Such ruthless killings for political benefits passed off as jihad is bound to have very adverse impact on others. Let alone others even right thinking Muslims condemn such acts as inhuman and totally un-Islamic.

In fact as far as the Koran is concerned the concept of 'jihad' has nothing to do with violence. The Koran does not use this word in any sense of war at all. It is much later usage with which we are not concerned here, it is highly regrettable that not only non-Muslims even Muslims in general think that the Koran uses the term jihad for war and that it is duty of Muslims to wage jihad (i.e. in the sense of war) in the way of

Allah. The word jihad unfortunately has been so misused in the history of Muslims that even an Arabic dictionary *Al-Qamus al-'Asri* by Elias Antoon (Cairo, 1972) gives its meaning as 'militancy, fighting' and *jihad ft' sabil al-din* as 'holy or religious war'. This is how original meanings are distorted through popular practice.

The word jihad is derived from the root 'jahada' and means to exert, to strain, to endeavour and to exert oneself. Similarly the word *'juhud'* means ability, power or strength and also strenuous or utmost efforts. Again it is from this that the word *ijtihad* has been derived which is used for strenuous efforts to re-interpret some Islamic doctrine or utmost creative efforts to apply Islamic teachings to new situations.

However, when the Koran uses this word jihad it has religious implication in as much as it is a struggle which is an act of worship (*'ibadah'*) for which Allah will reward the *mujahid*, i.e. one who strives in the way of Allah (*fi' sabi lillah*). Thus it becomes a religious act performed selflessly only to please Allah and not for any selfish desire. Thus it will not be jihad, though great deal of efforts might have been made, if it is for some personal ends. Any trace of selfish interests will disqualify it for any religious merit and it will not fall within the category of jihad.

We will quote some of the verses from the Holy Scripture of Islam to substantiate our point. Thus we see in 22:78 'And strive hard (*wa'ahidu*) for Allah with due striving. He has chosen you and has not laid upon you any hardship in religion—the faith of your father Abraham.' Had *jahadu* here meant 'war' it would not have been followed by words 'has not laid upon you any hardship in religion.'

Another important verse in the Koran in this regard is 9:24 which is as under:

Say: If your fathers and your sons and your brethren and your wives and your Kinfolk and the wealth you have acquired and trade whose dullness you fear, and dwellings you love, are dearer to you than Allah and His Messenger and striving (jihad) in His way, then wait till Allah brings His command to pass. And Allah's guides not the transgressing people.

This verse which uses the word jihad also implies striving for Allah's sake with ones wealth and every thing one has. He should be ready to sacrifice all the interests to promote a higher purpose in life before which everything one has becomes insignificant.

Agasin in the verse 22:52 the Koran says:

> So obey not the disbelievers, and strive against (*wa jahidhum*) them a mighty striving (*jihadan kabird*).

It is to be noted here that striving here is described as *jihad kabir*—a mighty striving because in adverse circumstances one has to make very great efforts to spread the message of truth. At times such efforts may require to face aggression from the forces of falsehood or those of unbelief and one may have to battle to defend oneself. But we will throw more light on this aspect little later. It is also to be noted that the above verse begins with the words 'So obey not the disbelievers.' which implies that one should not listen to those who do not believe in truth and should strive in mighty way to fight untruth through ones efforts. There is no reference to any kind of violence in the verse neither from the side of disbelievers nor from the side of Muslims but only to mighty efforts to contain untruth.

There is another verse in the Koran (60:1) which is important from our viewpoint. It says, 'If you have come forth to strive (*jihadan*) in my way to seek my pleasure, would you love them (unbelievers) in secret? And I know what you conceal and what you manifest.'

We learn from commentators that this verse was revealed shortly before the Prophet (PBUH) conquered Mecca. The Prophet had not set out from Medina with any intention to invade Mecca. His earlier expedition to Mecca also ended in peace of Hudaibiyah rather than entering the holy city by force. Finally when the Prophet (PBUH) entered Mecca after this verse was revealed he entered quite peacefully. There was no bloodshed and no revenge killing though the unbelievers of Mecca had severely persecuted the Prophet and his followers. But the Prophet did not permit any revenge killing. He generously pardoned all those who approached him for amnesty. And all those who remained indoor were not touched. When one of the followers of the Prophet during this march to Mecca shouted that 'today is the day of fighting', the Prophet immediately corrected him saying 'No today is the day of mercy' and, as pointed out above, the holy Prophet did show mercy to his enemies in abundance.

There are similarly other verses in the Koran which use the word jihad and its derivatives but nowhere it indicates aggression against others. Thus in 9:19 the Koran says, 'Do you hold the giving of drink to the pilgrims and the maintenance of the sacred Mosque equal to (the service of) one who believes in Allah and the Last Day and strives hard (*jahada*) in Allah's way? They are not equal in the sight of Allah.' Here in this verse though a derivative of the word jihad (*jahada*) has been used but the whole context makes it clear that there is no reference to violence of any kind at all.

The verse 49:15 says, 'The believers are those only who believe in Allah and His Messenger, then they doubt not, and struggle hard (*wa jahadu*) with their wealth and their lives in the way of Allah. Such are the truthful ones.' Here too, one can see there is no reference to any kind of violence or war. It only implies striving hard with all sincerity in the way of Allah without any selfish motive and without entertaining any doubt about the mission of Allah and His Messenger.

It is even clearer in the verse 29:6 which says. 'And whosoever strives hard (*jahadu*), strives for himself. Surely Allah is Self sufficient, above (need of) (His) creatures.' Thus one who strives hard for truth it benefits his own self and this striving hard in no way benefits Allah. Allah only shows humans path of truth. In other words He guides them to the right path and for that they have to strive hard.

Thus in all these uses of the word jihad and its derivatives in the Koran it is clear that war is not implied. There are other words like *qatilu, qital,* etc., which have been used in Koran for war. Then the question to be dealt with is whether the Koran, approves of war or discourages violence in absolute sense. And also whether nonviolence in absolute sense is possible in all situations? We would like to throw light on these questions in what follows.

It must be made clear that Koran does permit use of violence in certain given situations but with some strict conditions. Firstly, it disapproves of any kind of aggression which it calls *'udwan. 'Udwan* can also mean transgressing or exceeding the limits. The concept of limits of Allah (*hudud Allah)* is very important. Allah has fixed limits for everything and anyone who transgresses these limits harms himself as well as the society he lives in. Adhering to these limits ensures a balanced, moral and ethical life, which is necessary for meaningful and purposeful life. Allah has fixed limits for use of violence too. Any use of violence transgressing these limits will seriously injure social life and the moral fabric. The concept of limits is very important in Islam and anything transgressing these limits is considered sin. Thus aggression transcends the limits fixed by Allah and is thus sin in Islam.

We will throw light here on the verses permitting *qital* (war) for Muslims. It is to be noted and also as pointed out earlier the word for war in the Koran is *qital* and not jihad. There are several verses on qital in Koran but none permits war of aggression. The one such verse is as under:

> Permission (to fight) is given to those on whom war is made, because they are oppressed. And Surely Allah is able to assist them. (22:39)

Commenting on this verse Maulana Muhammad Ali says in his *Holy Koran* (Lahore, 1973):

> 'According to authentic reports, this is the earliest permission given to the Muslims to fight. There is nothing to show that this verse was not revealed in Makkah. On the other hand, it was owing to this revelation that in the well-known oath of allegiance taken at 'Aqabah, the Holy Prophet required a promise from the Madinah deputation that they would defend him against his enemies even as they would defend their own children. The words in which the permission is granted show clearly that war was first made on the Muslims by their opponents: and secondly, that the Muslims had already suffered great oppression at the hands of their persecutors. The words of the next verse, *those who have been expelled from their homes,* may refer to the emigration to Abyssinia, or to the exodus to Madinah, which commenced soon after the 'Aqabah allegiance was sworn.' (p. 656)

Thus the verse and comment on it clearly shows that permission to wage war was granted only for defence and to ward off aggression by the unbelievers of Mecca and this was the earliest permission granted to Muslims to defend themselves. There is another similar verse in the Koran, which permits to fight in the way of Allah to deliver the oppressed from their oppressors:

> And what reason have you not to fight in the way of Allah and of the weak among the men and the women and the children, who say: Our Lord, take us out of the town, whose people are oppressors, and grant us from Thee a friend, and grant us from Thee a helper. (4:75)

This verse makes it abundantly clear that one must not hesitate to fight for the liberation of the weak, the old, the women and children who are being oppressed. This verse was revealed after many people who could afford to migrate from Mecca to Medinah migrated leaving behind those who had no means to do so and which included amongst others women and children who were being severely persecuted at the hands of the Kuffar of Mecca. These helpless people needed to be rescued from the clutches of their oppressors and this was not possible without lighting against them. This is another reason for permission to fight granted to Muslims by Allah.

Another among early verse requiring Muslims to fight is from 2nd chapter, i.e. 2:190 which says. 'And fight in the way of Allah against those who fight against you but be not aggressors.'

This verse clearly states that light only those who fight you and that do not be aggressors. This is the main outlook of the Koran as far as waging war is concerned. One has to light those who fight you is, one can say, the Koranic doctrine of war. Also, it is conditional that one should not be aggressor and one should not transcend limits.

Another verse in the Koran, which throws light on the conditions on which fight with the enemies is permitted is 9:12. It is as follows:

> And if they break their oaths after their agreement and revile your religion, then light the leaders of disbelief—surely their oaths are nothing—so that they may desist.

Thus another reason for fighting the leaders of disbelief is that they break the agreement after entering into it and also do not stop at that. They also revile the religion of Muslims. In Arabia of the time agreements entered into had great importance and breaking an agreement meant declaration of war as per the then prevailing tribal traditions. The above verse permitting fight with leaders of disbelief who break agreement and revile religion of Muslims should be seen in that sight.

The basic objective of the Koran is to establish peace and sustain it. This could be achieved in those days as today by entering into agreements with the opponents. The Koran specifically forbids war with those who do not break the agreement even if they are non-believers and refuse to accept Islam. Thus we see in the following verse a clear injunction in this regard:

'It may be that Allah will bring about friendship between you and those of them whom you hold as enemies. And Allah is Powerful; and Allah is Forgiving and merciful.

'Allah forbids you not respecting those who fight you not for religion, nor drive you forth from your homes, that you show them kindness and deal with them justly. Surely Allah loves the doers of justice.'

'Allah forbids you only respecting those who fight you for religion, and drive you forth from your homes and help (others) in your expulsion, that you make friends of them; and who ever makes friends of them, those are the wrongdoers.' (90-8-9)

Thus the above two verses from the Koran put forward the doctrine of war as far as Islam is concerned. Respect those who do not fight you for your religion and do not drive you out of your homes. Not only that do not fight them but show them kindness and deal with them justly as

Allah loves the doers of justice. Thus justice and peace is fundamental doctrines and maintain peace and do justice to those who are not Muslims but do not do any harm to you. Thus there is no question of waging war against others just because they are unbelievers and refuse to accept Islam.

The Koran also requires of Muslims that do not refuse any proposal for peace. Thus it says: 'And if they incline to peace, incline thou also to it, and trust in Allah. Surely He is the Hearer, the Knower.' (8:61) Thus it is against the commandment of Allah to reject in proposal for peace from the enemy. As indicated in the previous verse quoted above Allah can create friendship with the enemies. Thus ultimate purpose is to establish peace. War should be considered as an abnormal situation.

Some people quote the verse 9:29 to prove that Islam requires fighting all those who do not accept Islam and imposes *jizyah* on those who refuse to accept Islam. The verse is as under:

> Fighty those who believe not in Allah, nor in the Last Day nor forbid that which Allah and His Messenger have forbidden, nor follow the Religion of Truth, out of those who have been given the Book, until they pay the tax in acknowledgement of superiority and they are in a state of subjection.

Firstly, it has to be kept in mind that this verse is about the people of the Book, i.e. Christians and Jews. However, it should be read in conjunction with those verses quoted above which lay down a principle. It cannot be read in isolation. It is well-known fact of the Islamic history that the Jews who are among the people of the Book had frequently conspired with the leaders of unbelievers of Mecca despite the fact that the Prophet had given them full religious freedom through the covenant of Medina. They broke agreements repeatedly and it became necessary to fight them.

Now the Prophet (PBUH) received reports of the Christian power (Roman empire) preparing to wage war against the Muslims and to subjugate them. The above verse is related to this event. The Prophet set forth on what is known as *Ghazwa-e-Tabuk* the battle of Tabuk. However, when the Prophet came to know that the Roman Empire had still not mobilised its forces, he returned and did not proceed. This again establishes the principle that Muslims cannot take initiative in launching war against the enemy. It will constitute aggression, which is prohibited.

The above verse does not command Muslims to convert others at the point of sword or to wage war to convert others to Islam. The verse lays down that either they should follow their own religion of Truth

(*Din al-Haq*) or follow Islam and its teachings or pay *jizyah* after laying down arms for having committed aggression. *Jizyah* was enforced not to humiliate but to protect those who had laid down arms. It is quite clear from the context of the verse.

Thus it will be seen that peace is very basic to Islam. In fact as pointed out by many scholars and theologians Islam in Arabic means establishing peace as well as to surrender to the Will of Allah. It is this bounden duty of every Muslim to strive to establish peace. Real jihad (striving) is to strive for peace and justice in the world. One of the names of Allah is Salam (peace) and since Muslims are servants of Allah they are above all servants of peace. Their whole life should be spent in the service of peace to fulfil their religious obligation.

Also, one has to bear in mind that the Koranic injunctions about war should be situated in the sixth-seventh century Arabia and its tribal traditions. Absolute non-violence as demanded by some is an Utopia even now and much more so in the pre-Islamic Arabia. The Holy Prophet and his followers had to deal with actual situation as they faced. There were powerful enemies who were out to wipe out Muslims as is obvious from various verses quoted above. The Prophet himself left Mecca when there was real danger to his life and he had to leave the town in great secrecy and after careful planning. Even then the Prophet tried his best to maintain peace in Mecca.

When in Medina he entered into a covenant with Jews and idolaters and gave them full freedom to practice their respective religions. But even then the Jews resented the emerging power of Muslims and conspired with the unbelievers of Mecca and betrayed the Prophet and the community of Muslims. Some idolaters, on the other hand, entered into agreement with the Muslims and honoured the agreement and the Koran prohibited Muslims to fight them as quoted above. The peace of *Hudaybiyah* on most unfavourable terms to Muslims also shows convincingly that as far as possible the Prophet wanted to avoid war.

And if one takes note of all the battles the Prophet had to fight it will be obvious that all were forced on the Muslims. Various Islamic scholars and historians have given details of these battles to show that Muslims were not the aggressors. Sir Syed Ahmad Khan has given such details in his *Tafsir al-Koran* (volume II) while explaining the verses of the Koran on permission to fight. It will convince anyone that though Islam permitted violence for defence in given situation its transcendent vision is of peace and it is transcendent vision which is more important than what is permitted in a given situation. Peace and security of human life is most fundamental to the teachings of the Koran. The Koran says that 'whoever kills a person, unless it be for a man-slaughter or for mischief in the land, it is as though he killed entire humanity and whosoever saves a life as though he has saved entire humanity' (5:250). This is quite an eloquent statement of the Koran to show it is totally against bloodshed or even killing of a single innocent person without any cause.

There is no doubt that there is great deal of violence in history of Islam but it is due more to the vested interests undertaking wars for their own interests misusing some of the verses of the Koran rather than due to injunctions of the Koran. It is also to be borne in mind that there were more internecine wars in the history of Islam than against non-Muslims or for spreading Islam. It would be interesting to study al-Baldhuri's *Futuh al-Buldan* (Conquest of Countries) which mentions various pacts entered into by Muslims with non-Muslims to understand this. As there were wars between various Muslim rulers there were wars with non-Muslims for conquest and political hegemony. Some historians hostile to Islam project these wars as wars for spreading Islam. Such projection of history is, to say the least, quite simplistic and based not on a proper understanding of Islam but on hostility towards Islam. It is injustice both with Islam as well as history.

Similarly the jihadi groups among Muslims today are also doing great injustice to Islam by misusing some of the Koranic provisions in entirely different circumstances. Their urge for violence has nothing to do with Islamic teachings. It is either their impatience or their interests, which make them take up guns where problems could be resolved peacefully and democratically. One should not be misled by their conduct. Islam is and remains religion of peace. Islam wants its followers to devote themselves for peace and worship Allah who is peace embodied (*Salam*).

7
Koran and Other Religions

There is today the question of inter-religious problems in our increasingly globalised world. Never before so many religions coexisted together. Every nook and corner of the world today is religiously plural. At one time Europe was almost mono-religious and so was America and Canada. Today not a single country of Europe can be said to be mono-religious. America and Canada are highly diverse today.

While diversity is a strength in a democratic society it can also become a serious problem in many cases. Thus in almost all the countries we are experiencing inter-religious conflict to a lesser or greater degree. Those who promote conflict in the name of religion do so by quoting scripture and thus they try to hold religious scripture responsible for the conflict. Muslims hold non-Muslims as kafirs, Christians think all non-Christians are pagans and doomed to hell or some Hindus hold Muslims and other non-Muslims as malechhas (i.e. impure).

We would like to throw light here in this article on how Koran views other religions or those who possess no scriptures. Does Koran reject other religions? And who is a kafir? How do we define it? These are important questions and must be satisfactorily answered. Should one be tolerant or intolerant? Should one tolerate or respect other religions or reject them as false? The militant Muslims are extremely intolerant and reject all other faiths as false. They do not want to exist with other religions on equitable basis. Can such an attitude has any basis in the Koran? The militants of course think it has.

In fact as we have repeatedly maintained one has to have a methodology of understanding a scripture. A scripture should not be understood on selective basis and also should not be understood in literal way. It is often rich in symbolic and allegorical language. Also scriptures respond to historical needs and one must keep historical situation in mind in response to which those verses have been revealed. The orthodox or militant Muslims do not keep these things in mind and neither consider historical situation to which the scripture responds nor its allegorical language.

Koran, all 'ulama agree, believes in unity of religions, i.e. *wahdat-e-deen.* It accepts prophets preceding Muhammad (PBUH) as prophets sent by Allah and scriptures brought by them as revealed one like the Koran. Though these scriptures are revealed one but they think Koran has superceded them all and has finality over them all and the ones preceding them are of historical importance. They are no more valid. It is this attitude, which creates problem.

Here we have to examine the Koranic position as to whether such a position vis-Dis other religions is valid. It is true that Koran, according to Muslims, is a final revelation and Muhammad (PBUH) is a last Prophet. But there is nothing new in this position. Followers of all religions have such belief. The Jews do not accept Christ as prophet of God and Christians do not accept Muhammad as Prophet and Zoroastrians did not accept any other prophet after Zoarastra. The very identity of that religion depends on non-acceptance of other prophets.

To understand Koran it is important to note that part of it was revealed in Mecca and part in Medina. The social and religious situation in both the cities were very different. Mecca was a holy city for Arabs even before rise of Islam and had Quraysh tribe as most influential one and certain cans like Hashimites had leadership of religious establishment in their hands.

The Qurayshites were good diplomats and experienced administrators of affairs but had no written scripture or had no prophet or seer in their history. They only followed their tribal customs and traditions. In other words they did not possess any higher or divine truth. There were diverse traditions but no scriptural religion.

Medina, on the other hand, had different religious and social situation. It was religiously a plural society when Mohammad (PBUH) migrated to Medina. There were Jews, tribal Arabs like those in Mecca and Muslims as some tribal Arabs had embraced Islam while the Prophet was still preaching Islam in Mecca. When the Prophet migrated to Medina these three religious groups existed there. Also, Medina, while being multi-religious, was an oasis and had fertile soil. Thus socio-religious situation in Medina was thus quite different.

In Mecca the revelations deals primarily with moral situation and economic justice. In Mecca some were very rich and others very poor and this has created a social malaise and hence the Koran is greatly concerned with it in Meccan period (and this continues in the Medinese period also). The Meccan Surahs (chapters) show great concern for moral degradation and emphasises high morality.

Why the Koran strongly condemns idol worship and shirk (i.e. associating partners with Allah). Is this condemnation absolute and shows its intolerance towards idol worshippers? The orthodox would like to believe us it is so. But if one studies Koran very carefully and in all its complexity, one would realise Koranic position is not so simple as this. It is much more complex.

The Koran attacks idol worship for variety of reasons but not to show its intolerance towards idol worship as some would like to show towards Hindus in India. The Koran attacks idol worship as it had brought much moral degradation and superstitious beliefs. Those Arabs thought the idols were all powerful and their destiny was in their hands. They threw dice (*azlam*) before them to decide this or that way. Their total faith was in these idols as supreme power. These superstitious beliefs made them irrational and impeded their moral growth.

Koran points out that these idols cannot even create a fly, let alone control their destiny (see 22:73). Whereas Allah is all powerful and has created entire universe. Thus the argument is here on a very different plane. In India Dayanand Sarswati, the founder of Arya Samaj employed similar arguments against idol worship. He saw rats eating away the food offerings made to idols and he began to argue that these idols could not ward themselves from these rates, how can then they control destiny of humans.

Thus condemnation of idol worship as prevalent in Mecca was in response to the concrete situation prevalent there and to improve moral situation and create conditions for rational progress. Thus it is not idol worship which is being condemned but the consequences of such worship. The Indian Sufi Mazhar Jan-I-Janan had well understood this and maintained that there is qualitative difference between Arabs' idol worship before Islam and Hindus' idol worship in India. The Arabs worshipped idols as God while Hindus worship it as a means to God since Hindus believe in one God and consider God as nirgun and nirankar (i.e. without attributes and without shape) which is highest form of *tawheed*.

Koran also believes in freedom of conscience and declares *la ikrah fi' al-din*—2:228 (i.e. there is no compulsion in religion). This principle is more important and it is in keeping with this principle that Koran says in chapter 109 that unbelievers can worship the way they do and Muslims will worship the way they do. Thus chapter 109 and verse 2:228 lay down freedom of conscience and principle of co-existence between religions.

The Koran also exhorts believers not to abuse others' gods lest they should abuse Allah out of ignorance and it also states that for every people Allah has made their deeds fair-seeming (6:109) and it is Allah who will decide about their deeds. Thus leave final decision to Aliah and people should leave with tolerance and mutual cooperation. There are many verses to this effect in Koran see, for example, 2:148 and 5:48. Normally these verses end with excel each other in good deeds. The matter of worship, dogmas and beliefs vary and leave it to Allah to decide and it is for people to live in harmony.

Nowhere Koran teaches intolerance, much less bloodshed in the name of religion as many extremist Muslims and non-Muslims believe. As far as people of the book (*ahl al-kitab*) are concerned Koran requires Muslims to respect them and states that it is the duty of all believers to show equal respect to all prophets named or not named in Koran (see verses 150–2).

The word kafir means one who hides the truth and people of Mecca who opposed the Prophet (PBUH) and persecuted him were denounced as kafirs because they refused to accept the truth and actively opposed the Messenger of Allah. Since people of Mecca did not possess any scripture nor any prophet had come there was need for the message of truth which was brought by Mohammad but refused by the tribal chiefs of Mecca including Prophet's own close relatives and were condemned as kafirs. They refused to see the light of knowledge and wanted to remain stuck to customs and traditions harmful to the society.

That however does not mean that any non-Muslim will automatically should be dubbed as kafirs. Any non-Muslim who possesses truth brought be their own prophets and seers cannot be dubbed as kafirs as they possess their own truth. And the Prophet (PBUH) entered into alliances with Bedouin tribes who had not entered into Islam and the Koran exhorts Muslims to honour the treaty with those tribes. It clearly means that Muslims can form alliances with those people who are not believers in Islam.

II

Medinese Situation

The situation in Madina was somewhat different as pointed out above. There were three different religions present, i.e. Islam, Judaism and pre-Islamic paganism. The Prophet (PBUH) treated them on par and gave followers of every religion full freedom in keeping with the verse 2:256. It is popularly known as Mithaq-I-Madina. It was on the lines of modern multi-religious state in which people of all religions are free to practice their religion. Yet they constitute one political community.

Though Islam claims to be final religion, according to Muslims, superseding other religions, it never suppressed other religions. On the other hand, it allowed all religions to coexist. Some maintain that Islam clashes with other religions in its teachings and hence for Muslims those religions are not true and so how can it coexist with other religions. No one can deny that there are significant differences between Islam and other religions. For that matter no two religions can be same.

But coexistence does not require sameness, or even similarities. It requires tolerance and respect for others and the Koran precisely emphasises this. Its words *fastabiqu al-khayrat* (i.e. excel each with the other in good deeds) are very significant in this respect. This world is diverse because it is divine design and according to the Koran this diversity has been created to test us whether we can live in peace and harmony or act according to *fastabiqu al-khayrat* (5:48).

According to the Koran all places of worship—churches, synagogues, temples and mosques are to be protected as in all these places Allah is remembered (22:40). These places of worship are centres of divine remembrance whatever the way of remembering Allah. On no account Islam falsifies other religions but declares that Islam has come to reconfirm truth brought by other prophets of God. We confirm, Koran says, what exists before see 2:97, 3:3, 3:50, 4:47, 5:46 and so on.

Thus religion should not become cause of conflict, Also, great Islamic scholars have maintained that Koran promotes the belief in wahdat-i-din (unity of religion). From India the eighteenth century Islamic thinker Shah Waliyullah and twentieth century Islamic scholar Maulana Abul Kalam Azad have discussed the theme of unity of religion on the basis of Koran. In fact Maulana Azad has devoted one full volume of his Tarjuman al-Koran on this theme.

There should not be any tension between Islam and other religions. If there is tension it is not because of teachings of Koran but activities of Muslims and Muslim organisations, Islam does not even believe in aggressive conversion campaigns. It clearly lays down that you should call others to the ways of Allah with wisdom and goodly words and argue with them in the best manner (16:125).

Since there is no compulsion in religion no one can be compelled to convert and conversion campaigns often lead to tension between different religions. Even Prophet's duty is to deliver the message (of Allah) and no more. He should not despair if people do not accept. There are many verses to this effect, i.e. 3:20, 5:92, 5:99, 13:40, etc. Thus no Muslim should coerce or induce any one to convert. All he/she can do is to deliver the message or explain the teachings of Islam and leave rest to the person to decide, to accept or reject.

There are many Da'wah (mission) organisations who enthusiastically preach to on-Muslims and even compete in countries like Africa, with Christian missionaries leading to inter-communal tensions. But this is certainly not the requirement of the Koran. Koran stresses co-existence rather than competition with other faiths. And since Koran requires deliverance of message with wisdom and goodly exhortation, there should not be condemnation of any other religion. It will defeat the very purpose.

Koran being divine very well appreciates the fact that religious belief is matter of inner conviction and inner conviction can be created only through deeper knowledge and persuasion. Coercion cannot lead to deeper conviction and without deeper conviction religion has no meaning. That is why Koran advises believers to be extremely polite and convincing in the matter and it is better to be tolerant than engage in polemics. Religious polemics has no place in the Koranic teachings.

But such polemics did take place in history of Islam and we also find confrontation with other religions. However, that is not because of religion but more because of struggle for power. Religion often becomes effective tool for power. Though Koran accepts validity of religions of people of the book and message of Moses and Christ, there were clashes between Jews and Muslims and Christians and Muslims.

The Crusades also led to much bloodshed between Muslims and Christians but a deeper study will show that these were territorial and not religious wars. It is totally wrong to think that Muslims spread out with Koran in one hand and sword in the other to convert the world to Islam. There can be nothing more untrue than such a perception. This perception is a result of propaganda than reality.

In fact Sufis, who kept their distance from power structure coexisted with other faiths in perfect harmony. They had no ambition for power and hence understood the real significance of the hadith by the Holy Prophet that best jihad is speaking truth in the face of a tyrant ruler (afdal al-jihad kalimatu haqqin 'inda sultanin jairin). Those who have political ambitions try to prove that truth lies only in their religion and others follow untruth. Such polemics then generate bitterness and conflict.

One should always take care to distinguish between religious (theological) conflict and political conflict. We often confuse between the two and drag religion in political conflicts or settle political scores by invoking religious differences. If we can understand this difference much confusion can be removed. Today people often do not understand this difference and support those who exploit religious issues for political purposes and animosity results between two communities.

If Muslims understand the Koranic perspective for other religions they will have no feeling of hostility towards other religions, however different they may be. But the problem is Muslims themselves do not know the Koranic perspective and often they go along with the extremist Muslims who selectively quote the Koran to achieve their political ends. It is therefore duty of the moderate Muslims to challenge the extremists and put forward the correct Koranic perspective.

For this it is also necessary that moderate Muslims themselves should take pains to study the Koranic perspective first hand and spread it with the same sense of mission as extremists have. The moderates, however, are not able to develop such sense of mission and become drawing room critics. Surprisingly, they often support extremists by thinking that there is tension between Islam and other religions and peaceful coexistence is not possible or that there is conflict between the Koranic and other religions.

This means that extremist propaganda affects moderates themselves and this further strengthens extremists' hands. The media too is either highly prejudiced against Islam and hence takes extremists' claim seriously, or is ignorant about Koranic perspective and think Koran is hostile to other religions and all non-Muslims are 'kafirs' and that Islam totally lacks tolerance.

Islam is the second biggest religion in the world and if moderate Islam as per Koran is popularised, it will give tremendous boost to world peace. The terrorist violence has not only distorted image of Islam but also has resulted in disturbing world peace. Though what terrorists react by and large on what US rulers do but terrorist reaction is not the right way or does not have Koranic endorsement. Killing innocent people, whatever the reason, can never be endorsed by Koran.

The moderates will have to come out of drawing rooms, study the Koran seriously and spread its message of peace and harmonious coexistence with a sense of mission. Nothing less will help. In doing this we will not only be spreading message of Islam and but also strengthen world peace.

8
On Sufi Approach to Islam

Historically speaking sufism appeared in Islam towards the end of first century of the Islamic calendar. Some sufis of course maintain that the Prophet of Islam himself is the mainspring of sufism and they draw inspiration from him for their spiritual and devotional practices. Also, there is debate about the meaning of the word sufi. Some maintain that it is derived from the word suf, which means coarse wool as sufis used to wear coarse woollen overall. Some others maintain that it is derived from the Greek word meaning knowledge and wisdom. Whatever its meaning the word sufi has been widely used in Islamic history for a distinct set of doctrines and practices within the Islamic framework. This school of thought had wide following among the Muslims.

The sufi Islam, it is interesting to note, is love-oriented while the theological Islam practised by the 'ulama is mainly law-oriented. The sufi God is God of love whereas the concept of God in theological Islam is a punishing God for violation of Islamic law. It is for this reason that masses of Muslims have been greatly attracted by the sufi Islam than the theological Islam which has intellectual appeal and orientation. The sufi Islam, on the other hand, has spiritual and emotional appeal. While theological Islam is rigorous and rigid in approach the Sufi Islam is flexible and soothing to the soul. While theological Islam lays stress on practice of shari'a law, the sufi Islam lays stress on devotion to God.

It does not, however, mean that sufis are negligent of shari'a practices, at least not all. There are several schools within the sufi Islam. Some follow the shari'a provisions quite rigorously and there are some which are on the other extreme who do not give much importance to shari'a practices. And there are some who are in between and give importance to both devotion and law. In India Chishti school has been very popular and all major sufi saints in India have been from this school. The sufis of this school follow the doctrine of what is called *wahdat al-wujud* postulated by the great sufi saint Muhi al-Din Ibn-i-Arabi.

Ibn Arabi has exercised great influence on sufis of India as his doctrine of *wahdat al-wujud* is quite accommodative and flexible in many ways. According to this doctrine the real existence *wujud* is that of Allah whereas all of us are its manifestations. In fact entire universe is His manifestation. Thus such a doctrine leads to demolition of barriers between people of one religion and the other. This doctrine brought Hindus and Muslims together in India and helped evolve a composite culture. The Chishti saints followed this doctrine and thus came very close to people of other faiths in various regions in India.

The basic teaching of this school of sufi thought is what has been called *sulh-i-kul,* i.e. peace with all. Thus peace, friendship and love have been at the centre of this school of sufism. Maulana Rum whose *masnavi* (an epic poem running into several volumes) is considered by many as the Koran in Persian, puts great stress on love and peace in his *masnavi.* In one of his couplets he says you have come to effect union (between people) and not for separating them. He also says that dogs fight for the bones and the wise take the narrow meaning thereby that it is not dogmas which contain the truth of religion but it is essence of religion, its kernel which is important. Maulana Rum was one of the greatest sufi thinkers of Islam and he has inspired and continues to inspire generation after generation of Muslims and others. Maulana Rum's whole emphasis has been on love and union.

The Sufis also lay great deal of stress on meditation and reflection (*muraqibah*) which drew them closer to Indian traditions. But unlike Indian tradition they did not practice complete renunciation. They married and had children as per the practice (*sunnah*) of the Prophet but never went near the power centre. They kept their distance from power centres. The 'ulama, though not all, were generally drawn close to power centres and often did their bidding.

The sufis were closer to the people than to the rulers. In fact rulers were often tempted to be seen in their company to acquire some legitimacy. The noted sufi-cum-theologian Al-Ghazzali says that one should not look at the face of tyrant and unjust sultan and even if it becomes necessary one should turn ones face away while talking to such a ruler.

Nizamuddin Auliya was one of the great sufi saints of India during the sultanate period and he saw the times of several sultans but did not pay court to anyone. When he consistently refused to go to the court Sultan Jalaluddin Khalji sought an interview with Nizamuddin Auliya, which was politely refused by him. The Sultan then thought of visiting the *khanqah* (hospice) without informing the Shaikh (i.e. Nizamuddin). 'My house has two doors', remarked the Shaikh. 'If the Sultan enters by one, I will make my exit by the other.' (see Khaliq Ahmad Nizami. *Shaikh Nizamuddin Auliya*, Delhi. 1991, p. 105)

And when the Sultan planned a surprise visit to the Shaikh, Amir Khusrau, his celebrated disciple reported this to Nizamuddin Auliya and Nizamuddin left for visiting the tomb of his spiritual mentor Baba Farid at Ajodhyan to avoid meeting the Sultan. Thus it is obvious how sufis of the eminence of Nizamuddin Auliya maintained their distance from power centres. And it was for this reason that they were so dear to the common people. Though there are always exceptions to the rule most of the sufis maintained distance from rulers. They did not want religion to be misused by rulers. Religion, for these sufis, was not a means for acquiring power and influence, but it was meant for their spiritual needs.

These sufi saints were greatly respected by the common people as they assimilated local culture and even local customs. In other words they believed in acculturation. Baba Farid was among the great Chishti sufis of north India. He was great scholar of Persian and Arabic but he wrote his poetry in Punjabi language. In fact he is considered as the first Punjabi poet and his verses have been quoted by Guru Nanak in his Adi Granth. He is held in great respect by Sikhs and there is Baba Farid Chair in Punjab University-Chandigarh.

Thus Khaliq Ahmad Nizami writes about Baba Farid,

> Sheikh Farid's ideal of life flowed from his concept of religion which was revolutionary in its contents and dynamic in its potentialities. His God was neither a theological myth not a logical abstract of Unity, but an all embracing personality present in his ethical, intellectual and aesthetic experience and furnishing the inspiration for creating an ideal realm of values in a distressed and struggling world. It made him citizen of that Universal society in which God is the supreme Intelligence and all human beings His manifestations. He sought to reach the creator through His creation and identified religion with service of humanity. Again and again he emphasised the fact that faith in God means 'love of His creatures' (see K.A. Nizami, 'Shaikh Farid-ud-din Ganj-I-Shakar', in Gurbachan Singh Talib, ed., *Perspectives on Sheikh Farid,* Patiala, 1975, p. 30).

All sufis believed in non-violence and Baba Farid particularly so. He believed in non-violence as the only way to solve the differences in social life. Through his behaviour he demonstrated, maintains Nizami, that pacifism and non-violence is the cult of strong and not the defence of the weak. Nizami quotes a verse of Baba Farid included in the Guru Granth Sahib as under:

> Farid return thou good for evil,
> bear no revenge in thy heart:
> Thus will thy body be free of maladies,
> And thy life blest.

The Guru Granth contains 112 Shlokas of Baba Farid which he wrote in Punjabi. The burden of these Shlokas is divine love, need for purification of inner life, value of penitence in spiritual progress, ephemeral character of human existence and other similar subjects. 'Striking metaphors', says K.A. Nizami, 'mostly borrowed from the atmosphere around, add to the effects of these *Shlokas*. They seem to be the gushes of a heart overflowing with divine love and constitute a valuable treasure of the Indian historical heritage.' (*ibid.*, pp. 33-4).

Nizamuddin Auliya was his celebrated disciple and lived simple life and around whom thousands of people flocked. Nizamuddin Auliya respected local customs and traditions and never held other religions to be inferior to his own. One day when he was going along bank of the river Jamuna he saw some Hindu women bathing in the holy river and worshipping sun. His celebrated disciple Khusraw was with him and he said addressing Khusraw: 'do not hold these women in contempt; they are also worshipping Allah though in their own way'. And he recited a verse from the Holy Koran, in support of his view: 'For everyone has a direction in which he turns (himself), so vie with one another in good works.' (2:148)

Thus Hazrat Nizamuddin stressed here that it is not the method of worship, according to the Koran, but the good deeds which matter most. Thus the sufis respected the local rituals to promote love and friendship between the people. They did not pass the judgements of right and wrong. For them love and service were more important than the method of worship. The Holy Prophet is also reported to have said that it is more meritorious to feed a hungry widow than to pray whole night.

The sufi saints never dismissed other religions out of hand. Nor did they ask anyone to convert to Islam though thousands converted to Islam at their hands. They were seen as role model by the people. It was their character and devotion which attracted people to the religion they practised not any intellectual argument or even persuasion. Preaching Islam to others was not their mission. They showed equal respect to all high and low in the society. Many people from low castes who were treated with contempt by upper class and upper caste people flocked around sufis as they found respect for human dignity. This was one reason why large numbers of dalits have believed to have converted to Islam without even being asked to do so.

It is a great myth to say that Hindus converted to Islam on the point of sword. No ruler was interested in converting Hindus through coercion, as it would invite the wrath of Hindus. Let alone converting Hindus to Islam these rulers were not even prepared to ban their religious processions as it would anger the Hindus. It is for this reason that very few upper caste Hindus converted to Islam and only dalits did.

Many orthodox 'ulama differed from sufi ways and opposed their liberal attitude. It is well known that Abul Fazl and Faizee, both sufi brothers were persecuted by orthodox 'ulama because of their liberalism. It is later that they went to Akbar's court and Akbar was greatly influenced by them and became liberal under their influence.

The sufis never tried to even dissuade converted Muslims from giving up their pre-Islamic customs and traditions. It is for this reason that most of the Indian Muslims, particularly in rural areas and small towns even today practise with great enthusiasm all their local pre-Islamic customs and traditions. We will throw some light on this aspect little later. The orthodox 'ulama on the other hand engaged themselves in purifying Indian Islam of pre-Islamic influences.

Some 'ulama like Sheikh Ahmed Sirhindi better known as Mujaddid Alf-i-thani (the renewer of second millennium) vehemently opposed the sufi doctrine of *wahdat al-wujud* which maintained, as pointed out earlier, that real Being is Allah and we are all His manifestations. This approach resulted in bringing about greater unity among peoples of different religion, race and tribe. Sheikh Ahmad Sirhindi preached the doctrine of what he called *wahdat al-shuhud*, i.e. unity of witnessing. Thus he maintained that we are not manifestation of One Being but it is only an appearance, not reality.

Sheikh Sirhindi attacked many practices among the Muslims, which he condemned as un-Islamic. Thus in one of his letters written to a lady Sufi (letter from volume III, number 41) deals mainly with the pledge of women (*bay' at al-nisa'*) at the time of Muhammad. Sirhindi expresses his conviction that women are more prone to blameworthy actions common among men and then proceeds to describe the innovations common among Indian Muslims, chiefly women, in his time. Because of their utter stupidity women pray to stones and idols and ask for their help. This practice is common, especially when small pox strikes, and there is hardly a woman who is not involved in this polytheistic practice. Women participate in the holidays of Hindus and Jews they celebrate

Diwali and send their sisters and daughters presents similar to those exchanged by the infidels.'

The implications of the doctrine of *wahdat al-shuhud* were quite grave as it emphasizes the superiority of people of one religion over the other and for that reason that religion should be kept 'pure' and divested of all other influences. Thus the Sheikh spent his energies in purifying Indian Islam. However, his influence never spread among the masses. He had greater influence among a section of the Muslim ruling classes, nobles and courtesans. It is interesting to note that the Chishti saints had the greatest amount of influence in India. The other sufi schools remain confined to limited circles. The Chishti saints were popular because they were more liberal and accommodative in spirit. They accommodated others rather than rejecting.

The Chishti saints, on the other hand, not only accommodated but even adopted the customs and traditions of others. Take Meo Muslims, for example. The Meo Muslims, along with nikah also go for circumambulations around fire. They celebrate not only Eid but also Diwali with same enthusiasm and follow all customs and traditions prevalent in their area. They converted to Islam but never gave up their pre-Islamic roots. It is regrettable that even V.S. Naipaul never understood this. He condemns Islam in his books, particularly in *Among the Believers* that Islam while converting people robs them of their pre-Islamic culture. Unfortunately Naipaul never bothered to study any Muslim society from sociological and anthropological angle. He would not have otherwise made such sweeping statements.

Many sufi saints themselves adopted prevailing cultural practices without much hesitation. Sheikh Muhammad of Maharashtra, for example. He not only wrote on sufism in Marathi but translated sufi terminology into Marathi language. He was greatly respected in Maharashtra and was even compared with Gnaneshwar for his liberal compositions on sufi Islam in Marathi.

There is also the case of Hamiduddin Nagauri who was a sufi saint from Nagaur, Rajasthan. He became strict vegetarian and also always kept a cow with him. He in fact lived like a Hindu peasant does. He was disciple of the renowned Sufi saint Sheikh Moinuddin Chishti of Ajmer. Hamiduddin Nagauri wrote a code of conduct for sufis with the approval of his master. Some of the salient points of the code are as under: (1) one should not earn money; (2) one should not borrow money from others; (3) one should not reveal to anyone nor seek help from anyone if one has eaten nothing for seven days; (4) if one gains plenty of food, money, grain or clothing, one should not keep anything until the following day and (5) having fulfilled these conditions one should regularly fast during the day and pray during the night.

One sees that this is very close to practices of Hindu seers. Buddhist bhikus and munis. They did not condemn practices of others as the orthodox ulama did describing them as practices of infidels. Khwaja Hasan Nizami in his valuable book *Fatimi Da'awat-e-Islam* has given numerous examples of Sufis adopting the local customs, rituals and traditions. He quotes various instances of certain sects of Islam like the Niazaris and others even adopting the symbol of Om as when written in Sanskrit with slight variation it resembles 'Ali, as written in Arabic. The Imamshahi sect even projected Ali, the Prophet's son-in-law as the 10th incarnation of Vishnu. (see Khwaja Hasan Nizami, *Fatimi Da 'wat-e-Islam,* Delhi, 133S ah).

Khwaja Hasan Nizami describes various rituals around the grave of sufi saints which were borrowed by the sufis from the local Hindu rituals of temples. He says that the circumambulation around the grave of a sufi shaikh was nothing but circumambulation (*parikrama*) around the idol in the temple. The ritual of offering *sandal* and flowers to the grave, he maintains, has been borrowed from similar practices among Hindus. The idol has been replaced by the grave of a sufi Saint. Hasan Nizami describes all these rituals adopted from Hindus in detail in his above book.

Hasan Nizami also describes in some details a Hindu sect called Pranami Panth which is half Hindu, half Muslim. He even met their Mahant Maharaj Rangi Lal in Saurashtra (which was then known as Kathiawad). Their holy book is called *Qulzum Sarup* Generally it is referred to by common people as *Kullum sharif* (*Kalam Sharif*). The Khwaja says that this Book contains shlokas from Geeta as well as verses from the Koran and also some hadiths. There are also some extracts from other holy scriptures.

The Pranam Panthis are spread over several parts of India. Apart from Gujarat they are found in Bihar, Bundelkhand in UP, in various cities of Punjab, etc. According to this Panth Krishna Maharaj and Prophet Muhammad are one and the same. First Krishna Maharaj appeared and then he appeared in the Arab world. It is Pran Nath Maharaj who was a disciple of Deepchand Maharaj who wrote *Qulzum Sarup*. Pranamis believe it is a revealed scripture. The Pranam Panthis are great devotees of Muhammad (PBUH) and call themselves as real believers and think Muslims are heretics. They also believe that the Prophet Muhammad is the last prophet. It is interesting that Pranamis apply *tilak* on their forehead and also wear *geneo* (sacred thread).

We do not want to go into details of this interesting sect here. What it shows that there are several such sects, which adopted beliefs and practices from Islam and Hinduism in India also selectively from other religions. The reality is very complex. The sufi approach to Islam was very flexible and accommodative. Thousands in India became Muslims because of such an approach. The 'ulama who adopted rigid ideological approach never succeeded in converting people to Islam.

Thanks to these sufi saints that our culture at popular level is a composite culture. There is no doubt that the ruling classes also collaborated with each other and created composite culture but at the people's level it is the sufis who created composite culture and even composite religious rituals as examples of Meos and Pranam Panthis show. There never was communal polarisation as we have today.

9
Love in Sufi Poetry

Ghazal poetry in Arabic/Persian and Urdu in general and sufi poetry in various genres is basically, a love poetry. Ghazal, which is an Arabic word, has several meanings, one of which is to talk to ones beloved. Many Sufis wrote in ghazal form and many others used other forms like *masnavi* (duet). Sufis belonged to many *silsilas* (different schools) of thought. These schools differed on certain issues but were one on core issues.

Islam as such became part of ruling establishment and hence in popular and even theological stance, came to be associated with power and hence general people began to believe that in Islam religion and politics cannot be separated. This formulation, though not correct, became people's belief. This association with power politics began to influence religious outlook.

As there was complete legal vacuum in Arab society before Islam, a whole new legal system had to be worked out based on Koranic pronouncements and Holy Prophet's sayings and doings (called Sunna). And since political rule had to be based on some written law, Islamic legal corpus called sharia developed by several Imams, both Sunni and Shi'ah, became central to Islamic establishments.

The Sufis, on the other hand, were basically spiritual personalities and did not like association with any political establishment and wanted to spend their time on matters spiritual, controlling their desire, concentrating on inner discipline and spending their time on remembrance (dhikr) of Allah. Though they did not renounce world altogether as renunciation of the world is not preferable (though not forbidden), their involvement with matters worldly was minimum.

Psychologically speaking when you want to concentrate on someone, you end up developing unbreakable attachment and this leads to intense love of, and involvement with, that person. And in case of Sufis, that person was none other than Allah. Thus sufi poetry is full of love of

Allah. And to express their love of Allah, Sufis had to use existing genres of poetry, i.e. ghazal or masnavi.

And traditionally love in poetry represented love of a human beloved. Sufis also had to use existing human terminology while expressing their love of Allah. In other words, Allah had to be personified though Allah is beyond all our perceptions and cannot be likened with human form. Thus in sufi poetry though beloved appears to be human but it is due to constraints of human language and actual beloved is Allah. Thus one finds sufi poetry deeply immersed in love of Allah.

Thus it will be seen that there is basic difference in the concept of sufi's and theologian's Allah. While Sufis stress love of Allah and invoke this love again and again, central to theologian's Allah is fear. A theologian always asks us to fear Allah and consequences of disobedience, sufi asks us to love Allah and be immersed in love of Allah.

This difference is quite understandable. A theologian, directly or indirectly, is associated with ruling power and has to be concerned with maintaining order in the society and those who are entrusted with enforcement of law and order; he has to create fear of authority. This probably explains why theologian is so concerned with fear of Allah as Allah also personifies authority.

The Koran was of course contains both types of verses—fear of Allah and love of Allah as the situation of Arab society was very complex. There was no ruling establishment and society allowed often licentious behaviour within the limits of tribal customs and traditions. However, new commercial relations which were breaking tribal customs, needed to mind more complex social order and hence Koran and Sunna met this demand by giving clear legal instructions.

In a tribal society where social order was the last thing on their mind, a strong centralized state structure emerged within few decades of Prophet's (PBUH) death. The legal structure of Islam also developed in this political atmosphere and hence its emphasis on fear of Allah.

The sufis, on the other hand, as pointed out, were more concerned with inner spiritual being and hence their priority was love of than fear of Allah. Though fear of Allah was not totally absent in them, priority was of love, not fear. Thus we find the popular legend about Rabi'ah Basri, a noted woman sufi saint, that one day she was seen carrying bucket of water in one hand, and a burning rag wrapped around a rod, in the other.

When someone asked her Rabi'ah why are you carrying water in one hand and fire in the other, she replied she wants to put out fire of hell with this bucket of water and so that people do not worship Allah for fear of hell and to set fire to paradise so that people do not worship

Him for greed of paradise. Thus the message was that Allah should be worshipped for pure love, nothing else.

Unfortunately today due to political struggle between a section of Muslims and Western powers, particularly represented by the USA, violence and fear has come to be associated with Islam. This uni-dimensional approach to Islam has done all the damage to an understanding of the rich and complex world of Islam. Islamic civilization is far too rich and carries various trends within it.

Scholars like Professor Huntington by writing *Clash of Civilizations* has created one-dimensional Islam to be condemned as promoting violence and terror. Thus in the Western world scholars like Huntington have done more damage to Islam to fulfil US political ambitions. One needs to focus on other aspects of the rich heritage of the world of Islam. Sufi Islam is an Islam of love and universal humanity. We must come out of our obsession of political Islam. Political Islam is advocated and practiced by a small section of Muslim elite whereas Sufi Islam inspires the silent majority of Muslims. The silent majority of Muslims is as much victim of political Islam.

We would throw light, in this article, on sufi Islam and its doctrine of love. The great Sheikh popularly known as Ibn Arabi who was born in Spain (ad 1165) and died at the ripe age of 76 in ad 1240 was founder of famous sufi school known as School of Wahdat al-Wujud (Unity of Being). The real being, according to this school is one and entire creation is His manifestation. This is most universal in its outlook and demolishes all barriers of religion, race and nations.

The Sheikh-i-Akbar (the Great Shiekh) as he is known as, was a great poet and profuse writer and said to have left some 800 works, though not all authenticated. Love was central to his philosophy and understanding of religion. Thus he writes in one of his poems: I believe in religion of love. Whatever direction its caravans may take. For love is my religion and my faith (*hubbi dini wa shari'ati*).

In one place he writes:

> Now I am called the shepherd of gazelles,
> Now a Christian monk,
> Now a Zoroastrian,
> The Beloved is Three, yet One;
> Just as the three are in reality one.

In his poem 'My Heart Can Take on Any Appearance' he writes: 'My heart can take on any appearance. The heart varies in accordance with variations of the innermost consciousness. It may appear in form as a gazelle meadow, a monkish cloister, an idol-temple, a pilgrim Kaaba, the tablets of the Torah for certain science, the bequest of the leaves of the Koran.

My ditty is the debt of Love, I accept freely and willingly whatever burden is placed upon me. Love is the love of lovers, except that instead of loving the phenomenon, I love the Essential. That religion, that duty, is mine, and is my faith. A purpose of human love is to demonstrate ultimate, real love. This is the love which is conscious. The other is that which makes man unconscious of himself.

Yet in another poem 'While the sun's eye rules my sight', he says:

> While the sun's eye rules my sight, Love sits as sultan in my soul,
> His army has made camp in my heart
> Passion and yearning, affliction and grief,
> When his camp took possession of me I cried out as the flame of desire burned in my entrails.
> Love stole my sleep, love has bewildered me, Love kills me unjustly, and
> I am helpless, Love has burdened me with more than I can bear
> So that I bequeath him a soul and no body.

Thus we find many more such verses penned by Ibn Arabi which indicate that love is most fundamental in his understanding of relations between human and the Ultimate Being. He clearly distinguishes between phenomenon and essential. He reaches for Essential, not phenomenon. Phenomenon is bound to vary but essential is one. Ghalib, the great Urdu poet, who was also essentially a sufi in his approach, says in one of his verses: '*Nahin kuch subh-o-zunnar ke phande meinh geerai, Wafadari men hai sheikh-o-barehman ki azmaish*'.

It means there is not much in the knot of rosary or thread (which a Brahmin wears) but real trial of Sheikh (a Muslim priest) and Brahmin (a Hindu priest) is in their loyalty to what they believe in, i.e. God. Rosary, a Muslim symbol and thread, a Hindu symbol, differ in form but the Essential, the Ultimate Being, whom they worship, is One and their trial is in not carrying a rosary or wearing a thread but in their steadfast love or loyalty to God.

This was approach of Sufis to religions. They were not enamoured of the form but were concerned with the contents. Maulana Jalaluddin Rumi, who is known for his seminal work called Mathnavi M'anavi which many Muslims considered as Koran in Persian, also lays emphasis on love. He was, to begin with, a great 'Alim and a jurist, had place of honour in the court of Quniya, a town which his father migrated to.

The Maulana was greatly revered as an 'alim and jurist. He had thousands of disciples who would regularly attend his sermons. But once he came into contact with a sufi Shams Tabriz from Syria, it all changed. Shams Tabriz caste his spell on him and he was completely transformed from an 'alim and a jurist issuing fatwas to a sufi absorbed and immersed in love and leading life of ecstasy.

Afzal Iqbal, a noted scholar of Islam, writes in his *Life and Work of Jalaluddin Rumi*, 'A person who was once considered the last word on religion by his own generation, and who had, according to his own light, ruled out music as undesirable, had now become so enamoured of it that he threw all "decorum" to the winds, listened to music with rapt attention at odd hours of the day and danced in ecstasy.'

Afzal then quotes his son's description of his father Rumi: (translation from Persian verses)

> Day and night he danced in ecstasy,
> On the earth he revolved like the Heavens.
> His (ecstatic) cries reached zenith of the skies,
> And were heard by all and sundry.
> He showered gold and silver on the mutriban (singers); He gave away whatever he had.
> Never for a moment was he without music and ecstasy,
> Never for a moment was he at rest.
> There was an uproar (of protest) in the city,
> Nay whole world resounded with that uproar.
> (They were surprised that) such a great Qutb and Mufti of Islam
> Who was the accepted leader of two Universes?
> Should be raving like a madman in public and private.

The people turned away from religion and faith (on his account). And went crazy after love.

Such was the impact of Shams Tabriz that a great mufti and 'alim turned into a mad mendicant. Such was the appeal of love of Allah on the person of Jalaluddin Rumi that 'alim and theologian of Rumi's standing had now very different view of religion, from legalistic sharia centred to spiritual love centred. It was a great change indeed and it was Rumi's meeting with Shams Tabriz that the world was rewarded with Mathnavi full of gems of wisdom.

The transformation was so complete that the Maulana addressed Muslims as follows:

> What is to be done, O Muslims? I do not recognize myself
> I am neither Christian, nor Jew, nor of Gabr, nor Muslim.
> I am not of the East, nor of the West, nor of land, nor of the sea;
> I am not of Nature's mint, nor of the circling heaven
> I am not of earth, nor of water, nor of air, nor of fire;
> I am not of the empyrean, nor of the dust, nor of existence, nor of entity.
> I am not of India, nor of China, nor of Bulgaria, nor of Saqain.
> I am not of the kingdom of 'Iraqian, nor of the country of Khorasan.
> I am not of this world, nor of the next, nor of paradise, nor of Hell.
> I am not of Adam, nor of Eve, nor of Eden and Rizwan'.
> My place is placeless; my trace is Traceless;
> 'This neither body nor soul, for I belong to the soul of the Beloved.
> I have put duality away; I have seen that the two worlds are one;
> One I SEEK, One I know; One I see, One I call.
> He is the first, He is the last, He is the outward, He is the inward;
> I am intoxicated with Love's cup, the two worlds have passed out of my ken;
> If once in my life I spent a moment without thee,
> From that time and from that hour I repent of my life.
> If once in this world I win a moment with thee'
> I will trample on both worlds;
> I will dance in triumph forever.

This poem is of great importance to understand Maulana Rumi's philosophy and his being drunk with love. It is a fundamentally different view of religion. When religion becomes theologians' play and dogmas rule our lives, and we seek power-reducing religion to be a mere instrument of our quest for power, rather than quest for truth, we have all the complex problems on hand including hatred and violence.

One may argue, however, if as Maulana Rumi says in the above poem, human beings loose all their identities and are immersed in ocean of love, how can one live? If one has to live conscious life on this earth, we need certain identities, certain distinctions and certain goals. How can we function? What Maulana Rumi says is mere utterance of a mendicant absorbed in love of God.

True, absolutely true. But if we reflect on Maulana's utterances we will find great relevance in our life. If Maulana is immersed in love of God and looses all sense of identity and duality, we too are immersed in this world and give excessive importance to identity and duality and result is so much conflict, so much violence in the name of these identities. These identities and interests linked up with these identities have caused so much havoc in the history of the world.

Apart from other major wars in the past in last century alone we saw two world wars causing death of millions of people. Are such identities leading to such barbarism worth its while? Yes, we all cannot become mendicants, we have to live in this world and identities are important but Maulana makes us conscious of limitations of these identities and wants us to remember we all have emanated from that Ultimate Being and will return to it. This also should never be lost sight of.

And this approach which Rumi and Sufis of his ilk preached is so close to what we have come to know through science about our Universe. It is so huge, so large, its dimensions expanded over billions of light years, beyond all our imagination and we human beings, like tiny specks on this earth which is nothing more than tiny dot, even smaller than that, and still we fight so fiercely for worldly possessions, to grab other's properties, other's territories.

If we remain even slightly drunk with love of that Ultimate Being Who has created us all we will love all His creation and not destroy even a speck of those who co-exist with us. Our sense of identity should also be inclusive of our sense of non-identity, we should also remain conscious of non-duality between this universe and its creator, we can shed so much hatred and destructive actions.

Also, we get such one-sided view of Islam, Islam of political world, Islam of violence and war. There is need to know this Islam too where power plays no role, only love and complete identity with the Creator remains at the centre stage. In our over-politicized world, rich contributions made by highly revered Sufis, philosophers and scientists, have been totally forgotten or deliberately avoided.

Our view of Islam is so one sided that any alternate view based on love and peace, is disbelieved. Here I have quoted from most respected Sufis followed by millions of Muslims to draw attention to this alternate Islam. On ground, it is this Islam which is followed and becomes deep source of inspiration for vast masses of Muslims throughout the world, irrespective of the country they live in.

Let us hope slowly this alternate Islam will displace political Islam from space in media and world would come to know more and more of this Islam of peace and love. Of course media will not easily yield space to this alternate Islam. That remains our main problem.

10
Religious Diversity and Tolerance in Islam

Diversity and tolerance are considered the very basis of modernity as one of the modernity's fundamental principles is individual and community rights and also, as modernity implies democratic rule, tolerance and right to pursue any ideology or religion assumes great importance. The western countries consider themselves as role models for democracy and freedom. Former american president, george bush, after 9/11 attack often used to say why (read muslims) are jealous of our democracy and freedom?

Most of us believe in this myth that West stands for freedom of conscience, democracy and liberty. And in theory it is quite correct. But is it is in practice? First of all let us ask one question did they ever consider non-whites, non-Europeans as equal and entitled to equality and liberty? The history tells us no. The white superiority was always underlying assumption and the blacks (now known as African-American) were always discriminated against. Even Jews, until Second World War, did not enjoy equal rights. They were always discriminated against and forced to live in ghettoes, apart from what Nazis did with them.

Also, until Second World War when the Western world was mono-religious and mono-cultural its tolerance for non-Western religions and cultures was never tested. It is only when economic migrations began from the erstwhile colonial countries that West began to experience what they now call multiculturalism and Western society became multi-religious and multicultural.

It was then that strains appeared and we saw number of cases of prejudice and discrimination against non-white, non-Western people migrating to the West. The most recent case is of Switzerland voting to ban minarets for Muslim mosques. In the poll held 57 per cent Swiss people voted against allowing minarets to Muslim mosques. In Switzerland close to four million people are Muslims.

It is heartening that the *New York Times* editorially condemned this proposed ban. It is worthwhile to quote excerpts from the editorial which was published on 30 November 2009, immediately after the referendum in Switzerland: 'Disgraceful. That is the only way to describe the success of a right-wing initiative to ban the constitution of minarets in Switzerland, where 57 per cent of voters cast ballots for a bigoted and mean-spirited measures.'

Further the editorial says, 'But the vote also carries a strong and urgent message for all Europe, and for all Western nations where Islamic minorities have been growing in numbers; and visibility, and where fear and resentment of Muslim immigrants and their religion have become increasingly strident and widespread. The warning signs have been there: the irrational fierceness of official French resistance to the shawls and burkhas worn by some Muslim women; the growing opposition in many European quarters to Turkish membership in the European Union.'

The New York editorial is, indeed the voice of sanity in the growing intolerance in the Western world towards Muslims in particular and, non-Western cultures and religions, in general. We would again like to reiterate here that in principle West does stand for equality, freedom of conscience and human rights which most of the Muslim countries have yet to learn. But, as we will show herein below that Islam also stands for tolerance and respect for other culture and faiths and believes diversity is creation of Allah but test really comes in practice.

It is also true that terrorist attacks in some countries, and especially after 9/11 has intensified hatred against Islam and Muslims but then in Switzerland, the Muslims have been peaceful and there have been no instances of such attacks and it appears quite irrational that people of Switzerland should display such intolerance towards their peaceful minority. However, the signs were in the air.

I had delivered a lecture on Islam and non-violence way back in 2004 in Zurich which was held in collaboration with the local church. When question-answer session began the journalists present there said how Islam can ever be non-violent and peaceful. I said I have based my speech on the Koranic text and anyone can verify what I have said but the journalists did not seem to be convinced. They kept on arguing until the church official intervened. What these journalists must have been writing about Islam is obvious. In modern society media plays very important role.

This is further borne out by the TV debate between noted Swiss Muslim intellectual and my friend Tariq Ramadan and Oskar Freysinger on ban on minaret. It became evident from the debate that the real issue was not minaret, but Islam itself. Dr. Patrick Haenni, a researcher at Religiouscope, who believes that religion, not politics, was the core of the initiator's discourse through a perspective full of misconceptions and stereotypes.

The ban on burqa in France by the Government is another instance of this intolerance for non-Western religions and cultures. This writer is no advocate of burqas covering entire body and face from head to toe but the question is not one should wear burqa or not, more fundamental question is of individual right and choice? Whatever reason for wearing burqa, personal conviction, social or peer pressures or identity issue, does one have right to wear or not? Should one ban it outright?

Here I would like to narrate an interesting experience. I was lecturing on secularism in the University of Bukhara and in the audience were mostly young women dressed in skirts as Western women do. During the lecture two burqa clad women (wearing burqa from head to toe) entered and sat down. After my lecture was over some of those women stood up and agitatedly said sir, why should we not thrown out these two women (wearing burqa)? I was shocked at the aggressive tone of these agitated women.

I enquired why do you want to throw them out? These women (all of them Muslim) said why are they wearing burqa and why do they cover themselves? I said I ask you one simple question suppose all these women were clad in burqa and two of you had come wearing skirts and with modern haircut and if they had asked why not throw these two skirt-wearing women out, what would have been your response?

I said throwing out or banning a practice is not the solution but to dialogue with each other and to understand each other. They then appreciated my viewpoint and sat down quietly and we continued our discussion. Thus to accept the other, as other is (not with prescriptions) is the essence of democracy. Prescription for the other violates the very spirit of others' rights and dignity which is the basis of modernity. Now it has been universally accepted that it is not only individual rights which are important but also group rights of minorities as well are equally important.

The West, whatever its principles and values, is yet to come to terms with non-Western others. Also, it should not depend on the doctrine of reciprocation but group rights should be absolute. I remember in U.K. there was debate in eighties how Muslims treat Christian minorities in Muslim majority countries. Do they give them equal rights and freedom of religion? If not, why do they expect such rights in Western countries?

This reciprocative approach contradicts the very spirit of democratic values and principles. These values and principles are absolute and no conditionalities could be prescribed. Of course there are complex reasons for the growing intolerance towards Muslim minorities in the Western world. As everywhere the rightist forces thrive on hatred of the other and the ban on the minaret in Switzerland is also the result of rise of rightist politics. The Muslims in India too have experienced it when the BJP tried to come to power through hate politics of Ramjanambhoomi.

In France too, ban on hijab came under the regime of Sarkozy who is a known rightist. Secondly, the rising number of immigrants also creates fear in the minds of original inhabitants of the country and, in order to press the issue, these numbers are highly exaggerated. Muslims, both by way of migration and birth, are the fastest growing minority in the Europe. Thirdly, most of the Muslim migrants are non-whites, many of them blacks from African countries and here both religious as well as racial prejudice combine and intensify hatred and intolerance.

In France, for example, most of the Muslim migrants are from former French colonies and hence happen to be black. Discrimination against them and their marginalization totally alienates them and this alienation finds expression through complex ways through aggressive behaviour or overemphasis on their identities which in turn further intensifies their alienation.

And, if this is followed by economic crisis as Europe is undergoing these days, the majority fear against the emigrant other' becomes even more aggressive, born out of fear and the rising tide of rightist forces in such circumstances further aggravates it. Also, the US policies in the Middle East has resulted in intensifying extremism in a section of youth in the Muslim countries resulting in terrorist attacks such as 9/11 which incites even more hatred against Muslims in the West.

What is the way out then? Where to stop this vicious circle of action and reaction? It is for sure that we cannot control all the factors. But it is also equally certain that we need a wise political leadership who is not after power but the welfare of people. Democracy ideally speaking is for people's participation and for their well-being. However, like other political systems, democracy too, has become means of grabbing power by certain groups and classes. Also, it tends to be majoritarian, i.e. heavily tilted in favour of racial, religious or linguistic majority. There has been hardly any exception to it in the world.

Certain Muslim countries who swear by Koran as their constitution also flagrantly violate Koranic provisions. Koran gives certain ideals and values for governance, an idea of the desirable society. It says diversity is Allah's creation and must be respected and celebrated. And this diversity includes linguistic, racial and religious and human beings, whatever religion, race or linguistic group they belong to, must be accorded equal dignity and which means all of them should enjoy equal rights.

However, you will not find any Muslim country swearing by the Koran as the book of Allah implementing these ideals. You find discrimination on the basis of religion, even sects, language and ethnicity. You very much find discrimination for example in Saudi Arabia, against non-Arabs, non-Wahabi Muslims and other ethnic and racial groups. One finds discrimination in Iran against Sunni Muslims, Arabs, Bahais and non-Persians.

In Pakistan one finds discrimination against certain linguistic groups like Baluchis and Sindhis. It is dominated by the Punjabi majority. Not only that there is sectarian violence between Shi'ahs and Sunnis besides Christians and Hindus. It is the Punjabi majority which rules the roast. One has yet to see any Muslim country which does not violate injunctions of the Koran while swearing in by it as one has yet to see any Western democracy not violating injunctions of their own constitutions enshrining ideals and values of modern democracy.

As long as the goal remains power, this is bound to happen. Another bane of the situation is the current rise in rightist forces which arouse emotions of people on the basis of religion, race and language. Again no country is an exception to it. Education system itself, which prepares children and students is controlled by, in most, if not all cases, by rightist elements.

The Netherlands is also undergoing severe problem of anti-Muslim tirade. One politician made a film called *Fitna* and refused to take it back. Also, a Muslim fanatic murdered a film maker from the Netherlands who caste a slur on Islam and this further led to anti-Islamic surge there. I met a professor of Islamic studies from the Netherlands in Germany who spoke on Islam. The seminar was on progressive Islam.

I was stunned by his anti-Islamic outpouring. It was nothing short of hate-Islam speech. When we protested the organizers maintained that all views are allowed to be expressed from this forum. May be it was so. But what was worrying was that the person was teaching Islam in the Netherlands. If such Islam is taught in universities of a country what mindset would be generated? One shudders to think.

Media is no exception. While it must be made clear there are honourable exceptions and some newspapers and TV channels which are quite objective or tend to be so but then such papers and channels are, more often than not, popular. They are read or watched by serious kind of people. Popular media tend to be prejudiced. Also, media is often owned by certain interests and it is not committed to the cause of objective reporting.

And media plays a most crucial role in democracy. I would say if media plays a responsible role, rising above all interests, modern democracies would be far more conflict-free than they are today. And in answering the question raised above media provides one of the crucial factors. Despite all the laws made by the state, media behaves the way it wants to as various state organs fail to implement the laws.

It is true we cannot have ideal democracy as the German philosopher rightly points out ideal is not real and real is not ideal, still one has to try to come as close to ideal as possible. Even such efforts are lacking in modern democracies. Invariably it is powerful interests which determine the shape and direction of things and there is always tension between vested interests and the ideals and interests seem to win.

Of course if the conflict remains manageable it is one thing but disaster takes place when it goes beyond manageable proportions. The attack on 9/11 and subsequent attack on Afghanistan and Iraq took this conflict between Islam and the West beyond imaginable proportions as here too very powerful interests were involved. However, it would be wrong to consider it a self fulfilment of Huntigntonian prediction of 'clash of civilizations'. It was, instead, a clash of political interests on both sides.

It is interesting to note that Huntington's book received such media attention in the West precisely because certain interests in the West wanted such a book written to promote conflict. Of course things may not have gone as planned but to an extent those interests were served but at a great social cost. It greatly sharpened prejudices in the West against Islam. And this has been going on for quite some time now.

Since Muslims began to immigrate to the Western countries in the post-colonial period the anti-Islam prejudices began to acquire sharper edge. Rushdie's book *The Satanic Verses* in the eighties and the support it received in the West was also part of this process. The enthusiastic support was not for the sake of freedom of opinion. There was a purpose behind it. The Islamic revolution had occurred in Iran which was anti-West in its thrust and made Iranian oil beyond Western powers. Thus the West adopted an anti-Iran posture and when Khomeini, for his own political compulsions, issued a fatwa against Salman Rushdie, swords were drawn on both sides and the West lent unqualified support to Rushdie in the name of freedom and Muslims stood by Khomeini's fatwa. It was neither freedom nor Islam but who will dominate Iran and its oil, the West or the people and rulers of Iran.

All these developments through the eighties culminated in the 9/11 attacks and everything was complete for anti-Islamic prejudices in Western countries and media. As far as Arab oil is concerned the clashes are likely to continue and will go through different phases. It reached its culmination during Bush regime's unqualified support to rightist policies and outright adventure in the West Asia.

However, since it crossed critical limits in conflict management Obama took over the reigns of administration. But it would indeed be too much to expect that Obama would resolve the conflict. But yes, certainly he may succeed in managing the conflict a shade better and he appears to be sincerely trying. He is far from free agent as many think. His hands are tied by so many uncontrollable factors.

The Al-Qaeda and Taliban issue is not here to disappear in a few years. Afghan people are fiercely independence loving and even the Moghuls failed to subdue them, much less totally aliens like Americans. American policy makers should study the history of the Afghan rebellion much more seriously than they have done. US jackboots cannot crush Afghans. Obama has to an extent realized this and though he is sending more forces but had also promised to withdraw by 2011.

Withdraws or not but certainly the solution does not lie in trying to crush Afghans but to resolve it through dialogue and accommodation which again is not easy. The US is also not in Afghanistan just to wipe out Al-Qaeda and Taliban but to control rich gas and mineral resources in Central Asia. It did not invade Afghanistan for nothing. And as long as the US wants to control rich resources of Central Asia it cannot find accommodation with Afghan Taliban and as long as the Taliban issue continues anti-Islam prejudices will remain strong as ever.

It is also absolutely necessary to solve the Palestinian problem if one desires peace in West Asia. While Afghan Taliban are more concerned about peace in their region, Al-Qaeda is more focused on West Asia and to solve both the problems sans the US interests in both the regions is asking for let us say impossible. Should we despair then? Not really. But it is a challenge which few politicians can succeed in facing.

The Muslim countries too will have to seriously contemplate policy changes and have to make concerted efforts to project a peaceful Islam on their part. They will have to fight powerful interests and confrontationist mindsets on their part. The rulers in the West Asia have to go for modernization, changes in their education system and promoting a spirit of understanding and dialogue with the other.

King Abdullah of Saudi Arabia is wiser than his predecessors and following strategies to contain extremist elements in his own country. Like Obama's his hands are tied too. In Pakistan the military establishment is too powerful to be contained easily and for quite sometime to come civilian rule will not be able to ascertain its independence and Pakistan is very crucial for peace in Afghan-Pakistan region.

Well, while working for greater understanding let us understand these challenges too.

11
Salafishm (Wahabism) and Sufism: Is There a Real Conflict?

Salafism or Wahabism, also referred to as cult of Ahl-e-Hadith is supposed to be directly opposed to the sufi strain of Islam. In India too the two sects are opposed to each other though here, due to democratic secular polity, nature of conflict is not very aggravated or violent. The partisans of both the ideologies apart, it confuses many Muslims as to what are their differences about and why they condemn each other?

The word salafi means what pertains to our forefathers—*aslaf,* i.e. we have strayed from the pure Islam practiced by our early ancestors and must be restored. According to the ideologues of Salafi Islam, our practices should be based only on the Koran and Hadith, not on any *fiqhi mazhab* or school of jurisprudence like Hanafi, Shafi'im, etc. Hence they are also known as Ahl-e-Hadith as they base all their juristic decisions on the Koran and Hadith.

The Salafis strongly condemn Sufi Islam as corrupt and destructive of all that Islam stands for. To visit sufi mausoleums and to pray and invoke intercession (*shafa'at*) is totally against Koran and Islamic teachings. Only Allah's name could be invoked, not of anyone else not even of the Prophet (PBUH), let alone of any sufi saint. One cannot pray even on the Prophet's grave or recite the Koran facing the Prophet's grave. To invoke intercession, according to the Salafis, amounts to *shirk* (associating partners with Allah which is great sin).

Those who are supporters of Sufi Islam disagree with these views. They argue intercession cannot amount to *shirk* as intercession does not elevate a person from human to deistic status, human beings remain human beings though one has achieved perfection (*insane-e-kamil*) through ones spiritual perfection. They quote Hadith in their support. In Hadith literature, according to the supporters of Sufi Islam, the Prophet Mohammad (PBUH) has been described as *Shaft' al-mudhnibin,* i.e. intercessor on behalf of sinners.

Here in this essay it is not our intention to support this or that ideology which has torn the Muslim world apart and caused much challenges, even violence. Our intention is to understand both the strains and understand the factors which gave rise to these ideologies among Muslims. It is certainly not easy to reconcile the two but understanding the underlying factors can probably pave the way for better appreciation of both the schools of thought.

The Sufi Islam

Before we understand the origin of Wahabi or Salafi Islam we must first understand the origins of Sufi Islam and its need for Muslims. One also has to understand why the Sufi Islam acquired tremendous popularity in the Islamic world and remained dominant for centuries. The Salafi Islam originated in Najd area of Hijaz now named after the Saudi dynasty Saudi Arabia as an ideology as late as the eighteenth century.

What are reasons of tremendous popularity of Sufi Islam? Let us remember religion, and any religion for that matter, basically fulfils two human needs—moral and spiritual. Most of the great religions of the world have originated in the times of great moral degradation. When greed, crass materialism, war, pillage, loot, plunder and ruthless exploitation begins to rule, a reformer, a prophet and great moral thinker appears on the scene and either through divine revelation or his own thoughts tries to restore morality in the society.

Such a person does not normally rely on rational thought alone but also anchors his teachings deep into his inner spiritual resources. All great religious founders resorted to what one can call deep encounter with ones own self and searched for truth deep inside. It is this encounter with ones own self or solitude which provides resource for abiding truth and that appeals to the people. Mere rational thought, however philosophical or exalted it may be, will not have deeper emotional impact on people.

Rational thought, it may be noted, has its own significance and performs great social functions and ensures human development and progress and so there is no question of lessening its importance. But it appeals to the intellectuals and engineers and architects of society and scientific thought. However, either they are averse to or simply not interested in what is human the deeper emotional self and its potential.

They are explorers of macrocosm, not microcosm. Their interest is in what is out there, not what is in here. The sufis, mystics and bhaktas explore their inner self and for them self is more important than the whole universe as universe is much more important to intellectuals and philosophers and scientists than the inner self. The sufis and mystics maintain that one who has deeper knowledge of oneself (self) can have knowledge of God (Rabb). God cannot be understood only rationally but through deeper spiritual resources.

Spiritualism brings deeper conviction and inner solace and certitude—what Koran calls *iman* (faith). It needs both heart and mind to believe and hence, according to the Koran, those whose hearts are sealed can never believe. Belief has to be grounded in deeper spiritual forces and superficial rationality cannot achieve deeper conviction. The sufis and mystics spend years fighting great impediments encountered in themselves and perfect their *nafs* through minimizing their desires and removing all traces of greed controlling acquisitive instincts.

Then they emerge as what we can call role models for the masses of people in the society and gather around them large number of followers. One more social function of religion is to provide solace to troubled hearts and minds. No amount of material wealth can buy this inner solace and these sufis become sources of inner solace for these troubled souls.

The sufis and mystics use rich cultural resources to achieve this purpose. Poetry and its powerful symbolic language on the one hand, and, music, on the other, provide spiritual tools which have great emotional appeal. Also, sufis assimilate different cultural values and express themselves through cultural values and language of the region they situate themselves in. This again greatly enhances their appeal to the masses of people.

Thus many great sufis happened to be from Iran and hence they wrote in Persian. The Persian poetry was greatly enriched by the sufis of Iran. They did not hesitate to use symbols like wine, cup of wine or sip bearer of wine (*saqi*) for spiritual purposes, giving it entirely new meaning and significance. Also, the sufis spoke a language of love, not of power. It is language of love which has emotional appeal, not language of power which reflects ambition and exploitation.

Thus it is rich cultural resources and language of love which tremendously enhances the appeal of sufi Islam. For example what Maulana Jalaluddin Rumi could achieve through his *Mathnavia Ma'navi* could not have been achieved through hundreds of tomes written by great scholars in terms of emotional appeal. The Mathnavi was even called Koran in Pehlavi language (i.e. Persian).

It is also important to note that Jalaluddin Rumi was as great a scholar of Arabic as of Persian. Arabic was the language of Islamic learning whereas Persian was the language of culture and administration and Maulana Rum chose Persian for writing his Mathnavi precisely because it was the language of the people and their cultural expressions were in that language and it was this powerful cultural too that made Mathnavi popular over the ages.

The Indian sufis, on the other hand, also wrote either in Persian or even in regional languages like Brij, Avadhi, Khari Boli, Bengali, Marathi and in Urdu and used symbolism of local culture. Also, since they spoke the language of love there was no rejection of the other, only acceptance. But ideological puritans, on the other hand, speak language of rejection, one who is not purist, is not acceptable. Thus they narrow down their circle of followers. One who does not believe in their ideology is not a believer and hence a kafir.

Also, the Sufis, through assimilation of local cultural symbols, even rituals made it easy for the local masses not only to flock to them but also convert to Islam which became much nearer to their way of life. In India, the rituals around sufi mausoleums bear close resemblance to those of a Hindu shrine replacing the idol with a sufi grave. Conversion should not result in cultural rupture. Culture is much closer to ones heart than any intellectual belief.

There is another dimension which one has to take into account for origin, development and popularity of sufi Islam. Islam did not remain confined to the Arabian Peninsula with scarce cultural resources but spread far and wide with highly developed cultures and civilizations like those of Iran and India, besides others. While Islam impacted cultures it was also in turn impacted by them and new composite strains of cultures developed in these regions. Both Iran and India developed highly enriched composite cultures due to the entry of Islam.

It was this composite and enriched culture which using all native and foreign cultural resources that sufis adopted unhesitatingly. Thus it made easier for the people of those regional composite cultures to identify themselves with sufis and their creative endeavours like poetry, music and in some cases even dancing in trance. *Mehfil-e-sama'* (the divine musical session) became an important institution in sufi Islam. The ulama opposed it saying music is *haram* (prohibited) in Islam. However, for masses it was an important means to be drawn towards sufis. Amir Khusro, Nizamuddin Awliya's disciple made very rich contributions to the world of sufi music.

Salafi Islam

The sufi Islam began, according to some scholars right from the Prophet's (PBUH) time as some of his companions, drawing inspiration from him, indulged in rigorous spiritual practices and *ahl-e-suffa* (those who sat on a place outside the Prophet's house and used tò practice very simple life). Some people consider them as the first sufis. Sufis were subsequently divided in several schools of thought one of which is known as Wahdat al-Wujud school. This school was founded by Muhiyuddin Ibn Arabi, a Spanish sufi of great eminence.

This school which believes in One Real Being and that all others are His manifestations, was most open and liberal and hence became very popular in India and attracted the maximum number of following. It produced great sufi saints who were highly revered by Hindus and Muslims a like. They were truly spiritual and role models for many. Among Arab countries too, Muhiyuddin Ibn Arabi and sufis of his school were quite popular.

However, after the decline of power and onslaught of Western colonialism, sufism lost its original thrust and vigour and degenerated into superstitious practices, amulates and charms— which sufis also encouraged. Such degeneration resulted in inaction and total submission to whosoever was in authority. Masses flocked to sufis or their graves not for any spiritual inspiration but for mere solace and seeking solution to their problems through charms and amulates or mere invocation of sufi saints.

This degeneration created its own reaction. This reaction came in its strongest form from Najd which was a predominantly Bedouin area with simple style of life with no complex cultural traditions like in Iran or India. Salafi movement was founded by Sheikh Muhammad bin Abdul Wahhab (1703-1792) of Najd. The name Wahabi movement draws from his name. He was educated in Medina. He was quite studious and acquired his expertise in Hadith from well known Muhaddith (scholar of hadith) Sheikh Muhammad Hayat Sindhi.

It is said once Abdul Wahhab was standing near the chamber of the Prophet and people were indulging in what were according to Sheikh Hayat Sindhi *bid'at* (innovative and false practices). This was, it is said, the turning point in Sheikh Abdul Wahhab's mind. He decided to purify Islam of all these innovative practices and founded his movement. Some highlights of his movement was firstly *tawhid* in its purest form without any traces of *shirk* (association of others with Allah), opposition to *taqlid* (blind following of any authority), invocations of saints (one does not need invocation of any living or dead person to seek nearness to Allah or visiting dead sufis' mausoleums and kissing their graves and praying there).

Thus it would be seen that Sheikh Abdul Wahhab tried to attempt ideological purity of Islam and such a purist Islam, it would be interesting to note can appeal more to desert Arabs which lacked rich and complex cultural traditions. It mainly spread only in these areas and could not attract followers in Iran, Central Asia, India and other parts which had such traditions.

One more factor is important in this respect and that is political. As we all know the colonial period had begun and the Arabs were under domination of Turks and the British had established its foothold over Egypt. There was a power struggle in the air. Sheikh Muhammad Abdul Wahhab was acquiring popularity in the Najd region and could influence the local ruler of the region Amir Muhammad bin Saud and this gave political power to the movement. Thus the religious appeal of Sheikh Abdul Wahhab and political power of the Saudi family made the Salafi movement a power to be reckoned with.

Slowly the Saudi power increased and it captured whole of Najd, the Karbala and even temporarily Mecca. This began to ring alarm bells in Turkey, Egypt and alerted the British that they may loose hold over the region. Political conspiracies began and Sheikh Abdul Wahab's movement was labeled as Wahabi movement to give it a bad name. When a religious movement takes resort to political power it also has to face certain political consequences.

However, we do not want to go into the political history of the movement, its defeats and victories, neither do we want to pass any judgment on its religious merit or otherwise as our main aim is to attempt to explore the socio-religious roots of the movement and its appeal or otherwise. Salafi movement, as pointed out, did not arise with political ambitions but with a zeal for ideological purity. Sufism and its various practices were seen as a deviation from pure Islam and as a compromise with its concept of *tawhid*.

It should also be noted that zeal for ideological purity in any religion or political movement leads to extremism sand denunciation of all those who do not agree with them. Also, the concept of such purity appeals only to small number of people as in this complex world it is very difficult to ensure such purity. And ordinary people see no great need for such purity as their very existence demands compromises on every step.

Moreover such ideological purity and extremism in its advocacy, besides limiting its appeal, also makes it unsuitable for peasant and non-tribal cultures which tend to be much more complex, ritualistic and dependant on vagaries of nature. Islam could not escape the local hues and traditions of peasant cultures when it spread to these regions. Also, these regions produced much agricultural surplus extracted from peasants which in turn produced a leisurely class consuming this surplus which indulged in creating high culture, philosophy and abstract concepts.

Many sufis were greatly attracted, like other Muslim intellectuals and philosophers by the philosophy of neo-Platonism, and spiritual practices which helped them understand ones inner self. The Muslim ruling classes were engaged in extending and consolidating their rule and thus constantly engaged in warfare which created revulsion among those who were intensely religious.

Thus they withdrew themselves from political Islam and concentrated on spiritual Islam. Thus they became much more tolerant and open to other religions and cultural traditions. Salafis, on the other hand, reversed this trend, gave preference to political Islam and associated themselves with political ruler to survive. Rejection of others leads to isolation and isolation needs external props to survive and need for political support,

Should then hostility continue between *Salafis* and Sufis? I do not think such a course could be advisable. While the Salafis have to realize that total rejection leads nowhere and only to extremism, the advocates of Sufi Islam should understand that Sufism is much more than mere visiting graves and indulging in charms and amulates. Sufism is nothing if not intense religiosity and spiritualism.

The ideological purity of Salafism and tolerance and inclusiveness of Sufi Islam must be wedded together to make our world more livable. We live today in a multi-religious and multicultural world no matter where we live and exclusivistic trends would only lead to extremism. Peace and tolerance is possible only if we accept others rather than reject them. Inter-religious dialogue and understanding will ensure harmonious co-existence whereas extremism will bring nothing but peril for all of us.

King Abdullah has also realized this and has begun an initiative to start inter-religious dialogue. It is very welcome initiative. We must abandon old positions and adjust to our own realities without compromising the course of fundamental values and principles. Love, compassion and tolerance have enriched all cultures throughout human history and we need these values much more than before.

In India though there is no struggle for power between Barelvis (advocates of Sufi Islam) and Deobandis (advocates of Salafi Islam) but polemics continue between them. This leads us nowhere. Coexistence, while respecting each others positions and doctrines, is the only way out. India is a secular democracy and allows full religious freedom and every Muslim sect could subscribe to its own doctrines and dogmas and hence there is no need to denounce the other.

All Muslims, however, must unite to denounce the terrorist and al-Qaeda violence. Killing innocent people is most irreligious act. Only vested interests and those in pursuit of power would encourage such acts, never a religious person for whom religion is a great resource for peace and security of everyone. Let us look inside us and see are we really religious in this sense?

12
Is Islam Compatible with Democracy and Modernity?

Because of certain happenings and because there happens to be monarchy or dictatorships in most of the Muslim countries it has been concluded that Islam is not compatible with democracy and also with modernity. Some even maintain that very Islamic culture is a stumbling block and cannot permit democratic polity and modernistic society. To maintain this amounts not only to misunderstanding religion but also society, history and social forces at work.

If this logic is to be accepted then Christianity will also come under cloud as the Christian Church also opposed democracy, secularism and modernity until eighteenth century. A great struggle ensued between church and princely rulers on one hand, and between church and secular elements in the society, on the other. It was finally only during nineteenth century that democracy and modernity became acceptable to Western society.

However, even some well known scholars and orientalists have often accepted such superficial view of Islam and Islamic society. The Western media partly for political reasons and partly for ignorance of social and material forces at work, also has been a great instrument of propagating such views about Islam and Islamic societies. In order to understand reality one has to bring to bear not only religious, but also sociological, political and historical view of reality. It requires deeper insight into social processes and working of societies.

Recently a debate took place on a web page and 10 questions were circulated to be replied by the participants. These questions were: (1) Whether Islam and democracy are compatible; (2) Can sharia laws with their harsh punishments and democracy go together; (3) Is it possible in Islamic countries to separate religion and state? (4) Can Islam support individual rights, i.e. human rights?; (5) Has United States contributed to hampering democracy in countries like Saudi Arabia, Egypt, etc.; (6) Is Islam opposed to modernity and refuses to come to terms with it; (7) Could religious texts be used as blueprints to structure modern society;

(8) Do women hold inferior position in Muslim society? (9) Can equality for women be ensured only through secular laws; (10) Is Islam tolerant and progressive? Islamic countries ban music and TV, cinema posters, etc.

We will try to answer these questions one by one. As stated before to understand the problem it is not enough to see what is happening in Muslim countries today and ascribe it to religion and religious teachings. Religion may appear to be a dominant cause but often it is not. Much happens behind the cover of religion and religious teachings. One who has penetrating insight into socio-political affairs would know what role religion and other forces play in a society. There are all sorts of interests, particularly political and economic which are more determinative than any thing else and while exercising ones judgement one should not ignore the role of these forces. One also has to remember that there is no single interpretation of religion. It generally has multiple interpretations. And ones interpretation is deeply influenced by ones socio-political inclination and ones bent of mind. The contemporary forces also play an important role in interpretation of religion. Contemporary Islam is being interpreted in multiple ways.

Also one should keep in mid the role of history, historical forces and culture. Certain cultural formations also play important role. Culture, in turn, is not determined wholly by religion and religious teachings though it does play part therein. For understanding contemporary socio-political set up one can hardly ignore the role of culture as well as that of historical heritage.

With these preliminary remarks I would throw light on the questions detailed above. The first question is whether Islam is incompatible with democracy. It is certainly not. In fact even if one goes by religious text the Koran lays emphasis on what it calls *shura'* (consultation) (3:159, 42:38). Even the messenger of Allah is required to consult his people in worldly matters and Muslims are required to consult each other in their secular affairs.

Now it is true such consultation and modern day representative democracy may not be exactly similar. However, the spirit of modern democracy and the Koranic injunction to consult people is same in spirit. New institutions keep on developing and human beings, depending on their worldly experiences keep on changing and refining these institutions. The Koranic text not only gives the concept of *shura'* (democratic consultation) but does not support even remotely any concept of dictatorship or authoritarianism.

Some people try to use the Koranic verse 4:59 to justify obedience to any kind of authority including a monarch or a caliph or a military dictator. It is certainly not the spirit of the Koranic verse. One has to see it in historical background. The verse is addressed to Bedouins who were nomads and were not habituated to submitting to any authority. The Prophet used to send his representatives to these Bedouin tribes and they will refuse to follow their instructions. The verse thus exhorted them to obey these authorities. One cannot justify submission to illegitimately constituted authority. And, if this verse is read in conjunction with the verses 3:159 and 42:38 it would mean one has to submit to properly and democratically constituted authority. An authority has to be legitimate and properly constituted.

In contemporary world the concept of *shura'* should mean democratic process and constitution of proper democratic institutions of which elections are a necessary requirement. In Islam any authority forcibly constituted or acquired by power of swords or arms can have no legitimacy whatsoever. The institution of monarchy or military dictatorship did not exist during the prophet's time at all. These are subsequent developments and were legitimised by the 'Ulama in order to prevent anarchy. Thus 'Ulama conferred some legitimacy on monarchy, not in the light of Islamic teachings but only to prevent anarchy. Some of them also became part of power structure and their pronouncements had no Islamic legitimacy. One sees this today in most of the Islamic countries. The 'Ulama in Saudi Arabia are very much part of monarchical power structure and legitimise everything the Saudi rulers do.

Thus the absence of democracy in Muslim countries is by means on account of Islamic teachings or incompatibility of democracy with Islam but due to host of factors political, historical and cultural. The imperialist powers, firstly of Europe and then those of United States also play their own role. The early Islamic democracy breathed its last within thirty years of the Holy Prophet's death. The institution of monarchy crept in under Roman influence. It is important to note that the capital of Islam had shifted from Medina to Kufa in Iraq and then to Damuscus in Syria which was once under Roman Empire. Mu'awiyah who siezed power without consent of Muslims was functioning from Damascus and adopted Roman monarchical ways. Thus deeper historical and cultural forces must be taken into account to understand the political institutions in many Muslim countries today. The US and British interests also play their role in shaping things in these countries. In many Islamic countries including the Saudi Arabia. Egypt and other Muslim countries there is deep urge for democracy and popular government among the people but it is frustrated by heavy hand of authoritarian rulers. Islam in no way comes in the way of establishing democracy in these countries. It is powerful vested interests both internal and external, which do not permit democracy to be established.

The next question is of implementation of sharia law in Muslim countries. Many theologians and their followers believe sincerely of course that problems confronting their countries and societies can be solved by enforcing sharia laws and the punishments prescribed therein. Also, they believe these laws must be enforced as they were evolved by the early jurists (*fuqaha'*) without any rethinking.

This is certainly not the spirit of the Koranic injunctions. Many Koranic verses were revealed in a particular situation and while applying these laws that has to be kept in view. The fundamental principle is to prevent crime and crime can be prevented in number of ways. At times harsh punishments become necessary and at times reformative efforts more relevant. The Koranic injunctions about crimes like murder, theft, robbery, rebellion, rape and adultery are understood carefully it becomes quite obvious.

For example, the verse on cutting off of hands 5:38 is immediately followed by verse 5:39 which says, 'But whoever repents after his wrongdoing and reforms. Allah will turn to him (mercifully). Surely Allah is Forgiving, Merciful.' Thus emphasis is on reform and repentance, not on harsh punishment. It may be awarded only in extreme case. Also, if it is read in conjunction with the verse 5:33 where punishment for 'those who wage war against Allah and His Messenger and strive to make mischief in the land is that they should be murdered, or crucified, or their hands and their feet should be cut off on opposite sides, or they should be imprisoned', it should become obvious that one must distinguish between ordinary and ultimate crime. When for mischief in earth or waging war against Allah and His Messenger could be imprisonment as well, how can the punishment for mere theft could be cutting off hands.

It could be interpreted as metaphorically as well, i.e. cutting off of hands means taking measures which will prevent him from committing theft in future as cutting off tongue means silencing some one, not literally cutting off tongue. Also, one must keep conditions in Arabia at the time. This was the traditional punishment meted out at that time and also some tribes indulge in crimes for their survival. The Koran used prevalent punishment and also added the concept of reform and repentance and talked of Allah's Forgiveness and Mercy. A criminal, if repents and reforms should be forgiven and shown mercy. Thus the Koran accepts the prevalent punishment but also improves upon it. The real purpose of the Koran is not to give harsh punishments but to reform the criminal but not to spare him if he persists despite better opportunities in life.

Another question relates to separation of state and religion. It is true Muslims in general believe that in Islam religion cannot be separated from religion. This belief has acquired almost a status of doctrine among Muslims. However, it has no such doctrinal position in the Koran. In fact it has been pointed out that Koran does not even give any concept of state, only a concept of a just society.

However, in Arabia there was no state at the time of appearance of Islam and the Prophet laid down a bare framework of administration of newly emerging society. There was no paid police, army or bureaucracy during his time. It was during the time of 2nd Caliph Umar that a register (*Diwan*) of paid army soldiers was started. Thus it was mere historical coincidence that a state structure came into existence along with a religious movement. The sharia law has such status in Islam as in Arabia as there was total legal vacuum and Islam provided, for the first time a cohesive and logical legal structure. This legal structure was provided in total legal vacuum. It was great development. Hence sharia law acquired very high status in Islam.

So integration of state and religion is historical coincidence rather than religious doctrine. Over period of time sharia law which was result of dynamic process became stagnant. Some modern scholars tried to infuse the principle of dynamism by invoking the institution of ijtihad but did not succeed much in view of total stagnation in Muslim countries. The authoritarian rulers in Muslim countries find legitimisation only by seeking support of the 'Ulama and 'Ulama insist on retaining the Sahri'ah law as inherited from the past. If sharia law is rethought or re-interpreted keeping in view the modern conditions, the orthodox 'Ulama fear loosing grip over power structures. Thus such collaboration between authoritarian rulers and orthodox 'Ulama has resulted in total social, political and legal stagnation in Muslim countries.

Though in given circumstances it may not be possible to attempt total separation between state and religion in Muslim countries as this has become integral part of historical legacy, one should begin by taking gradual steps in that direction. There cannot be any universal recipe as much will depend on concrete conditions in each Muslim country. But an overall Islamic moral framework has to be retained as had happened in many Western countries including USA where an overall Christian moral framework has influenced law making. There are few countries in the West, which have discarded such influence totally. Among Muslim countries Turkey has achieved separation of state from religion. It also has to be borne in mind that forcible imposition of modernisation and separation of state and religion has failed in Muslim countries like

Afghanistan during thirties and in Iran during Shah's time. Such attempts resulted in Islamic revolution and imposition of sharia law from above.

Individual Rights

Individual rights are very fundamental to functioning of any liberal democracy. In fact the concept of individual rights or human rights has evolved along with evolution of democratic power structure. Since there is no full fledged democracy in any Muslim country there is no respect for individual rights and many authoritarian rulers in Muslim countries reject the very concept of human rights denouncing them as western and secular in origin.

Thus one has to struggle for democratic power structure in order to usher in the concept of individual rights in Muslim countries. The Human rights activists in Muslim countries like Saudi Arabia. Egypt etc. are dubbed as western agents, persecuted and thrown into jails. As a result of this anyone who holds different political opinion faces persecution. Some who advocate change in sharia laws in view of changed conditions or attempt to re-conceptualise Islamic philosophical doctrine face severe persecution. Thus there is no respect for individual rights and individual dignity. It will be possible only when democratic culture prevails. For that there is basic need for democratic polity.

Freedom of conscience and freedom of speech has never been denied by Koran or the Prophet. The Prophet never suppressed individual freedom or discouraged differences of opinion. He even said that difference of opinion in Islamic ummah is matter of grace and mercy. However, with evolution of feudal and monarchical culture differences of opinion were not permitted and ruthlessly suppressed. During the early Abbasid period a controversy raged whether the Koran is created or co-eternal with God. The Abbasid who supported the Mu'tazilah viewpoint that Koran is created forcibly suppressed the other point of view that Qur'a' is co-eternal with God and flogged person of Imam Abu Hanifa's'stature for holding views contrary to those of Mu'tazilah. This authoritarian culture has not changed in Muslim countries until today. Many profound scholars of Islam had to leave for western universities from countries like Egypt, Pakistan and other Muslim countries.

It is for this reason that in no Muslim country today one has good tradition of social or physical sciences. For these sciences to flourish one needs liberal democratic culture. The Muslim countries would remain far behind in these fields if authoritarian power structures are not demolished and replaced with democratic ones. Unfortunately there is no such movement in sight. The United States has always propped up corrupt and authoritarian rulers in Middle East who suppress freedom of expression and these countries remain totally dependent on the west in every respect. They cannot develop even like India has developed. No Muslim country can boast of any modern scientific discovery.

Islam and Modernity

In fact democracy and modernity go hand in hand and one can hardly be modern without being democratic. One can say that there are authoritarian models of modernisation like China and Singapore but on deeper reflection it will be seen that democratic model is far more congenial to modernisation in all spheres including social sphere. Modern social sciences cannot flourish in authoritarian regimes though natural sciences might.

However, lack of modernity in Muslim countries is not on account of Islamic teachings but more due to its medieval interpretation. Islam cannot only come to terms with modernity but its teachings were quite modernistic if one goes by the Koranic pronouncements. Koran encourages pluralism if one goes by the verses like 5:48,6:109. 60:8, etc. All these verses are quite supportive of pluralistic social structure. In fact earlier the Islamic societies were much more pluralistic than any other societies throughout medieval ages. The Koran not only recognises validity of other faiths but also makes it incumbent for Muslims to respect equally all past prophets and one who does not is not true Muslim. The verses 4:150-152 are clear proof there of.

Intolerance in Muslim societies today is more political than religious. Islam is not intolerant of any other religion including that of kufr (unbelief) if it agrees to co-exist peacefully and harmoniously. Thus Islam and pluralism always go together. In fact it was in Europe in medieval ages that non-Christians were not tolerated. Islam today of course needs to be freed from intolerant theologians who are close to authoritarian power structures, which is at the root of their intolerance.

Religious Text and Modern Societies

It is true religious texts pose some serious problems for modern society. But it need not be so with all religious texts if they are appropriately interpreted, at least not with Koranic text if it is understood in its real spirit. But at the same time one should not obstruct democratic social and political structure if some text is problematic. The religious text were revealed or evolved in very different social background and one must take today's relevance into account. One need not reject religious text but examine its suitability or otherwise for modern societies.

Status of Women

It is true that Muslim countries treat women as inferior to men and try to justify this treatment by quoting from the religious texts including Koran. But they quote very selectively from Koran to prove women's subordination to men. Koran, if approached holistically promoted equal status for women. The verse often quoted by theologians to show inferior status of women is 4:34 and ignore verses like 2:228. 33:35 and several others or try to explain away them as merely promoting spiritual equality. It is far from true. The Koran taken as a whole is far more supportive of equality of sexes. The modern Islamic scholars are totally rejecting orthodox interpretation of the verse 4:34 which was done in an atmosphere wherein male superiority was considered as quite natural, social and biological. I have discussed this in details in my book *Rights of Women in Islam*. It need not detain us here.

But one has to wage serious struggle to promote sexual equality in contemporary Muslim societies wherein Muslim women suffer several disabilities. Again, it should be a part of democratic struggle. One can break stronghold of conservative 'Ulama only in a tolerant, pluralistic modern democracy. It is not Islamic teachings which come in the way, it is orthodox 'Ulama on one hand, and authoritarian power structure, on the other, which come in the way. Koran, in fact, can become a great asset for promoting sexual equality. For that we need not only modern interpretation of the Koranic text but also female theologians fully conscious of their rights.

The Prophet of Non-Violence

The title might come as a surprise for many readers as the Prophet Muhammad (PBUH) has been very frequently projected as the Prophet of violence by media and religious extremists. A Danish cartoonist even showed bombs in his turban. But here in this paper I want to show the Prophet (PBUH) was indeed a Prophet of non-violence. For this I would not fall on traditional sources as Maulanas and muftis (who give religious opinion) but use Koranic values and discuss circumstances in which the Prophet lived. And on these grounds there are no disagreements among Islamic scholars. First of all a question what is non-violence and is absolute non-violence possible? It is crucial to discuss these questions if we want to form opinion about any personality whether he is violent or non-violent. Also, in order to be non-violent what are crucial pre-conditions? Can non-violence be practiced in any given circumstances? Also, can non-violence depend on one person's philosophy?

Let us take these questions now. What is non-violence? Nonviolence is not mere act of non-aggression. A meek or a person totally lacking courage can also apparently be non-aggressive but this meekness or lack of courage becomes a store of aggression within him or her and strikes in devious ways including conspiracies and even can deliver mortal blow. Thus absence of violence cannot be treated as non-violence.

Non-violence is based on deeper inner conviction of a person even if he cannot control all forces operating around him. We must remember that a non-violent person without such deeper conviction cannot be truly non-violent person. This is a crucial point here. A person without such deeper conviction may not ever resort to violence if circumstances do not so dictate to him and a person with deeper conviction about non-violence may, in certain extreme circumstances, have to resort to violence. We have several examples of this in history.

This leads us to second crucial question: Is absolute non-violence possible in society? I think answer, contrary to my desire, is in the negative. Society around us is an extremely complex entity. Around us operate highly contradictory forces which go into dictating themselves on us. As it is said human beings are neither absolutely free to act nor totally dependent on others.

A human being is a complex mixture of freedom and unfreedom. To the extent there is unfreedom our deeper conviction also cannot help. Thus whether a person is non-violent or not will have to be judged by his/her deeper conviction and to an extent what strenuous efforts he/she put in to check violence and simply not by whether one succeeded in creating non-violent society.

Thus a modern historian knows even persons like Mahatma Gandhi who undoubtedly had very deep conviction for non-violence failed to create non-violent India and Independence accompanied by partition saw unprecedented violence. Yet he is known as apostle of non-violence. Much before him Christ, who is known as price of peace and love, ended violently himself nor his followers except for first three centuries during which there were highly persecuted minority, remain peaceful and even Church participated in crusades bringing about killing of thousands of innocent people or Church even allowed burning at stakes of all those who deviated from the Church fiats.

Also, the question whether one can create non-violent society out of one which is based on acute injustices and unequal distribution of economic resources? Of course one can certainly launch non-violent struggles to achieve the aim and that is what it should be, but the question is those whose interests are hit would remain non-violent allow you to achieve your aim. Certainly not. Many peace activists who worked ceaselessly for non- violent struggle were killed at the hands of vested interests.

All this is not to argue even for moment that we should resort to violence and give up non-violent, peaceful struggles. Far from it. But it should be accompanied by deeper understanding for various forces working in the society and the extent they can go to ward off all threats to their interests. I would like to stress here that nonviolence as a value, is absolute, not ensuring it in the society—society as a whole which is beyond our control.

To create a non-violent society we have to create a just society and creating a just society itself evokes at times rivers of blood as it happened in Muslim history (which do not refer to as Islamic history which creates needless confusion). As we will see all this was deliberately or otherwise, though to be result of Islamic teachings and some Muslim scholars and historians are no less responsible for this. Jihad became much misunderstood word right from beginning of Muslim history.

In the light of all this let us now turn to the Prophet (PBUH) of Islam and examine his convictions and his struggles and understand him whether he ever preached violent revolution or tried to employ violent methods to bring about transformation of Arab society. As I pointed out above, I am using here interpretative historical, social and political analysis to understand this rather that traditional sources which often Muslim scholars do.

We must divide the Prophet's struggle in two main phases and others before me have done that. First is the Meccan phase from his birth to his migration to Medina which became his ultimate resting point. Second phase is his stay in Medina until his death. Some point out that Meccan phase was of peaceful nature and that of Medina of rather violent nature. I do not agree with this categorization of one phase being peaceful and the other violent. Basically as far as the Prophet (PBUH) there is no such contradiction. Contradiction is of circumstances, not of choice.

As we all know non-violence is not possible without truth. Truth and non-violence are non-separable from each other. And there is complete unanimity among Muslim scholars, historians and non-Muslim historians that the Prophet's reputation was that of being very honest and trust-worthy (amen). Thus a truthful person cannot become violent at any stage of life. He was as peaceful and nonviolent in Medina as in Mecca though of course in Medinese state circumstances changed drastically which we will take note of. Any discussion without proper social and political context becomes bereft of its roots and at best remains doctrinal. The Prophet, when he appeared on the scene at Mecca was in his prime youth and very sensitive soul.

He was greatly distressed to see Meccan scene—complete turmoil, social anarchy, sharp class differences between poor and dispossessed on one hand, and powerful international business corporations owned by some tribal and clan chiefs. They were indulging in international trade exchanged at Mecca. Slavery added to the acuteness of the scene. Women were at their worst except some powerful elite women.

The Prophet was so distressed by this scene that he began to retire in a cave—known as a cave of Hira on the fringes of Meccan city and would contemplate seriously on the Meccan scene. But he was no mere recluse. He wanted to actively intervene in the situation and as Muslims believe he got a revelation from Allah to show the way. It was his wife Khadija, who accepted him as a prophet and congratulated him.

The Prophet (PBUH), who was otherwise leading a peaceful life with his wife and four daughters, now began preaching his divine message and all the hell let loose. What the Prophet preached can be summarised as follows:

1. Unity of all human beings and unity of all tribes across Arabia which was causing so much conflict and bloodshed. Intertribal unity was greatly needed. Thus he preached ukhuwwah (brotherhood-sisterhood as the word is inclusive of both the genders). This could best be realized by tawhid (oneness of Allah). It became basic doctrine of Islam. So many gods and goddesses were source of all kinds of inter-tribal conflicts and superstition at the cost of direct rational thinking.

   To relieve distress of the poor, orphans, widows slaves and other weaker sections of society and several Meccan chapters and verses of Koran are proof enough of this He wanted to bring about redistribution of wealth to realize social peace and gave us the institution of zakat (though Koran did not set its quantum, the Prophet said it should be two and half percent of ones wealth at the end of the year.
2. Uplift of women by giving them dignity and individual rights. He wanted to bring about social revolution in this respect. What we say 'empowerment of women' was achieved by the Prophet but later, as usually happens sabotaged by powerful and conservative Ulama. What Koran did to enhance empowerment of women was indeed revolutionary.

3. To establish just, peaceful and non-violent society through these means and give every human equal dignity and rights irrespective of ethnic, religious, linguistic or cultural differences. Since the Prophet's teachings deeply disturbed the vested interests in Mecca who were engrossed in accumulating profits, neglecting all their tribal social obligations and perpetuating gross injustices. Also, a section of youth and the poor enthusiastically flocked around the Prophet (PBUH), these powerful traders and tribal chiefs gathered together to silence the Prophet. When they failed they approached his uncle Abu Talib who, according to tribal tradition, was his chief protector.

When Abu Talib conveyed to him what those tribal chiefs wanted he replied: if they put sun in one hand, and moon on the other and ask me to shut up, I would not. When Abu Talib saw his deep moral conviction he assured his nephew of full protection and give him full liberty to preach his ideas. Not succeeding in that the tribal chiefs started insulting the Prophet, mocking him and persecuting, in many cases of weaker unprotected sections, severely.

One of his followers was an Ethiopian slave Bilal Habshi who had embraced Islam right in the beginning. He was one of his most loyal followers as he saw in the Prophet a great liberator of slaves. The Prophet too, never neglected him and often showed preference to him above more powerful and richer of his followers. He appointed him as his mu'addhin (caller for prayer) which was great honour to which many of his companions were aspiring for.

However, the Prophet never retaliated against his and his companions and followers persecution. He and his followers were urged to bear all this with patience. In fact one of the Koranic surahs of Meccan period dwells on virtues of patience and makes it inseparable part of truth. Truth and patience go together, it says (chapter 103 Al-Asr) in both Meccan and Medinese chapters the virtues emphasised are: truth, justice, humility, patience, compassion, wisdom and piety. Also emphasized is suppression of feeling of revenge and anger. Revenge and retaliation were main ingredients of tribal behaviour and had already led to years of bloodshed among Arabs.

All of these virtues lead to non-violent conduct, in fact is most essential part of it. The Prophet showed greatest forbearance in the Arab history who desisted from retaliating at any stage. When faced with gross brutalities he would often retire to himself, reflected deeply and came out with peaceful solution. When prosecution became unbearable in Mecca both for him and his companions and tribal chiefs plotted to assassinate him while sleeping, he decided to migrate to Medina in the dark of night.

He bore all tribulations quietly, some suggest because the Prophet and his followers were a minority and dare not to fight back in Mecca. This is gross distortion of Prophet's very character. He was meticulous follower of peace and non-violence. Had it been so he could have easily not only conquered Mecca earlier than he did could have taken revenge from his persecutors, killing them and shedding blood after he did. He did not order killing of any of his foe or persecutor which was allowed by tribal tradition.

When he migrated to Medina he was welcome very enthusiastically as he went there primarily as peace-maker. The inter-tribal feud had robbed Medina of peace for last forty years. He succeeded in ending this feud and establish peace between the two tribes on principles of justice and fairness to both. Thus he entered Medina as an ambassador of peace and hence got enthusiastic welcome.

In Medina situation was entirely different partly under the Prophet's control and partly beyond him. He emerged in Medina as great moral, spiritual and ethical teacher who not only brought about unity among the people of Medina but also guided them in every walk of life. Another great virtue of the Prophet was his humility. He described himself as 'abduhu was rasuluhu, i.e. as servant of Allah and His messenger. He never tried to place himself above others. When he was constructing his house and mosque he himself took part, like others in constructing it. He used to say I am not above you except as a messenger of Allah. A great teacher and so humble! Some Arabs tried to bow down before him. He strictly prohibited them from doing so and said you should bow before none except Allah.

But there were certain things beyond the Prophet's control. The Prophet's (PBUH) migration to Medina gave rise to another kind of hostility among the Jews who handled trade and often functioned as arbitrators to whom the Arab tribes would refer their disputes to. The Prophet's migration changed this situation. The Jews lost their pre - eminent position and over and above this their monopoly of trade was broken which hurt them deeply. Many of the Prophet's companions like Abu Bakr, Uthman and others were expert traders and since they also came along with the Prophet, began trading and thus Jews' monopoly was over.

There in Mecca, the tribal chiefs were very angry that the Prophet escaped and is now preaching in Medina. They had vowed either to silence him or eliminate him. They had failed in both these projects. So they decided to pursue their animosity right in Medina. The Prophet was very alert to the situation. Soon the Meccan chiefs secretly established contacts with the Madinese Jews and prepared to attack Medina. The Prophet in apprehension of possible attack had sent some of his followers to keep an eye near a place called Badr which was possible site of attack.

Meanwhile the Prophet had entered into a covenant with all tribes including the Jewish tribes known as *Mithaq-e-Madina* and guaranteed full freedom of faith, traditions, culture and security life and property. The Jews too had full freedom to follow their religion and all traditions without any interference from any. Only condition was that if Medina was attacked all will defend it together. It was wonderful document as modern as Union or national and international declarations of today.

By this covenant Jews were obliged to join Muslims if Medina is attacked by the Meccans. And Meccans did attack Medina and Jews had advance information of it as they were in secret negotiations with the Meccans. The Jews did not defend Medina and a hostile situation arose between Jews and Muslims. The battle of Badr took place in which 313 Muslims defeated about 1000 Meccans which was great humiliation for them.

The Prophet (PBUH) cannot be in any way responsible for this battle. He left Mecca so as to avoid any violent conflict and even in Medina he and his companions were not left in peace by the vested interests.

Of course there are some vague, even dark areas about the fight between Jews and Muslims. As far as Jewish betrayal and conspiracy with Meccan is concerned it is beyond doubt. However certain narratives in Ibn Ishaq, Tabari, primary sources for the Prophet's life, have recorded certain events which need to be critically looked at. They have uncritically accepted certain Jewish historical narratives accusing the Prophet of killing more than 700 Jews after the battle of Trench (Khandaq) in which the Meccan Jews openly collaborated with the Meccan enemies of the Prophet (PBUH).

There is no place to go into details of this here but suffice it to say that this whole episode does not accord with the character of the Prophet. One psychological reason for accepting this uncritical narrative by early Muslim historians is that they wanted to establish their superiority over their enemies who betrayed them. Moreover it does not accord well with the Koranic description of the event, Islamic historians and scholars need to look into it very seriously and make critical appraisal of it. Unfortunately all scholars, Islamic as well as non-Islamic, keep on quoting from Ibn Ishaq, Tabari, etc. without seriously subjecting it to critical analyses in the light of modern historical researches.

The Prophet of Islam, it must be noted never resorted to wars of aggression. There is specific prohibition in the Koran for war of aggressions. The Koran specifically says, 'And fight in the way of Allah against those who fight against you but be not aggressive. Surely Allah loves not aggressors.' (2:190) The Prophet of Islam never violated this Koranic doctrine and this 2nd chapter was revealed in Medina, not in Mecca. This is clear that war of aggression is not acceptable to Allah in any case.

I would like to give two major examples of non-violent way of resolving highly complex issues which establish the Prophet as a major exponent of peace in a region like Arabia which had witnessed blood baths on minor issues. And their revenge and anger never came to an end. One example is that the Prophet, though head of a proto-state, never raised any army throughout his life. All the fights he was forced to fight was done by voluntary participation and hence came to concept of martyrdom—dying for a higher cause. Had Prophet had any aggressive intentions and seek political power, he could have raised an army. Also funds for weapons, etc., was collected through donations from his followers, never by any public tax.

Zakat money as clearly described in Koran was meant for distribution to the poor and weaker sections of society and was never spent on was preparations. Prophet never accepted zakat for himself or his family. It was prohibited to him. Only a person of non- violent intentions will desist from raising army while being surrounded by powerful and highly resourceful enemy.

Second proof of Prophet's peaceful intentions is what is called in Islamic history *Sulh-e-Hudaibiyah* (Peace of Hudaibiyah). Before he performed his last Hajj after conquering Mecca peaceful he intended to perform Hajj a year before. He was apprehensive of armed resistance by the Meccans so departed for Mecca with defensive preparations. He was stopped, as expected at Hudiabiyah on the way and asked not to proceed. Though the Prophet was fully prepared to take Meccans on, he instead started negotiations with the representative of Meccans. He accepted all these terms in the interest of peace including deleting Messenger of Allah, from his name. This angered some of his followers but he persisted and avoided unnecessary bloodshed. This peace agreement favoured Muslims ultimately and next year the Prophet could enter Mecca very peaceful without shedding a drop of blood. There cannot be greater proof that peace and non-violence was not only teaching of the Koran but embedded in the very character of the Prophet (PBUH).

To conclude I would like to make few observations:

1. Violence in Prophet's life was highly contextual and no one like the Prophet had any control over it. Whatever violence took

place was result of vested interests from Mecca and Medina not only not to allow peaceful preaching of Islam but also inflicting violence on the Prophet and his followers.

2. There is no difference in Meccan and Medinese period as far as Prophet's approach is concerned. The Prophet followed consistently policy of peace and non-violence in both the phases. Whatever contradiction we find in Meccan and Medinese period is of the situation, not doctrinal, much less intentional.
3. The Koran had to permit defensive violence without which Muslims could not have survived at all. Thus absolute non-violence can only be doctrinal and cannot work in a highly complex world full of different interests and people who want to dominate. Absolute non-violence can be applied in a different world which is perfectly just and full of people willing to coexist without contradictions and evil intentions. Such a world has remained Utopia so far.
4. Islam is not a political ideology but a civilizational force with strong spiritual and moral doctrines. Its main aim is to exalt the human beings to highest levels of spiritual and moral conduct. Allah has created human beings in best of mould (fi ahsan-e-taqwim) but they descend into lowest of low to fulfil their ambitions and desires to have more and dominate others.
5. The Muslims must understand that Islam will emerge in its best only when they pursue these higher values, not power. Pursuit of power caused enough bloodshed and is still causing in the Muslim world. Islam has great civilizational potential and has given great civilization to the world.
6. And they can call the world to way of Allah only through wisdom and good upright conduct.

13
A Critical Look at Koranic Verses on War and Violence

Certain verses of Koran are repeatedly quoted by the critics and enemies of Islam to show how Islam is intolerant of its opponents and wants them to be eliminated. Also since the days of crusade the West has projected image of Islam as 'sword in one hand, and Koran, in the other'. This image has stuck in the minds of thousands of non-Muslims throughout the world. It got fresh lease of life after 9/11 and spurt of news reports and articles in media and TV news channels on terrorism and Islam. It is, therefore, necessary to have a critical look at these verses.

Before we deal with these verses we wish to make two comments which are very necessary. Firstly, the critics and opponents of Islam deliberately ignoring hundreds of other verses which are on tolerance, forgiveness, humane treatment of enemies and so on. Besides that in the Prophet's (PBUH) life too there are several events which could be model for anyone to imitate. However, critics and opponents of Islam are deliberately quite selective in picking up certain verses out of context and quote them to show intolerance of Islam towards its enemies. In some cases it is deliberate, in others, perhaps out of ignorance. But more likely it is deliberate.

Secondly, the Muslim theologians and jurists also must share the blame. They still continue to imitate the medieval jurists (fuqaha') in giving doctrinal status to war and violence. It was understandable in medieval times when wars were considered quite legitimate and were resorted to by all sides Christians and all others. Even then as we will see further, Islam had permitted violence with certain reservations and conditions. Thus violence or war never had doctrinal status in Islam. It was permitted only for defence, never for aggression. The Koranic position is clearly stated in 2:190. This verse has doctrinal status.

According to this verse two conditions are required to be fulfilled for war: firstly it should be in the way of Allah, not for any personal ambition, revenge or territorial grab. Secondly, it should be strictly in defense, not by way of aggression as Allah does not love aggression and aggressors. I do not think any other religion or ideological system before Islam had laid down any such conditions restricting wars. Sword was considered decisive especially while dealing with opponents.

Islam, the critics should note, did not appear in vacuum; no religion does. Each religion carries birthmark of its concrete historical and social conditions. Islam appeared in Arabia of 6th and 7th centuries and ferocious tribal wars were order of the day in those days. The main preoccupation and challenge before the Prophet of Islam was how to restore peace in the society wherein violence was a norm, not an exception.

Prophet's hands were forced by the circumstances. He also had limited choices. When he and his followers were severely persecuted and faced with violence, they had to resort to violence as no other alternatives were available. Thus in one of the verses Koran says, 'And what reason have you not to fight in the way of Allah, and of the weak among the men and the women and the children, who say: Our Lord, take us out of this town, whose people are oppressors, and grant us from Thee a friend, and grant us from Thee a helper.'

The words of these verses show how helpless Muslims had become in view of oppression by enemies of Islam. Islam was, let us remember, a religion which not only confine itself to moral exhortations but also, in view of the given circumstances, a social revolution.

There were powerful vested interests who had accumulated great deal of wealth and their greed drove them to accumulate more and more totally neglecting the poor and other weaker sections of society. Accumulate, accumulate and accumulate as Marx says in Das Capital was their religion.

The Prophet (PBUH), a great lover of justice from pre-Islamic days (he had formed hilf al-fudul—to help the victims of injustices much before he was appointed a prophet) was deeply concerned with social justice as most of the Meccan surahs clearly point out. And when some one challenged these vested interests and that too, from their own class, they spare no efforts to wipe out that person, especially, if they fail to co-opt or buy off that person, or silence him in any other peaceful manner.

Islamic historians tell us that the rich merchants of Meccans offered the Prophet (PBUH) enough for him and his coming generations to live on but the Prophet replied if you put sun on my one hand and moon on the other, even then I am not going to give up what I am preaching. Thus the Meccan merchants, failed to co-opt or buy off him and then they declared an all out war against him and his movement.

Even then he advised his followers to remain peaceful and bear hardships and persecution but not to yield. His followers did and put up with severe persecution. Muhammad (PBUH), who was against idol worship as the very basis of his religion was *tawhid* (oneness of God) he declared that non-believers can continue to worship as they worship and for them is their faith and for me mine (chapter 109).

But real opposition was not, as far as the rich merchants were concerned, to way of worship as attack on their greed and accumulation of wealth in the face of great misery and poverty of people at lower rungs. They did not stand any check on accumulation of their wealth and they did not want to undertake any measures for poverty alleviation. The only method they knew was to co-opt or wipe out the opponents of their greed.

The verse 4:75 quoted above shows desperation of the situation. Persecution went beyond all limits of human tolerance and no other alternative was available. There was no democracy that one could sit on dharna or organize demonstration to get the grievances redressed. And we know even in democracy how police fires on demonstrators and kills several people or baton charges them brutally and severely injures demonstrators.

The Prophet even then chose another alternative, i.e. to migrate to other place which was more hospitable like Ethiopia first and then to Medina. However, the vested interests in Mecca knew that Muhammad (PBUH), with his powerful appeal to the weaker sections of society, would be a great danger for them and their trade caravans could come under attack. Thus they decided not to leave him in peace in Medina. His migration was not a good riddance for them. It was a different challenge, perhaps more difficult challenge now than before.

The Prophet (PBUH), on the other hand, in pursuance of justice and peace, entered into a covenant with Jews and pagans of Mecca and gave them equal rights and freedom to pursue their respective faiths. Not only this he called all those who were signatory to this covenant as one people (umma wahidah) with an obligation to defend Medina, if attacked by outsiders, especially Meccans. This umma wahidah comes very close to modern day concept of a nation bound by obligations of a constitution. This covenant was the constitution of Medina.

But what was feared did happen. Medina was attacked by powerful merchants of Mecca and the Prophet was forced to go for defense. However, it must be noted that there was no regular army and it was voluntary to participate in the battle. In the absence of any state structure neither Meccans nor Medinese had any regular army. Both ways participation was voluntary. But there was one vital difference.

The Meccan merchants were not only united but also had all the resources material as well as human. Also, they were defending their wealth and 'right' to accumulate without any social intervention. The Muslims in Medina, on the other hand, had severe problems. The Jewish tribes, though signatory to the covenant of Medina, were not only unwilling to fight but also willing to collaborate with the merchants of Mecca. They were resentful of intrusion of Mohammad (PBUH) and his followers in Medina. They had lost their privileged position as leaders due to intrusion of Muslims into that city.

Second great difficult situation for Muslims was lack of resources—both material as well as human. Thus we find several verses in the Koran imploring Muslims to donate generously and that Allah will reward them seven folds if they did. Yet another difficulty was that Muslims in Medina had either migrated from Mecca and left everything behind or belonged to poorer sections of society and had very little to donate. The Ansars of Medina (those who had embraced Islam from Medina) too were not well off and had little to spare. These were formidable challenges for Muslims.

But, as pointed out before, Muslims had little choice but to fight and in the battle of Badr they were hopelessly outnumbered also. There were only 313 Muslims as against thousand Meccans without proper weapons and line of supply. Still it was their faith and strong commitment (they had little to loose but their slavery, poverty and injustices) which ensured victory to them. They fought with great determination and strong resolve.

But this is not to glorify war and violence. It was forced on Muslims and they bravely faced it. Had Meccans not attacked them they would not have gone to Mecca to fight against them as it was clearly against the Koranic injunction. Even today when we talk of democracy, nations fight not only when attacked but even in anticipation of any such attack, or even forging false grounds. America attacked Afghanistan and Iraq, not because it was attacked by these two weaklings but by falsely forging documents that Iraq possessed 'weapons of mass destruction.'

Thus Koran neither glorifies violence nor makes it essential for a believer to resort to it as a religious duty. At best, permits it as a necessary evil in case of defending oneself against aggression. It should not be and cannot be elevated to the status of doctrine. I do not want to discuss here the question of jihad as much has already been written on it and suffice it may to say that jihad in all 41 verses of Koran that this word has been used, it no where means war.

But then critics quote some verses from the Koran to prove that it believes in violence against kafirs and requires believers to kill them wherever found. One of these verses is, 'They long that you should disbelieve so that you might be on the same level; so take not from among them friends until they flee (their homes) in Allah's way. Then if they turn back (to hostility), sieze them and kill them wherever you find them, and take no friend nor helper from among them' (4:89).

To many, the words 'sieze them and kill them wherever you find them' may appear very disturbing and they may argue that these words clearly establish that kafirs should be killed wherever they are found and also this established the fact that Muslims went out with sword in one hand and Koran, in the other. However, this interpretation of the verse ignores the fact that it does not describe normal situation but situation of active hostility. The following verse also makes it clear.

The verse which follows the above verse says, 'Except those who join a people between whom and you there is an alliance, or who come to you, their hearts shrinking from fighting you or fighting their own people. And if Allah had pleased, he would have given them power over you, so that they would have fought you. So if they withdraw from you and fight you not and offer you peace, then Allah allows you no way against them' (4:90).

This verse needs hardly any explanation that it clearly indicates war situation and situation of active hostility. It is also said in this verse that if they join those unbelievers with whom you have an alliance or they sue for peace then do not fight them. These verses do not apply to times of peace. Even in modern times, the nations at war treat each other as enemies and armies kill soldiers of enemy nation wherever found. There is nothing odd about it.

According to the second verse, even waverers are not to be fought or killed, if they refrained from fighting. Any civilized nation would approve of this and even applaud it. Unfortunately those hostile to Islam refuse to see even such obvious rules and attack Koran and accuse it of teaching intolerance against all non-believers.

It is also important to note that we should read one particular verse in conjunction with all other verses on the subject if we want to understand actual intention of the Koran. Koran nowhere teaches to go to war with those simply because they refuse to believe. Koran allows freedom of religion or freedom of conscience (2:256) and also emphasizes justice to the extent that justice must be done even if it goes in favour of the enemy. The verse reads as follows: 'O you who believe, be upright for Allah, bearers of witness with justice; and let not hatred of a people incite you not to act equitably. Be just; that is nearer to observance of duty' (5:8).

Another verse is 4:35 which also exhorts believers to be just even if it goes against themselves or parents or near ones. Thus how Koran can incite Muslims to kill any unbeliever simply because he/she is unbeliever. Also, there are other verses which clearly contradict such position. In this connection, the verse 8 of chapter 60 is also very important.

This verse tells Muslims that 'Allah forbids you not respecting those who fight you not for religion, nor drive you forth from your homes, that you show them kindness and deal with them justly. Surely Allah loves the doers of justice' (60:8). Is any further explanation needed? Those unbelievers who do not fight Muslims and do not drive them away from their homes; Muslims should behave with kindness and justice towards them.

Here again I would like to submit that we must distinguish between Islam as a religion, a belief system and Islam as a social movement, which was challenging powerful vested interests in Mecca and allies of powerful merchants of Mecca. Islam as a religion is spiritual and moral movement which exhorts Muslims to follow moral and spiritual teachings, but as social movement pitted against powerful vested interests and enemies, it allows them to meet the situation as in times of hostilities and wars.

The verse 60:8 is a moral and spiritual teaching, but what we find in verses like 4:89 and 4:90 is war like situation and one cannot teach in such a situation in a violence infested region like Arabia to surrender to the enemy at ones own peril. It would have been unacceptable. In Bible, too, one finds such contradicting verses. While as a moral teaching it talks of love and presenting another cheek if slapped on one cheek and also that one should sell ones coat to buy a sword.

Koran while requiring believers to fight if fought against also exhorts them to be just and kind and not to abuse others gods lest they should abuse Allah (6:109). The moral and spiritual teachings are eternal and teachings and exhortations about war or situation of hostilities contextual and will apply only in a particular context. To quote those verses as if they are eternally applicable is not correct. Or deliberate distortion of the Koranic teachings.

The concept of dhimmi (one whose responsibility to protect is on Muslims) is both moral as well as political. It is binding on Muslims to protect the dhimmis as if they would protect Muslims and to ensure complete freedom of faith and protections to their places of worship. The Koran itself guarantees protection to all places of worship whichever religion they belong to see verse 22:40 and it also says Allah has created a law and a way for every nation (5:48) and every one is free to follow one's own law and the way. There is no compulsion to follow anyone only.

Also, each one has ones own direction to pray and one should not quarrel over it but excel each other in good deeds (2:148). The Prophet himself was a role model in this respect. When a delegation of Christians of Najran visited the Prophet (PUBH), he made them stay in his mosque and allowed them to pray therein. They used to pray in one side of the mosque and the Prophet (PBUH) and Muslims on the other side. What better example of respect for others' faith?

When Tartars arrested Muslims, Jews and Christians and were willing to free only Muslims, Imam Ibn Taymiyyah, a great scholar of Islam told the leader of the Tartars that we will not accept freedom without Jews and Christians also being freed as it is our responsibility to protect them (ahl al-dhimma). What an example of fulfilling one's responsibility towards the dhimmis.

This is not to say that excesses have not happened in the history of Islam. Muslims have killed Muslims—most brutally as when Abbasids overthrew Umayyads they even dug out the graves of Abbasids and dishonoured—the dead. Similarly, the Kharijites (Khawarij), the extremists among Muslims considered permissible to kill all other Muslims who are not khawarij. Hajjaj bin Yusuf killed thousands of his opponents in Iraq and threw more than hundred thousand people into prison including women.

It will be naive to deny such excess in history, but responsibility for this cannot be inflicted on Islam, but on those Muslims who perpetrated these crimes against humanity. It is indeed quite wrong, as many scholars do, to foist its responsibility on Islam. Islam should be judged by its teachings, not by what happened in its history. Human action is not motivated by religious teachings in one's behaviour but by one's own vested interests and aspirations for power. One cannot blame a nation's constitution when some police officers commit atrocities on prisoners in lock-up.

Some Muslim scholars and theologians try to overlook, even, ignore these facts of Muslim history. It is as wrong to hold Islam responsible for what happened in Muslim history. We should be as fair and just in judging Muslims as judging non-Muslims. It is Koranic teaching as we have already referred to. This is also the dictate of unbiased scholarship and principles of higher criticism.

14
Islam, Democracy and Violence

It is not at all correct to say that Islam is incompatible to democracy. This myth is being spread by the supporters of authoritarian regime in the Islamic world. Kings, Sheikhs and military dictators are spreading such ideas, caring if Islam gets a bad name in the process. Islam does not come in the way of democracy; it is dictators and monarchs who come in its way.

We should remember, that the Koran does not give any concept of state but a concept of society. Koran wants to establish a just society and what other way could be better suited to establish a just society than a democratic society. Also the Koran emphasizes equality of all human beings and equal dignity for all despite different languages, colours and race and nationality. How can it be achieved except through democratic society?

The authoritarian societies negate all these and hence not democracy but monarchy and dictatorship is un-Islamic, not democracy. During medieval ages, the concept like equal dignity, gender equality and human rights were just non-existent and hence monarchy was quite acceptable. It is no longer so. The modern society is emphatic about human equality without any distinction and human rights and gender equality are of great significance and hence democracy is the only way out for Koranic concept of just society to be realized. Some people, especially radical Islamic groups do argue that the only just government could be through institution of khilafah. Let me say that the institution of khilafah has not been sanctioned by the Koran as pointed out above Koran does not recommend any form of government at all. The institution of khilafa was a result of historical situation. It was not even a part of Prophet's (PBUH) Sunna.

That is why there were differences among Muslims about the question of succession. Even most prominent companions of the Prophet (PBUH) were not sure about the mode of succession of the successor. Shias maintain that the Prophet (PBUH) appointed his cousin and son-in-law, Ali, to succeed him. But only the supporters of Ahl-e-bait agreed with this view while the others gathered in Saqifa while Banu Sa'ida to discuss the question of his successor. There was no unanimity, and after lot of suggestions and debates, Umar proposed the name of Abu Bakr and did bay'ah on his hand and others followed.

There was no unanimity in electing the Caliph. Many said the khalifah could be only from the tribe of Quraish of Mecca and Ansar of Medina who were from other tribes like Khazraj and Aus maintained that caliph should be from among them as they had helped the Prophet (PBUH) in Medina. It was also suggested that two persons be elected one from Quraish and one from Ansars. But this viewpoint was also rejected and ultimately Abu Bakr of Quraish was elected.

Then it was said that there could be only one caliph at one time but this concept also proved to be fragile as when the Abbasid defeated Umayyads, one of Umayyad's family fled to Spain and founded another empire there and at a time there came into existence two caliphs and when Buwahids captured power and caliph became merely a nominal head, caliphate turned into sultanate. The institution of Caliphate also lasted only for thirty years and Mu'awiyah captured power without any sanction from Muslims as in the case of first caliph and what is more he nominated his own son Yazid against the wishes of all Muslims and against the wishes of prominent companions of the Prophet (PBUH) many of whom were then alive.

All this clearly shows that the institution of khilafah was a tentative historical construct, not the result of any divine injunction either based on Koran or Sunna. Thus it cannot be argued that the institution of khilafah be restored and that is the only way out. Also, institution of khilafah, was after all more democratic than monarchy or sheikhdoms and dictatorship which have no sanction of any kind at all.

Also, in case of electing a caliph, tribal experience of the time was used, as successor to a tribal chief was elected by the members of the tribe. There was no concept of one-man one vote at the time. In the institution of modern democracy one man one vote is the tried and tested method for electing public representative. New historical experience has resulted in new methods of election. There should be no hesitation in excepting and assimilating new experiences. During the period of Khilafah many institutions were readily borrowed from Roman and Sassanid empire like keeping salary register for soldiers from Iran. Earlier, only share in the loot was given to those taking part in the fight.

Another question which is raised by Islamists is imposition of sharia law. They argue that in democracy there are man made (human made) laws and sharia law is divine law and this cannot be allowed in an Islamic state as only sharia law should be enforced. This is also an erroneous concept. sharia laws can be divided into two categories: 'ibadat and mu'amalat (i.e. laws pertaining to salah, saum, haj, etc., which are part of 'ibadat. Then the laws pertaining to mu'amalat which include relations between human beings and human beings. Laws about mu'amalat cannot be permanent. Of course, no changes can be made as far as sharia laws concerning 'ibadat are concerned but as for mu'amalat, laws cannot be permanent and parliament should be empowered to make laws in those respects. All modern democracies allow people to pursue their respective religions and do not interfere in their religious affairs. In all secular democracies also right to religion is a fundamental right.

Also, as far as 'ibadat is concerned, it does not require enforcement by any state but its importance lies in its voluntary nature. 'Ibadat pertain to ones heart and soul and real 'ibadat is one which is done most sincerely and from ones core of heart. It cannot be enforced. And it will cease to be 'ibadat if it is enforced by a state machinery. This is what Koran also maintains when it says there is no compulsion in matters of religion.

Thus no Islamic state is required even to enforce provisions of sharia. An Islamic state again would mean the majority of Muslim sect who live in that country would enjoy real freedom and those Muslims who belong to other sects would be persecuted. We see this right in the beginning of Islamic history. The Abbasids initially subscribed to the doctrine of createdness of Koran and all those who rejected this doctrine were severely persecuted. Even eminent Imam like Abu Hanifa was flogged for rejecting this doctrine.

In modern Islamic states, too, we see this phenomenon. In Saudi Arabia only Wahabi Muslims enjoy real freedom of religion. Those who do not subscribe to this doctrine are persecuted, or do not enjoy freedom like Wahabis to practise their religion. Similarly, the Shias are persecuted in Sunni majority states and Sunnis in Shiah majority states. In Iraq, a Sunni minority dominated and persecuted Shi'ahs and in Syria, Alawi minority dominate over Sunni majority as it wields political power.

Real freedom of religion is possible only in democratic state where all enjoy equal rights irrespective of caste, creed and colour. Large number of Muslims today live as minority in various secular democratic states in various Asian, African and Western countries and enjoy right to freely practise their religion. Thus, it is not correct to maintain that you need an Islamic state to practise Islam freely.

Every democratic state permits sharia laws pertaining to personal laws like marriage, divorce, property, inheritance, etc. In secular India too, Muslims are completely free to practise these laws. Indian Muslims refuse any reform in their laws and state does not insist on that though in many Muslim countries these laws have been reformed.

Now, the question about criminal law is whether it would be permitted in a secular democratic state to be permitted. The answer is certainly no. In India, the British had abolished Islamic criminal laws in nineteenth century itself, and enforced a criminal code drafted by their parliament. The Muslim Ulama agreed to abolition of the Islamic code and agreed to enforcement of common criminal code. Today, in the modern world, many Muslim majority countries have also taken similar steps. Criminal punishments are largely contextual. In the tribal Arab society, certain punishments were thought to be more effective and hence they were recommended. The main purpose is to prevent crime and nature and extent of punishment can certainly change. Also, there is provision for tazir punishment also in Islam and the rulers did enforce tazir punishments too. So it is not a matter of principle whether hudud laws are enforced or not, containing illegal activity is of utmost importance.

Thus, it is seen that a secular and democratic state is equally good as long as it permits Muslims to practise their religion. It is also important to note that the Indian Ulama voluntarily opted for a secular state as opposed to an Islamic state in the form of Pakistan, in 1947, when India was divided. They vigorously opposed the creation of a separate Muslim country and preferred to have a secular, democratic and multi-religious, multi cultural country. And who knew Islam better than the Ulama of Darul Ulum Deoband.

An Islamic state itself, as pointed out before, is a historical construct and not a Koranic concept and hence it is in no way obligatory for Muslims to set up an Islamic state. Those who argue in favour of Islamic state cannot produce any argument from the Koran and Sunna. In every country there are certain forces who adopt majoritarian aggressive postures and want their religion to be associated with the affairs of the state. In India, for example, a section of Hindus want India to become Hindu Rashtra (i.e. Hindu nation) but secular Hindus resist that demand.

In any religious state all citizens of different religious persuasions cannot enjoy equal rights and no modern state can allow this. The very essence of modern polity is that all citizens irrespective of their religion should enjoy equal rights. Maulana Maududi of Jamat-e-Islami of Pakistan had argued that no non-Muslim can become head of the state or prime minister of Pakistan. He or she cannot even hold any key post in the government. In secular states as well, no person from minority religion will find it easy to become head of the state but theoretically it is possible. In India—a Sikh, a non-Hindu became a prime minister and three Muslims could become president of the country.

Another objection raised by many Islamists is that in a secular democratic state, human rights are sacred and the very concept of human rights is un-Islamic. This is also not in keeping with the Koranic teachings. Firstly, most of the Islamic countries, with few exceptions have signed the UNO's Human Rights Declaration. Some countries did not sign the declaration on the basis that one who renounces Islam cannot be put to death as freedom of religion is a fundamental principle of human rights.

However, as pointed out above, Koran itself upholds right to freedom of religion and the Koran pronounced it much before modern world realized its significance. It is very strange that now some Muslims in contradiction to Koranic principle, of which they should have been justly proud, reject the doctrine of freedom of religion as modern Western and hence unacceptable. The sharia rule that one who renounces Islam should be given death sentence is highly controversial and there is no unanimity on this among Muslim jurists. Maulana Aslam Jairajpuri, for example, disagrees with it and advances several arguments from Koran and Sunna to

In fact freedom and faith go together. One cannot genuinely believe in any religion unless one is completely free to accept or reject it. If one is forced to accept a religion it cannot be accepted by his heart and soul. He may accept it outwardly but his heart and soul may resent it. It is precisely for this psychological reason that Koran made principle of freedom of religion so important. The sharia provision for death sentence was more for sedition than for renouncing religion. It was feared that a Muslim living in an Islamic state, if renounces Islam, he may join hands with the enemy and conspire against Islamic state. Punishment for sedition throughout the world is death.

The fear of sedition was genuine because Muslim states were surrounded by Christian states and there was direct political, (though not religious) confrontation between the two and hence anyone renouncing Islam became a possible ally for the Christian state. The crusades are well-known from 11th to 13th century. That period of confrontation between Muslims and Christians was most intense. Thus death punishment for renouncing Islam makes sense during that period. This context must be kept in mind, but in the long run the Koranic doctrine of freedom of religion must be upheld.

As for other principles of human rights, even the most orthodox Muslim cannot object to them. For example, equality of all human beings is very central to Koranic teachings too. Human dignity is sacred in Islam as well. Gender equality is also clearly enunciated in the Koran. Moreover, women have been given equal rights for contracting marriage and husband and wife have been described as each others garment. All these are enshrined in declaration of human rights issued by the UNO. Muslim countries like Saudi Arabia which did not sign Human Rights' Declaration also did not object to these provisions.

Those who argue that implementation of sharia is an obligation of Islamic State should understand that sharia evolved gradually and there were great deal of differences among the Muslim jurists on many issues. Thus sharia, as one Islamic scholar Prof. Muhammad Mujeeb maintained, is a human approach to divine injunctions. That is very apt description of sharia laws as evolved by many eminent jurists during first four centuries of Islam.

The great Urdu poet Iqbal from Indian subcontinent also maintained that every generation of Muslims should be entitled to will be the right forum to do so. He also maintained that *ijtihad* is the dynamic principle in Islam and *ijtihad* becomes necessary in changed conditions in modern society. Thus a democratic society with an elected parliament would be a better institutional arrangement for making sharia more relevant to our contemporary world. Many new issues have arisen which need use of ijtihad quite urgent.

And where Muslims are a minority and live in secular democratic state should evolve their own forums to bring about necessary changes. Today more Muslims live in minority situation than in majority and hence they would have to evolve their own institutions to do *ijtihad* with the cooperation of Ulama and modern scholars. No secular democratic state can stop them from attempting these creative changes in their laws. All this has to be done within the framework of Islam. No changes can be brought outside this framework if they are to be accepted by Muslims at large.

To accept democratic state would be far more beneficial to Muslims and would enable Muslims to practice their religion faithfully and fearlessly than in so-called Islamic state where sectarianism and fundamentalism will prevail. A democratic state is much better guarantee of genuine freedom of religion than a state based on any religion. This seems to be contradictory but in fact true.

Thus we must properly educate Muslim masses and prepare them for acceptance of democracy in Islamic world. They should be made aware that those who oppose democracy in the name of Islam are really serving certain vested interests rather than Islam. Islamic world is still reeling under the impact of feudal and medieval forces who serve their own interests in the name of Islam. Islam is quite compatible with democracy. It is the interests of rulers of Muslim countries which are not compatible with democracy.

Indonesia, I said in my lectures, has achieved democracy after a long spell under dictatorship and it must be protected at any cost and all religious minorities also should be guaranteed full freedom to follow their respective religion. Tolerance of differences is an important principle of democracy and due tolerance should be shown to all different religious opinions as well. It will not violate any Islamic principle at all.

15
Hindu-Muslim Unity through Religion?

For democracy, all secularists agree, secularism is a must and unity in diversity in countries like India is possible only through secular polity. Religion, in secular democracy should be at best a private affair and religion should have no role as far as politics and affairs of state are concerned. And Nehruites also maintained that schools supported by the government should not teach religion and education should be strictly secular.

Of course, Gandhians had different viewpoint from this. Gandhians did not de-emphasize religion while supporting secularism and secular democracy. Rather they believed in promoting religious values with a proviso that one should respect all religions equally. Then there are those who reject religion altogether and for them secularism means atheism and religion does not have any role in any sphere of public life. Thus these are different shades of secularism, i.e. Nehruvian, Gandhian and atheistic.

However, none of these models seem to be succeeding. Nehruvian model should have been more successful as it partly meets the Gandhian approach, and partly the atheistic. However, the way political class is behaving, i.e. only interested in power, not in principles and values it failed as it neither remained Nehruvian in spirit nor Gandhian, much less atheistic. In traditional society like India, Gandhian model should have had a greater chances of success, but even Gandhians did not follow those principles or practice them entirely.

What is now happening in the name of religion is purely communalism—gross misuse of religion for political purpose. The Sangh Parivar (i.e. those belonging to the family of BJP, a saffron party) taking advantage of majoritarian ethos politicized Hindu religion and communalism infiltrated both political and educational institutions and deeply polarized society on religious basis. Hindus and Muslims and other communities who had lived together for centuries and had influenced each other, began to lose warmth of relationship; began to hate each other. Spawned by the vitriolic propaganda by the Sangh

Parivar even Christians, who gave so much to modern Indian society, are under attack from Hindu fanatics and are, like Muslims, are feeling intensely insecure.

It is in these circumstances that my elderly friend Mr. Prakash Narain is passionately advocating revival of religious values and spirit in modern India—the religion of tolerance and compassion. I wonder at his passionate efforts at this age (he is more than 90 years old) to infuse true spirit of religion, especially Hinduism, among people and revive brotherly and sisterly relations between Hindus and Muslims.

He wants religion to be taught in schools so that people develop the spirit of humanity. He is against atheistic secularism and wants his message to reach large number of people. He has written a book whose tentative title is Indian heritage -Oneness in Masses of Hindus and Muslims through Vendanta, Vahdat and Vivayka. He tried his best to get the book published but for variety of reasons did not succeed. He has now put it online and wants Hindu and Muslim masses to read it.

He has been in touch with me for a long time. He lives in New Jersey, USA and corresponds with me through e-mail. We met once briefly in New Jersey, when I happened to go there for some lectures. I found him quite sincere and enthusiastic. He is sincerely engaged in promoting his mission. He approached number of people seeking support for his project and still continues to do so. I fully endorse the spirit of his efforts and it is of immense value today in contemporary India, wherein communalism, is being injected in public life.

Prakash Narain's efforts is like those of Darashikoh in seventeenth century India. Darashikoh, who was appointed heir apparent by Emperor Shahjahan, wrote a book majma'ul Bahrayn (Co-mingling of two Oceans Hinduism and Islam) and tried to show that Hinduism and Islam are complementary and not contradictory to each other. Since he was himself a scholar of Sanskrit and of Hinduism in addition to that of Islam, he compared teachings of both the religions to prove his point. He also translated Upanishads into Persian and called it Sirr-e-Akbar. He would have proved a great boon for India had he succeeded to the throne of India. But it was not to be.

Prakash Narain, who, is making herculean efforts to promote unity between Hindus and Muslims in contemporary India, may not be a scholar of Islam as Darashikoh was of Hinduism, but he had the benefit of studying under a Muslim teacher during fifties in the last century, and certainly imbibed the true spirit of Islam and learnt Urdu and Persian as students in those days had to learn. It infused into him the right spirit of Hindu-Muslim unity. That partly explains his passionate commitment to his project.

He complains that Nehruvian secularists banned study of religion in schools and thus deprived Hindu students of knowledge of true Hindu religious spirit. But, on the other hand, Muslims showed the wisdom of teaching their children Islam through network of madrasas. Hindus, on the other hand, in their enthusiasm for 'secular' education, closed down all their pathshalas and deprived their children of religious education.

Narain, therefore, passionately advocates that Hindus also be given chance of studying their religion in schools and thus chance to imbibe true spirit of their religion which in turn would help strengthen spirit of Hindu-Muslim unity. I think he says so under the strong influence of his vision of religion as a means of strengthening Hindu-Muslim relations. But even if Hindu religious studies are introduced, real question is who will control it? Will it be controlled by noble souls like Prakash Narain or those who want to promote Hindu-Muslim animosity through misuse of religion?

Is religion, as rationalists often maintain, a source of conflict? Or a resource for peace as persons like Prakash Narain feel? I have my doubts that given the contemporary situation in India where majoritarian rather than democratic ethos prevail due to communalization of politics, whether teaching of religion would indeed help? Had it been so, Gandhism would not have failed. Most of the Gandhian institutions, though not communalized, but certainly Hinduized have lost Gandhian spirit of equal respect for all religions.

The RSS, today, has much greater control over most of the educational institutions, in many cases even over professional institutions than the government. What Prakash Narain says was advocated by profound Gandhians like Pandit Sunderlal and Bishambarnath Pande with whom I had worked for several years for promoting communal harmony. Both Pandit Sunderlal and Bishambarnathji were profound scholars of Islam along with Hinduism. Both of them were passionately committed to Hindu-Muslim unity.

But unfortunately Hindus could not produce any other Sunderlal or Bishambarnath as Muslims could not produce any other Maulana Azad or Zakir Husain. Both Maulana Azad and Zakir Husain were soaked in Islamic tradition and yet were great champions of Hindu-Muslim unity. As Sunderlal and Bishmbarnath had imbibed best of Hinduism, its tolerance, its universality, Azad and Zakir Husain too represented best in Islamic values. However, subsequent generations lost these traditions.

Today, as Prakash Narainji would also agree with me, religion is being used to promote political benefits and such politicized religion can never represent best of its tradition. But one may argue, and rightly so that Nehruvian secularism too lost its real spirit and secularism itself has been reduced to 'psuedo-secularism (though I am not using it in the sense in which L.K. Advani of BJP uses it. Indeed secularism too has lost its secular spirit. Secularism, like religion, itself has been 'politicized' in the wrong sense.

Reasons are many. In this age of globalization and consumerism to talk of values and principles, is to be outdated. Today's generation is achievement-oriented and is naturally obsessed with achieving at any cost. Both politics and capitalism are highly competitive and compels not to excel but to achieve and achieve at other's cost. Now not only individuals compete but also communities and castes.

Our education system is itself part of the problem rather than part of solution. The education system controlled by politicians infuses conformism, on one hand, and competitiveness on the other. Also, education system is being used to create sense of belonging to one religion and one particular caste and then identities so created are used for promoting identity-based politics. Education system, if it has to be really education in true sense, must create a critical rather than conforming mind and spirit of cooperation and compassion rather than competition.

In this achievement-oriented age who will think of values like compassion and cooperation? Prakash Narain can succeed in his objective only if our education system is transformed and is used to promote best values in religion. His Vedantic vision can come into being only when our politicians first change their own vision and accept visions of persons like Gandhi, Azad, Pandit Sunderlal, Prakash Narain and others like them.

The prevailing atmosphere in the country and the way our education system has been tempered with and controlled by powerful vested interests, negates all such expectations. However, one should not despair and I believe to despair is to be a disbeliever (kafir). We must remain hopeful and strive in keeping with our conscience and it is in this sense I admire Prakash Narain's efforts. His optimism, vision, and his efforts to realize what he thinks is worthwhile for humanity is indeed very valuable.

I would now like to throw light on what Prakash Narain believes could help promote Hindu-Muslim unity in India. Firstly, I must say Prakash Narain is a devout Gandhian. He writes in Author's Note 'My above experience made this book necessary to reach Mahatma Gandhi's spiritual India of 400 million (now over a billion) of eight religions that alone can save India. Mahatma Gandhi's India secured us freedom. We must get rid of our avivaykee and bideshi (i.e. unwise and foreign-oriented) mind in just three years. We can start replacing this with a powerful vivaykee mind as that of Mahatma Gandhi by the defined and detailed strategy in chapter 5 of this book.'

What the author means by vivaykee mind is wise spiritual mind based on Vedic values and one which is aware of spiritual heritage of India. He considers Nehruvian model of secularism as bideshi and Gandhian secularism as swadeshi (of Indian origin). Nehru according to Prakash Narain was under Western influence and he preferred Western model of secularism over Indian model and hence was avivaykee and must be rejected.

One may find it difficult to agree with the author all the way as everything foreign may not necessarily be bad and rejected. Similarly, everything foreign is not good to be uncritically imitated. I think Nehru was not among those who rejected everything Indian and accepted everything Western. A critical reading of Nehru would show that he too was very much Indian in ethos and was proud of Indian spiritual heritage but impatient with empty ritualism and superstitious approach to religion. Nehru was also Gandhian in his own way. Gandhi considered him more suited for Prime Ministership than Sardar Patel and others as he combined both modern scientific approaches with what is spiritual.

Anyway one may not delve deeper in this controversy as the book written by Prakash Narain is much more than this. Prakash Narain is also a fervent advocate of religious education for Hindu children in schools—of which they are being deprived in independent India. According to him, it is necessary to teach Hindu children Vedic teachings to empower and spiritualize their minds. He feels, 'Without knowledge of dharma for conviction in faith in the reality of God as our constantly available succor—no Hindu has security a human being requires to live in love and virtue.'

Well, many would agree that our education needs more spiritual content in the form of values so that we can produce students with strong foundation of values like tolerance, respect for other faiths, proud of Indian composite spiritual heritage, truth and compassion for fellow human beings. These values can be imparted through teaching of one or also through comparative religion to inculcate respect for other faiths as all religions stress more or less same values.

But in government funded schools, in a secular democracy, no single religion can be taught as it would lead to legal and constitutional questions. Either those desirous of teaching one religion like Vedic religion or Islamic education opf for privately funded schools or essential teachings of all religions through carefully drafted syllabus could be taught tendemically. I agree with Prakash Narain that today our education system is too competitive and materialistic totally ignoring spiritual aspects of life promoting values.

Also, there has to be emphasis on creative and dynamic relationship between reason and wisdom. Reason is a double-edged sword and can be used both for creative and destructive purposes. Wisdom, on the other hand, is based on combination of reason and values and is superior to reason. Also, reason is more theoretical and deductive, whereas wisdom is more practical based on years of human experience. Our education system is more reason than wisdom oriented. We must relate our reason to our values and collective spiritual heritage and in a way it amounts to marry Nehruvian model to Gandhian one.

That Prakash Narain is not a bigoted Hindu but a man with universal outlook is amply borne out from his book. The very essence of this book is unity of all religions, a theme so necessary for our polarized country today. We are divided along religious lines as never before due to sectarian politics being pursued by a section of politicians with great gusto. Apart from Dara Shikoh, referred earlier, Maulana Azad also devoted first volume of his commentary of Koran to the theme of unity of religion (wahdat-e-Din). Prakash Narain has made similar attempt from Hindu scriptural point of view.

I think the most valuable chapter of the book is 4 in which the author discusses commonalities between Tulsidas Ramayana and the Koran. It is quite a detailed chapter. The purpose of the chapter in author's own words, 'This chapter is based on the search in the Holy Koran for quotations that accord with the basis in Sanatana Dharma, for understanding and mutual respect between Hindus and Muslims.'

The whole chapter is full of quotations from Ramayana and Holy Koran. Of course, since Prakash Narain, does not know Arabic, he has used Abdullah Yusuf Ali's English translation while quoting from Hindu scriptures originally in Sanskrit. Since Abdullah Yusuf Ali's translation is universally accepted by Muslims, one can accept what the author quotes from the Holy Book of Islam.

He makes a significant observation which will help dispel many misunderstandings. He says, 'With these handy definitions we realize that Dharma is roohaneeyat or spirituality and not religion. Religion also includes rituals, individual, family and social regulations, customs and visible practices. These have no bearing upon roohaneeyat (spirituality) in our religion. Religion is mazhab not roohanyyeyat alone.

Maulana Azad too makes a distinction between Deen and sharia which differs from religion to religion since sharia depends on cultural values and practices, customs and traditions. I do not know whether Prakash Narain has read Maulana Azad or not—most probably not—but he too draws similar conclusion and makes distinction between Dharma and religion. Dharma, according to him, is pure roohaneeyat.

If we develop this kind of understanding, we can greatly reduce our differences and easily build bridges between polarized religious communities in India. It is not only the question of reading this book. It is important to read this book along with Maulana's volume on wahdat-e-Deen. If read together it can really be much more effective. But even more important is to refashion school syllabi on these lines.

In these days of hate politics, it is increasingly important to read such works which try to build religious unity on the basis of religious scriptures. Yes, there are other interpretations of religion and many who have aversion to religion or consider religion as root of all evil may deride such an approach. Well they may do so. But those who can indeed make distinction between Dharma (Deen) and ritualized religion, can appreciate the efforts to build unity on the basis of spiritualism.

This work was done in medieval ages by Sufi and Bhakti saints and they greatly succeeded in building bridges across religions. They also richly contributed towards our composite culture. We need to re-emphasize those efforts. An attempt is also being made through our constitutional secularism but it is not enough. Constitution is after all a legal document based on certain modern fundamental rights.

We also need to supplement these efforts through promoting spiritual values as our people are soaked in religious practices and traditions. We need to make multi dimensional efforts to keep our people united. After all our democratic polity is competitive and in multi-religious countries like India religion provides the fault line of division and competition takes place along this fault line. In secular democracy, religious and cultural diversity should provide enriching public experience but political competitiveness has reduced it (diversity) to our weakness rather than our strength.

However, books like these are usually written in English and reach only a few chosen people whereas there is great need to make them available in Hindi, Urdu and other Indian languages, so that they have much wider reach. That is however, another problem. What is important for me is that still we have people like Mr. Prakash Narain around who try passionately to promote unity among the people of diverse faiths.

I congratulate Prakash Narain for writing this book and trying to promote it, not to make profit or earn name and fame but fulfil a mission in life. I am in touch with him for few years now, and I have seen his passion, his restlessness to get across this message of unity. Though we may differ on some points here and there but that is least important. His passion for unity of Hindus and Muslims is something to be experienced. And I am his great admirer in this respect.

I can only pray for the success of his mission as this is also my mission in life. Inspired by his passionate desire to promote unity and spiritual values, I have joined hands with him in my own humble way.

16
Democracy, Elections and Minorities in India

The general elections in India are about to take place within three months and all political parties are readying themselves to draw up their winning strategies. Elections are like a day of judgement for political parties. And, they have to stand before their voters and render account of their deeds and misdeeds. They have begun to woo their voters once in five years again. They have to woo different castes and religious groups and reconcile their conflicting interests in the context of the complex Indian reality.

The Muslims constitute 15 per cent of Indian population and play crucial role in the victory or defeat of the political parties. In the two big northern states of UP and Bihar, no political party can win without Muslim support. The Congress once used to win both these states without much problem as the Muslims voted for it for four decades after the independence. However, it lost both the states as the Muslims withdrew their support. UP was lost as soon as Rajiv Gandhi laid foundation stone of Ram Mandir in Ayodhya after instructing the district magistrate to open the lock of the Babri Masjid for the Hindus to worship Ram. The Congress has not been able to rehabilitate itself again in the eyes of the Muslims.

The Bharatiya Janata Party (BJP) once rode to power in the UP on the 'wave of Ram Mandir', but such waves cannot be generated again and hence the BJP has met with its speed breaker. During those hey days it was even said, 'we do not need Muslim votes', but it set up its own minority front, promising heaven to them, through some Muslim members like Shah Nawaz and others. It is also projecting Naqvi as its spokesman.

But the BJP does not want to give up its mool mantra (basic formula) of Ram Mandir to woo hard core Hindu votes. Rajnath Singh, its President, said that it would construct Ram Mandir if it came to power and even would persuade its National Democratic Alliance (NDA) allies to agree to pass a law for constructing the mandir. Even Advani asked what was wrong in constructing a mandir. Once they demolished Babri Masjid and committed a wrong; then what is the harm in committing a second one by constructing mandir on the site of Babri Masjid?

The election calculus shows that the BJP would find it extremely difficult to increase its present tally in Parliament. 'The Terror Card' did not pay even immediately after the Mumbai attacks in November; and the BJP lost the election in Delhi. Thus 'terror card' no longer arouses emotions to be electorally exploited. The BJP had found one more card when prices began to rise, but as its ill luck would have it, the rise in index fell to and has almost stabilized at below 6 per cent. And raising 'Ram issue' is flogging a dead horse.

Thus whatever its electoral acrobatics, the BJP will find it very difficult to increase its tally of seats won over the last general election in 2004. Moreover, what the lumpen elements of the Sangh Parivar have done in Orissa and Karnataka will hardly help its image. Those who sympathize otherwise with the BJP will also find it difficult to defend its violent attacks on Christians and women. There was a time when some Christian leaders had begun to join the BJP, but after the Orissa events even leaders like Fernandes will be hard pressed to defend the BJP. The BJP has thus increased its opponents.

There is tough competition between Mayavati the present Chief Minister and Mulayam Singh Yadav, the leader of the Samajwadi Party in the UP for the Muslim votes. Mayavati, in order to win over the Muslims, has promised 25 per cent tickets for the Lok Sabha elections for the Muslims. It is, no doubt, for the first time any party has taken such a step. The Muslims of the UP should welcome it and the Congress has a lesson to learn from it. It is a known fact that the Congress has never done justice to the Muslims in this respect.

However, while welcoming Mayavati's step, the real question is: how many Muslims will be given the tickets, how many seats will be winnable ones and what her party will do to see the Muslim candidates win? Also, what will be the stature of those Muslim candidates? These are important questions. It is difficult to expect Mayavati to give ticket to those who have some stature of their own and are independent by nature.

Mulayam Singh Yadav has entered into a friendship pact with Kalyan Singh who has the notoriety of overseeing the demolition of the Babri Masjid on 6 December 1992 as he was then the Chief Minister and had felt proud over his misdeed. Muslims have hardly forgotten this. Mulayam Singh claims that he has done so to wipe out the BJP from the UP. But this strategy is likely to misfire or backfire as far as Muslims are concerned.

Let not Mulayam forget the fate of the Congress in the UP, after it laid the foundation stone of the Ram Mandir in Ayodhya. Mulayam made Kalyan apologize for the demolition of the Babri Masjid under pressure from the Muslims, but the way Mulayam has expressed his solidarity with Kalyan may backfire. The Congress has also expressed its displeasure for this newfound solidarity of the SP leader with Kalyan Singh, but that only has provoked Mulayam Singh to ask the Congress to mind its own business, and he even said that he andKalyan Singh are farmers and, what is more pehelwans (wrestlers)! It is surprising, even enigmatic, that a shrewd politician like Mulayam was making such statements!

The way Muslims are reacting to the alliance with Kalyan Singh, shows it would be hardly politically wise for Mulayam to shake hands with Kalyan, if he is interested in Muslim votes in the U.P. After all he may not have the last laugh in this complex game of politics and electoral arithmetic. Mayawati may have the last laugh, after all. If the Muslims of UP vote for Mayawati, both the BJP and the Congress may not gain much in UP. The Congress may, perhaps, gain marginally but the BJP will not benefit even that.

In Bihar, BJP has no independent base at all. It is beholden to Nitish Kumar, the present Chief Minister of Bihar, who is unhappy that the BJP is creating problems for him by raising Ram issue again. Nitish Kumar is Bhumihar. Yadavs are not his electoral base. He also got two Muslims working for the OBC Muslim cause nominated to the Rajya Sabha. However, that may not mean much electorally, in, complex caste politics of Bihar Muslims.

However, it appears Nitish too does not have brighter chance and may not be able to improve his tally of seats won over 2004 elections. He has failed to deliver his promises and the Koshi flood disaster may prove a millstone a round his neck. The BJP may not be able to reap much depending on Nitish Kumar, who is the only support for the BJP in Bihar.

It will be seen from above that Muslim votes, like other non-Muslim votes, are now determined by regional politics. For quite sometime Muslims have been voting for the regional parties, and the Congress has only some regions like Maharashtra, Andhra Pradesh, etc., where the only alternative happens to be the Congress. It is a healthy development that the Muslims are less swayed by emotional issues and have realized that it would be a political disaster. But, for that matter, even, some Hindus, at one time, were swayed by the Ram Mandir issue, and the OBCs (Other Backward Classes) by Mandal Commission issue; and these two issues brought some crucial change in Indian politics and both issues were highly emotional in nature.

As the Muslims have now come out of that emotional phase, they should bargain hard with regional parties, and the aim should be: (1) to isolate and defeat communal forces and (2) to extract promises of implementation of economic and educational benefits along with proper share in political power for Muslims. For this they must shun emotional rhetoric altogether and have to be hard bargainers.

It is important to note that since the Muslims began to vote for regional outfits in UP and Bihar, the epicenter of communal violence has shifted to Maharashtra, and Maharashtra has emerged with the dubious distinction of a state with highest communal incidents in the last few years. The government's own statistics show this. The media have also reported these statistics. There are other dilemmas too for the Muslims in Maharashtra.

These incidents have taken place during the Congress regime, especially during the chief ministership of Vilasrao Deshmukh. R.R. Patil of the Nationalist Congress party also failed to handle the communal riots properly. Dhule is its worst example. But again the only alternative to the Congress in Maharashtra is the Shiv Sena-BJP alliance which Muslims cannot opt for. There is no other regional party here like in U P, Bihar, etc.

It is indeed a very challenging situation for Muslims in Maharashtra. Again separate political party of Muslims is no solution. It is a remedy worse than the disease. Besides voting for clean secular candidates in whichever constituencies available, the Muslims should go for frank dialogue with the present Congress leaders, preferably at the Central level. Regional leadership often colludes with the Shiv Sena and was under the awe of Bal Thackeray. Even Sharad Pawar, Bhujbal and other Congress leaders met him, touched his feet and had dinner with him.

In democracy, only hard bargain pays, nothing else. Our elections are based purely on caste and religious identities, nothing else. The weight of minorities must be felt by the political parties.

17
Modernity, Its Discontent and Religion

Modernity was greatly celebrated during colonial days of nineteenth century throughout the world, especially in African and Asian countries colonized by European countries. It was hallmark of superiority of West over East. West was considered most modern, rational in its approach and technologically far more superior whereas Asian and African countries superstitious, irrational and ignorant and backward.

Most of the intellectuals, mainly product of Western colonial education felt ashamed of their ignorance and backwardness and lack of rationality and science and tried to reform their societies by spreading modern approach among their people. However, there was vertical division in these societies between those who refused to modernize and preferred their orthodoxy and those who considered modernization a must and celebrated modernity.

Almost all religious communities in colonized countries faced this vertical divide but more particularly the Muslims. We are more concerned here with Muslim communities in the colonized countries. Muslims were comparatively slow and more resistant to modernization as the Muslim societies were deeply embedded in feudal values and religious orthodoxy.

Muslim intellectuals who came under the influence of Western education and modernism, welcomed modernity but had to adopt cautious approach between religious orthodoxy and Western modernism. They had to rely more on their religious text to keep pace with their societies. But those societies which took to industrialization and modern business and commerce found modernity more easily acceptable.

Muslim societies, deeply embedded in feudalism and feudal values, as pointed out above, could not go for modern industrialization, business and commerce and hence modernity did not appeal to them

or beneficial to them. Muslims were often criticized for refusing to change and modernize and even their religion Islam was blamed for it. Muslims still face this criticism though we have gone into post-modern era.

Modernity, however, did not prove to be unmixed blessing for Western countries, let alone for Eastern countries of Asia and Africa; due to the powerful vested interests who used modernity for their own benefit. Modernity generally came with the capitalist system. In fact, modernity was product of industrial system based on capitalism. It was Marx who developed great insights into functioning of modern capitalist system and wrote powerful critique of capitalism.

Capitalism was based on profiteering on one hand, and on cutthroat competition, on the other. The Western countries colonized Asian and African countries in search of raw materials and markets for their product. Modern machines produced on mass scale produced more than the demand of the domestic markets and they lacked raw materials as well. Thus colonial countries became rich source of raw material on one hand, and provided huge markets for their industrial products.

It was this competition for markets which led to two World Wars resulting in killings of millions of people. These wars gave great impetus to armament industry, so much so that in the post 2nd World War era, no American government could defy what came to be known as military-industrial complex. All American policies were fundamentally influenced by this military-industrial complex. This unholy alliance depended mainly on sale of armaments on huge scale and consequently had to be promoted in Asian and African countries.

This is not to say that modernization itself was responsible, but what was worth emulating in the entire modernization project was hijacked by powerful interests whose only concern was accumulating profits. That is why I maintain that modernity is not an unmixed blessing for humanity. It has its darker side too. Here we are discussing modernity, not as values, but as an instrument to promote certain interests.

Modernity essentially represents important values like rationality, objectivity, respect for human reason and human values and conformity with fact. It was this respect for reason, and not authority, that led to progress of science and technology through which West acquired superiority over Asian and African countries. The modern bourgeoisie in the West challenged the authority of the Church and succeeded in establishing superiority of reason, the hallmark of modernity.

Reason is the highest value in modernity. It relies solely on reason and has no respect for any tradition. The Afro-Asian societies were based, on the other hand, mainly on respect for tradition whether they conformed to tradition or not. However, sole reliance on reason without wedding it to values and without making reason and values two sides of the same coin, reason can and does become problematic.

Reason is a two-edged sword without values and this is what happened with modernity when powerful vested interests, mainly capitalists hijacked modernity for their own purposes. Modern weapons and modern technology developed by the Western countries were used for enslaving Afro-Asian countries and these countries were reduced to mere sources of raw materials and markets.

Reason could be used for promoting science, technology and deeper understanding of universe but also for developing disastrous weapons which cause great destruction. Humanity saw this destruction in the two World Wars. But it was reason again which developed pure science and we could understand infinite vastness of our universe and how it evolved and our extremely limited understanding of our universe changed. Koran says it is the 'Ulama, i.e. those who know, those who are scientists, who deeply reflect on the creation of Allah who can really worship Him.

Rationalists disregard importance of faith and values and begin to worship reason. They do not appreciate limits of reason. This attitude developed among rationalists as reason was totally disregarded and devalued in traditional societies and those who accepted reason and challenged superstitions or traditional authority were severely persecuted.

Also, unscrupulous elements had exploited faith for their own benefits, rationalists came to reject faith as blind and irrational. Thus as modernity solely relied on reason and ridiculed faith, traditionalists blindly held onto faith in the traditional authority and rejected reason. Thus both rationalists and faithful became exclusive categories. There was no meeting point. Thus faithful became blind and derided reason and rationalists dubbed faith as blind.

This mutual exclusivity caused much greater problems. Sole reliance on reason can give birth to discontents just like sole reliance on faith can make one lose touch with reality. We find interesting debate in Islamic history between Imam Ghazzafi and Ibn Rushd (known as Averros to the Western world). Ghazzali was also a rationalist at one time. He even became atheist at one stage of his development. However, he soon discovered reason does not lead to inner peace and meaning and significance of life. He turned then to faith (though as is evident from his writings retained elements of reason too) and attacked philosophers like Ibn Rushed. He wrote a book, *Tahafut al-Falasifa* (Bewilderment of Philosophers).

Ibn Rushd replied to Ghazzali's *Tahafut al-Falasifa* by writing *Tahafat Tahafut al-Falasifa*, i.e. Bewilderment of Bewilderment of Philosophers). Thus, this lack of mutual understanding lead to exclusivistic attitudes. Ghazzali was in search of inner peace and reason creates more doubts and raises more questions and leads to discontentment. Faith which depends on authority, gives inner contentment.

Modernity has thus led to discontentment in two ways: one, since it has been hijacked by capitalists it leads to more inner discontentment as it is hell-bent upon selling its products and creates illusion of 'material happiness' but fails to create one as more consumption leads to still more consumption; two, rationality lacks faith and for inner peace one needs faith which provides 'final' answers and hence inner contentment.

Thus neither rationality (i.e. modernity) nor faith alone can be without problems. For centuries—faith in authority created total stagnation and superstition. No change or progress became possible. Human beings entertained so many superstitions about creation and about our universe. Diseases thrived and mortality became high.

Similarly reason too failed to satisfy many questions though it too became absolute and wanted to displace faith altogether. Thus many questions about meaning and significance of our universe could not be answered by reason alone. Reason, in a way, gave rise to its own superstitions. Reason claimed all the space which so far faith had occupied. Blind faith also led to exploitation of ignorant human beings and now modernity too, in the form of emphasis on material happiness which also led to discontentment.

Thus, either way, dilemma remains and there is no solution in sight. But discontentment of modernity has far acceded that of faith. As religion has been hijacked by priesthood (reducing it to mere rituals devoid of values) and other vested interests like politicians with which priesthood often (though not always) collaborated, in case of modernity, too, it has been hijacked by powerful vested interests and it has become almost a part of capitalist system.

Capitalism is highly exploitative and reason has been made a powerful instrument for exploitation to promote profiteering. Today, modernity cannot stand on its own and has become almost an adjunct of capitalist system. Capitalism, in our own times, is promoting limitless consumerism. It has used reason to promote consumerism in various ways which leads to more and more violence.

Colonial violence was also part of capitalist expansion and led to wars and bloodshed. The colonized countries had to struggle hard, in most cases violently (India was an exception to a great extent) to free themselves from colonial bondage. However, in several newly freed countries, Western capitalist powers managed to install puppet governments and thus people could not enjoy fruits of freedom.

Thus, on one hand, ritualized religion and capitalist-based modernity created more discontent in the modern world. Democracy, though very necessary for ensuring freedom to common people, has also been hijacked by vested interests. In most of the countries in Asia and Africa, we find today one ethnic group or one religious group at the throat of the other. Ethnic, caste and communal violence is rampant in most of the democratic countries in Asia and Africa today.

All modern means are being used to exacerbate these differences including means of modern mass communications. Mass communication with its most modern techniques is a powerful instrument to promote prejudices and misinformation. Twenty-first century has already witnessed unprecedented violence. Attack on New York towers and resultant wars in Afghanistan and Iraq and consequent terrorist attacks has already killed millions of people during the first decade itself.

Modern technology, again a part of hijacked modernity, has produced weapons of mass destruction. During medieval ages, a sword could kill one person at a time. Today, modern technology has produced such weapons which can kill thousands at a time merely by pressing a button. Whole cities can be blasted out of existence. America invaded Iraq (to grab its oil) and tried all its latest weaponry on the poor people of that unfortunate country. More than half a million people perished.

Terrorists, not product of Islam as usually propagated, but a violent response to much greater violence being perpetrated by the Super Power, is also killing thousands of innocent human beings. These killings, it appears, has no end. Communally and ethnic violence within a nation states and wars internationally has robbed out modern world of peace and tranquility.

The important question is can we free religion on one hand, and modernity on the other hand, from clutches of vested interests? It is a difficult and complex problem. What we need is a creative synthesis of religion and modernity, but to get it accepted is itself very difficult. Religion in its spiritual sense and modernity with emphasis on reason can be very liberative for human beings.

Islam, many people would not believe, was such a creative blend of the two but unfortunately it lost its liberative thrust in the hands of vested interests, particularly the feudal ruling class and medieval values. It was very difficult for Islam to escape this fate. However, now is the time to rediscover the Koranic Islam though, as pointed out, it would be very difficult to make it acceptable.

Islam today is so encumbered with medieval practices and web of cultural and traditional practices that it is very difficult to disentangle it from this complex web of medieval culture and ruling class interests. I would like to throw some light as to why the Koranic Islam could be really so liberative. I do not think war against terror can ever succeed without rediscovering this Islam and also without disentangling modernity from the clutches of capitalist interests.

Koran, through the Prophet (PBUH), addressed itself to rid the society of its ills. Mecca was in the primitive stage of capitalist accumulation and so Koran strongly denounced accumulation of wealth and luxurious living. It created sensitivity towards the suffering weaker sections of society. It offered the ideal, considered most modern, of human dignity. No human being should be disrespected or robbed of dignity given by Allah.

It also gave awareness to its addresses that when it comes to human dignity both men and women are equal and one has no right over the other. Koran even avoided use of the word husband and wife, but called them zawjain (couples) so that man cannot claim superiority over his wife. It also sensitized believers to indignity.

Thus freeing slaves was considered most meritorious act and also exhorted believers that if they cannot immediately emancipate their slave immediately (though they should), until such time they should treat them as their equal in every respect. It was for this reason that many slaves were attracted initially to Islam and Bilal Habshi (an Ethiopian slave emancipated by his master after accepting Islam) became icon of these slaves.

Also, like modernity, it tried to do away discrimination between one ethnic or linguistic or national group from the other and declared colour, race, languages and nations are Allah's signs (Surah: Rum Verse: 22). Basic humanity and human dignity is above all these considerations. No superiority for one group, race, colour or language to any other one and declared that only distinction could be on the basis of taqwa (i.e. purity of actions and God-consciousness).

These were revolutionary declarations and humanity has failed to realize these ideals even in post-modern period. The Prophet of Islam (PBUH) faced stiff resistance from Meccan tribal chiefs because they were not prepared to accept such a revolutionary transformation of their society, which will fell in one swoop their status, their pride of wealth, their superiority of Arabic language and their belonging to tribe of Quraysh.

All this was not acceptable to them at all. They identified their ancestral religion with all their privileges and would not accept new religion as it was truly universal in believing in human unity beyond all tribal, linguistic and ethnic boundaries and what was worse for them, believing in socio-economic justice. In this new religion, neither language, nor race, nor colour of skin, nor wealth was guarantee to nearness of Allah but only piety, ethical and moral conduct. They did not mind demolishing physical idols kept in Ka'aba but were not prepared for demolishing idols of social, economic, linguistic, and ethnic pride. These idols were real object of worship which put them above others.

Modernity in this sense with due role of reason is hallmark of Islam from the beginning. But Muslims brought back all these idols installed in their hearts and never removed them. History of Islam shows, with passage of time, these idols carved out deeper and deeper niches. Ka'aba was purified of physical idols but hearts of Muslims were never purified.

Even today many Muslims have accepted modernity in superficial sense by accepting modern technology and like Western countries, have instrumentalized role of reason but has not accepted role of reason in fundamental and philosophical sense. Modern Western civilization is wholly materialistic and soulless, and hence modernity has created more discontents. Its hallmark is more and more consumption, bolstering material standards of life and hence fighting for others' resources leading to wars and bloodshed. America, though apparently modern and civilized, is most barbarious in waging wars on others territories with its ultra-modern weaponry.

Real modernity as expounded in Koran and also in other scriptures, does not use reason in instrumental sense but in fundamental and philosophical sense. It encourages cooperation, not destructive competition. It does not chase illusory goal of happiness based on consumption but promotes social justice, unconditional equality, inviolable human dignity and balanced approach to inner and outer happiness. Modernity cannot be judged through material progress alone. It is necessary but not sufficient.

Spiritual joy and material happiness must go together. Reason should not be devoid of values. Reason without higher goals, meaning and significance of life, is two-edged sword. Truth should not be mere conformity with facts but also beyond and above it, transcendent and all inclusive. Otherwise modernity will remain handmaiden of powerful vested interests which is what it is today and will generate more and more discontents.

18
Islam and the West—What Muslims should Do?

Muslims and the West seem to be on collision course. I read every day in Urdu papers about the conspiracies the West hatches to attack and destroy Islam. Western countries do something or the other which offends Muslims and results in protests, street demonstrations and at times results even in violence. Huntington's book, *Clash of Civilizations*, Rushdie's novel *The Satanic Verses* controversy, Taslima Nasreen's warm reception by European countries, Pope Benedict's statement about Islam, the Danish cartoons and now a member of the Netherland's parliament making a film Fitna—have all struck headlines. This new controversy has seized the Muslim world.

Some Muslims argue that West is enemy of Islam and keeps on attacking Islam and Muslims to serve its own agenda. Some even argue there is limit after all and how long Muslims can tolerate these attacks. They must act to stop this war against Islam. Many burn the flag of the country concerned or trample it underfoot, some give call for boycott of goods manufactured in that country and some even threaten to indulge in violence.

The way our newspapers report, we get an impression as if all in the West are hostile to Islam, and all Muslims are bent upon violent protests. But this is far from true. The Muslims should understand that all Westerners are not supporters of whatever some Westerners do, and Westerners should understand that all Muslims do not appreciate violent protests. It is also not true that Western governments patronize anti-Islam cartoons, films or novels. Nor governments of Muslim countries can be held responsible for violent demonstrations.

The matter in fact is very complex, and intellectuals on both sides should understand these complex issues involved and make constant efforts to promote proper understanding and smoothen mutual relations. Unfortunately, such serious attempts are not being made, or, even if made do not get proper projection in the media. I would like to make a few suggestions in this regard to be seriously considered.

First, we must mutually appreciate our cultural differences which are responsible for a great deal of misunderstandings between the West and the Islamic world. The West has by now a long tradition of secular democracy, freedom and human rights. The Islamic world is still not conversant with such concepts. It has not even ushered in to democracy; and there is no concept of secular democracy or human right in this part of the world.

Europe has undergone a long struggle against the Pope and the Church to win its right to criticize. The religion as propagated by the Church, the freedom of its press and certain other fundamental rights. There was a time when the Church did not tolerate any criticism or deviation from its theology which had the status of divine injunction. Deviationists were severely punished. Even by death or by burning them at stake. Religious persecution had assumed serious proportions.

Since the West had won the rights against the Church, after great sacrifices, it is not prepared to give them at any cost, and considers them almost, as sacred as the religious injunctions. It was because of this that philosophers like Bertrand Russell wrote a book like *Why I am not a Christian* and ridiculed in this book many doctrines propounded by the Church. Several books and articles were written attacking Christianity and continue to be written even today. Recently, a book has been published, which questions even existence of Christ. The author quotes several documents to prove that Christ never existed and what Church preaches is mere mythology.

Whether such a state of affairs is desirable or not is a matter of values to which one subscribes. Today in the West, especially in Europe, freedom, secularism and human rights have status of what religious doctrines had in the medieval age. And in democracy these rights have to be ensured without which democracy may lose its meaning. Now it can also take extreme forms, e.g. right to ridicule, right to mock at authorities, and political cartoons often make a caricature or mock at the false claims of political authorities.

Political cartoons are frequently used to ridicule political leaders. Now the question is whether cartoons can be drawn to ridicule religious leaders or not, and if so, can one draw cartoons of founders of religions, who are held in high esteem by their followers? It is of course a matter of ones perspective. Many would insist that it is sacrilegious to draw such cartoons and some would insist it is part of one's fundamental rights.

Salman Rushdie insists on his right to ridicule religious authorities, and mocks at Gabriel and Prophet's (PBUH) wives. The West defended him saying it is part of his human rights or fundamental rights. Western culture, as, it has developed over the last one century, promotes even sacrilege as part of one's rights as people in the West insist sacrilege is the ultimate right in democratic culture.

It is for this reason that the West defends persons like Salman Rushdie, or Danish cartoonist who mocked the Prophet and showed bombs in his turban. When Muslims protested more, papers in European countries published these cartoons in support of the right of the cartoonist. This led to even more protests in Islamic world. Similarly, Taslima Nasreen is perceived as one who is persecuted by Muslims and she is projected as a brave woman who must be accorded warm reception to appreciate her courage and fortitude.

When Muslims protest, the Western media dub it as act of 'fundamentalism' and 'religious fanaticism' and condemn it as unbecoming behaviour of enemies of media freedom. The West emphasizes on individual rights, and 'individual is at the centre of all rights'. There is no concept of collective rights in the Western culture. In democracy individual enjoys all the rights available in the Constitution. Also, there is concept of separation of Church and state which is quite central to secular democracy.

We would now throw light on what prevails in the Islamic world today, and why there is such sense of confrontation between Western values and values prevalent in the Muslim world today. The West, instead of outright condemnation of these acts, must try to understand value system of the Islamic world. This value system is undoubtedly more feudal than democratic. Individual rights are subsumed in community rights. There is no concept of full-fledged human rights.

Religion is sacred and divine and above any criticism including all its social and cultural traditions. Love and respect for tradition are universal and beyond the pale of any criticism. Often vested interests exploit this situation to their advantage and put many practices not remotely religious, also beyond pale of criticism. Even governments, declaring themselves as Islamic, try to shun criticism.

Once you declare something as 'Islamic', it becomes so difficult to criticize it and all sorts of vested interests, particularly the rulers, pass off their misgovernance also as 'Islamic'. Add to these low levels of secular education, and the picture becomes complete. There is hardly any awareness among Muslim population of the real issues. Also there is no open society and democratic governance.

As there is no democratic governance, there is no concept of human rights. Any such concept is limited to a few intellectuals who cannot air their views publicly. In one International conference in Morocco a couple of years ago, I met several Arab intellectuals who were highly critical of many traditional practices and autocratic governance in the Arab world. It gave me great pleasure.

II

Islamic World and Its Values

As is well known, Islamic world is yet to go through democratic revolution and hence there is no concept of individual and fundamental rights. There are various reasons for this which needs another article to discuss. It is important for the Western world to understand and comprehend this vital difference between two cultures.

Religion and religious values are quite central to Islamic countries or for Muslims who are living in countries like India. Though India is constitutionally a secular democratic country, it still lacks modern, rational and secular outlook. Indian society, too, despite political democracy, lacks what can be called 'social democracy'. Traditional religion has strong grip over the minds of the Indian people and much more so, in the case of the Muslims.

India, at least, has political democracy. Islamic world, by and large, does not have even that. In Islamic world, traditional religion and religio-cultural values reign supreme. There is absolutely no rational intellectual tradition spread all over society. Even if there are a few intellectuals who care for rational approach, they are isolated and are hardly heard with respect. Often they have to pay heavy price for their intellectual conviction.

It should suffice to give two examples as to how such intellectuals have to suffer. One example is of Prof. Fazlur Rehman, a noted Islamic scholar who was also believer in Islam and Islamic values. However, he had different understanding of the nature and meaning of revelation (he never denied revelation per se) and he also believed in rational approach to Islam. There was hue and cry when he published his ideas about the nature and meaning of revelation and he not only had to resign as director of an Islamic institution, he had to leave Pakistan and teach in Chicago University for one rest of his life.

Another example is of Abu Zayd Nasr, an Egyptian scholar who had studied in al-Azhar, the renowned Islamic University in Cairo and later taught there. He expressed his ideas about revelation (tanzil) and its interpretation (ta'wil); which were not in accordance with traditional thinking. He was tried in a court of law for sacrilege and the court ruled that he was no more a Muslim and hence his married wife became *haram* (prohibited) for him. Both Zayd Abu Nasr and his wife escaped and found refuge in Holland, and he has been teaching there ever since.

Both Fazlur Rehman and Zayd Abu Nasr were respected scholars of Islam but did not subscribe to traditional views about revelation and paid heavily for their views. Both were believers and had profound knowledge of their religion but were not conformists and so had to pay a price. Their views were considered sacrilegious and deviationist. In this atmosphere of total lack of freedom even within the framework of religious beliefs, one can understand the reaction of Muslim theologians and politicians (who always want to be on the right side of 'Ulama) if persons like Rushdie or Taslima Nasreen or Danish cartoonist, express their views.

The Westerners must understand that the whole value system in Islamic world is very different from their own. In traditional Islamic societies, religion and religious traditions are considered holy and beyond pale of criticism. Also vested interests exploit this for their own advantage. Often, even mis-governance is projected as 'Islamic' and any criticism is banned.

Add to this lack of any democratic values and awareness of human rights and low levels of literacy and the picture is complete. Most of the Muslim countries are governed by autocrats who are completely insensitive to people's rights and any movement for human rights is crushed. It will take long time to usher in democratic values in Islamic world. Entire education system is to produce conforming minds.

However, there are intellectuals who are critical of this state of affairs. I met many of them in an international Islamic conference in Morocco a couple of years ago. It was highly refreshing to listen to them criticizing lack of democratic rights in Muslim countries and the disproportionate role-played by traditional 'Ulama. However, this is limited to a few intellectuals and even these intellectuals are unable to publicly criticize their governments, or even 'Ulama in their countries.

Also, let Westerners know that religion and religious traditions are very much an integral part of people's lives in the Islamic world. These are not only sacred but lived traditions for them. The Western perspective is very different. For them, except those who belong to Church, religion is far from sacred. It is democracy and freedom of thought that is sacred. It is part of human rights to mock at religion. Thus these are two different worlds. They must appreciate this world view of Muslims. If they have intimate knowledge of Muslim world and their religious traditions and cultural values probably there will be no such confrontation.

Also, those Muslims who have migrated from Muslim world and live in Western countries, carry these cultural values with them, are greatly disturbed when they see their religious traditions being insulted. The film Fitna made by a member of the parliament of the Netherlands, is the result of such confrontation. Such people have hardly any intimate knowledge of Muslim societies, let alone of the Koran.

Some Westernized and secularized Muslims like Salman Rushdie, Hirsi Ali and others also take completely Westernized view and attack traditional Islamic values, and they are naturally lionized by Western media and projected as great champions of human liberty and human rights. This has created an atmosphere of Islamophobia in Western countries. What is needed is dialogue between representatives of these two value systems—Western and Islamic—to end the atmosphere of confrontation.

Films like *Fitna* are not going to make things easy. They would lead to further intensification of confrontation. There are rightist elements in Western countries who want confrontation, not peace between the two value systems. Maker of the film, *Fitna*, is a well-known rightist politician. He could not be persuaded even by the Prime Minister of the Netherlands not to make the film. He had definite rightist agenda.

What Muslims should Do?

As it is necessary for Westerners to appreciate Muslim cultural viewpoint, it is also necessary for Muslims to understand Western point of view and their respect for democratic values and human rights. While it is true that many Western scholars and media persons are rightist in their political agenda and attack Islam deliberately, there are many other who criticize Islam and Muslims as they feel many Muslim beliefs are undemocratic and anti-modern. They cannot understand why Salman Rushdie should be killed for his criticism or mockery of Islamic beliefs. It is his right to do so, especially in a Western country where the culture of democracy and human rights prevails.

Even while opposing views of Salman Rushdie, or Taslima Nasreen or Danish cartoonist, there is no need to get violent. Muslims must prove through our conduct that Islam is a religion of peace and tolerance and individual dignity. The Koranic teaching is not to abuse others or insult others. The Koran requires Muslims even not to abuse other's gods lest they should abuse Allah out of ignorance (6:109). Even if others attack out of ignorance we must be dignified in our opposition to their views of Islam.

Koran also says that even while debating with people of the Book, debate in the best possible manner. Thus Koran says, 'And argue not with the people of the Book except by what is best save such of them as act unjustly.' (29:46). Koran is saying all this when democratic culture or democratic rights were totally unknown. Even while disagreeing we must respect other's views. This is Koranic culture. Koranic culture is culture of tolerance. Tolerance is one of the best values of civilized people. Islam came to create a new human person. This human person is called m'umin by Koran and mu'min means believer—believer in best human values like justice, compassion, tolerance and wisdom.

As Muslims we must also reflect critically whether we seriously believe in these values. These values are so important that they represent Allah's names in Koran—Allah is just, compassionate and wise. If we believe in Allah, we must believe in these values and if we worship Allah we must practise these values making them a part of our lives. Then and then only we can call ourselves as believers!

Today Muslims are thought to be most intolerant and fanatic. Why? Should we not seriously reflect on this situation? All sorts of vested interests among us styling themselves as Muslims and leaders of Muslims often mislead us. Islam was torch bearer of 'ilm (knowledge) and we have become torch bearers of ignorance. Our 'Ulama (it means those who know) represent ignorance rather than knowledge. They acquire nothing but traditional knowledge of Islam and are narrow minded, sectarian and totally ignorant of the world they live in. They still believe that the Greek knowledge, once studied by their ancestors, is final and even sacred. This is what is taught under m'aqulat (rational sciences) in madrasas.

It is we Muslims who have made persons like Salman Rushdie, Taslima Nasreen, Hirsi Ali and others as great heroes of the Western world. Had Muslims not protested violently and issued fatwas to kill them, they would have been unknown entities. This way we have brought nothing but disgrace for Islam and Muslims. Some Urdu papers use word mal'un and mal'unah (those accursed by Allah) even while giving news about them. When Muslim media behaves so irresponsibly how can we expect Western media to behave with dignity? Disagreeing with their views, does not mean invoking curses for them.

There are selfish political leaders who want to cash in all such opportunities for their political interests. These opportunistic leaders exploit innocent Muslim religious sentiments for promoting their own interests. We have become emotional instead of rational. We instantly sacrifice rationality on the altar of emotions. In Koran, wisdom is the highest value and Koran says, those who are given wisdom have been given good in abundance.

Muslim intellectuals should also shed their fear and come out boldly for defence of Islamic values of tolerance and wisdom. If we really care for positive values of Islam we must oppose such opportunism as displayed by our politicians and ignorance and sectarianism displayed by so-called 'Ulama. The Prophet (PBUH) said that the best form of jihad is speaking truth in the face of a tyrant ruler. Time has come to speak out truth in the face of those who exploit Islam for their selfish ends. They are not really defenders of Islam but defenders of their own interests. Will we come out in defence of true Islam?

19
Islam, Globalization and Challenges

Much is being written these days on globalization and its effects as well as Islam and challenges of globalization. Yet much more is needed to be written to cover various aspects. Globalization has emerged as a major challenge for religions in general and Islam in particular. Before we deal with these challenges, we would like to throw light on the nature of globalization itself so that we can comprehend the challenge better.

I would like to assert here that globalization is nothing new. Right from known history there have been intercontinental migrations. Silk Route well-known in history was also sort of globalizing process. Then colonization of Asian and African countries in eighteenth and nineteenth centuries was also a phase of globalization. These phases of globalizations had distinct features and the current phase of globalization has its own features. In order to understand nature of globalization in the current phase, it is important to understand these distinct features. Then only we can understand the nature of challenges of the past and the present.

The nature of globalization when trade was carried out through silk trade route was of non-dominant nature. The trade caravans started from China and passed through India, the Yemen by crossing the Indian Sea and from Yemen it proceeded towards Eastern part of Roman Empire after crossing the desert called Rub'al Khali. This globalization also created certain challenges to Arabs which we would like to discuss.

Then the colonial powers of Europe colonized various Asian and African countries and this globalization was of very different nature from the one brought about by Silk Trade Route. Silk Route trade was participative, not dominating in nature. Each country participated in trade in their own way and contributed to trade. No country dominated over any other country. However, colonial globalization was of different nature altogether. The colonial powers dominated the colonized countries and deeply influenced the social fabric of the colonized country. It posed great challenges which we will discuss.

II

First we will throw light on challenges posed by Silk Route trade to Arab society in fifth and sixth centuries. It was this challenge posed by Silk Route trade which brought about birth of Islam. We would like to discuss this in some detail below.

The Silk Route trade also deeply impacted on social fabric of Meccan society in sixth century. The Meccan Arabs were expert guides for crossing the desert of Rub' al-Khali. No trade caravan could cross that formidable desert without their help. Thus the trade caravans wishing to reach Roman Empire had to cross this desert and these Arabs acted as expert guides. Mecca thus became a station on this international trade route and gradually a high centre of international trade and finance.

These Arab guides gradually became expert traders too and began to accumulate riches through profitable international trade.

Accumulation of riches deeply impacted tribal way of life and soon there occurred divide between rich and poor. A tribal society has no concept of private property except in animals and personal weapons and consequently has no concept of poverty. But this transformation from a tribal to trading society brought about dynamics of social change of its own and while some traders became rich, others were consigned to lower levels of social structure. A tribal society has no concept of social hierarchy and believes in equality of all and even tribal chief is first among equals, nothing more.

But division between rich and poor changed the whole social fabric, and the poor members of tribe were no longer treated as equal and they were forced to labour for the rich, often were used for loading and unloading the camels carrying trading goods. Slavery also developed and slave trade also took place as slaves were needed in Roman Empire and rich Meccans also began to keep slaves.

The tribal ethics underwent drastic change. Since in tribal society there is no concept of poverty, there is no question of neglecting the poor. But in newly emergent society not only poor came into existence but the rich began to neglect them thus violating tribal tradition. Thus, a social malaise developed and social tensions between rich and poor emerged. The lifestyle of the rich changed completely and the poor could not even meet their basic needs.

Muhammad (PBUH) was deeply disturbed by this social malaise and retired to cave of Hira to reflect over the situation. He began to receive revelation from Allah to guide him and the earliest chapters and verses dealt with this situation in Meccan society. These powerful verses strongly condemned accumulation of wealth (see verses 104, 107 and others). These verses exhorted the Meccan rich to take care of the poor, needy, orphans and widows what we can term in modern political terminology as weaker sections of society.

The Koran also made justice (including distributive justice) as central to the Koranic ethics and attacked lavish lifestyle of the rich. Thus Islam emerged as a strong political as well as spiritual movement in response to the impact of 'globalization' of its own time. 'Globalization' too was favouring the rich and accentuating differences between rich and poor and Islam's sympathy was clearly with the poor and the neglected sections of society on its margin.

Other countries were not deeply impacted by this international trade as India, Yemen and region of Roman Empire was feudal where such differences had already existed. It was Meccan society, which was structurally very different and was in the process of developing such economic classes. Thus Islam was embraced by the youth who were desiring change (in all revolutionary movements youth play and important role), slaves, and other marginalized sections of society. Of course, some rich traders too responded to it as they were also pained by marginalization of fellow tribals and wanted to bring about favourable change. Traders like Abubaker, Usman (who subsequently became political successors of the Prophet) embraced Islam readily and helped Islamic movement by generously donating their wealth for spread of the movement.

Thus it was that globalization brought about by this Silk Route trade between far-off China and region of Roman Empire via India and Yemen. Islamic movement soon reached these countries— parts of China, Central Asia, India, Yemen and conquered Eastern Roman Empire and Sassanid Empire in a course of a century. But though Islam deeply impacted the spiritual life of these regions, it could not leave deeper impact on political and social structure in these countries. The feudal politics co-opted Islamic politics and Khilafat, the representative model of Islamic politics, soon turned into monarchical model of politics so aptly discussed by Maulana Abul a'ala Maududi, the founder of Jamat-e-Islami in India, in his book Khilafat aur Mulukiyyat.

Thus Islam, after it spread in non-Arab regions of the world with advanced feudal political structure lost its revolutionary political impact and a political movement became an essentially other worldly spiritual movement. Thus social hierarchy prevails today in all Islamic countries though it is anathema to Islamic ethical as well as political teachings. Serious social and political inequalities prevail throughout Islamic world.

III

Thus seemingly innocuous trade between different countries in sixth century brought about a profound transformation in the region of Arabia which subsequently influenced our world. Thus globalization can throw up entirely new social movements and political structures. The globalization of second wave was colonial globalization as pointed out before. This globalization also had great impact on social and political structures of the colonialized countries.

Most of the Islamic countries from Algeria to Indonesia came under direct or indirect influence of colonial countries like Britain, France and Italy, etc. This phase of colonization seriously upset social structures and political outlooks. The colonized people were faced with the challenge of new culture and Western political as well as moral philosophy. Now the challenge was not only cultural and political but also that of science and technological inventions.

By nineteenth century, the European countries had developed far more superior technology and had made significant scientific discoveries. These discoveries had given great boost to rational and secular outlook, on one hand, and political philosophy of democracy, on the other. The colonized countries had not known these technologies and scientific discoveries and hence they developed inferiority complex. This colonization also led to developing a universal secular educational institutions thus creating an educated elite easily co-opted by the colonial country.

Thus colonized countries, in this second wave of globalization created deep divisions among colonized people—those educated and politically privileged and mass of poor people looked upon with contempt by the educated elite. The elite welcomed change, even Westernization and religious elite and unlettered masses opposing it. Nevertheless, colonial impact brought about democratic movements, administrative reforms, universal secular education and rational thinking. The colonial rule thus proved a blessing in disguise to a limited extent. None of the colonized countries had democracy. They were governed by monarchies including India. While colonial rule amounted to slavery, it also left its imprint on almost all spheres of life.

Thus challenges of colonial rule were a mixed bag. The colonial rule did not allow people of colonized countries to take independent decisions, it arrested economic growth and they could not free elect their own representatives. But at the same time as an impact of colonial rule, Islamic countries underwent beneficial changes in outlook and many reform movements were launched. Movements to revive early Islam also came into being. In Egypt Muhammad Abduh, a great Islamic thinker, reinterpreted many provisions of sharia and tried to reform Egyptian society. Many women writers took up the gauntlet and advocated reforms to improve the status of Muslim women.

Muhammad Abduh spent number of years in France and was highly impressed by level of education in that society and rational outlook of people of France. He started a magazine and named it Urwat al-Wuthqa along with Jamaluddin Afghani. Jamaluddin Afghani launched a pan-Islamic movement and tried to create unity among all Muslim countries to challenge Western supremacy. Jamaluddin was active in political sphere while Muhammad Abduh, his disciple, preferred to work for dissemination of education among Muslims.

In India Islam was undergoing an intellectual ferment and Sir Syed Ahmad Khan founded MAO College, which became a university in 1920. He also launched a magazine and called it tahzib al-Akhlaq and advocated social and religious reforms. He also tried to re interpret Holy Koran by writing a new tasfir in the light of new development in the world of science and scientific discoveries. Interestingly enough Syed Hamid, the then Vice Chancellor of AMU revived Tahzib al-Akhlaq and it is continuing ever since.

Justice Amir Ali, Maulavi Chiragh Ali, Maulana Mumtaz Ali Khan and others also advocated reforms in Muslim law in keeping with the modern times and made seminal contributions in that field. Philosopher poet Mohammad Iqbal wrote Reconstruction of Religious thought in Islam and invited Muslim intelligentsia to rethink on many Islamic issues. There was conflict of views between the conservative 'Ulama and reform minded Muslim intellectuals.

During the colonial period Islam was reviled by the Christian clerics and many Muslim practices came under attack from British colonial masters. New laws and new judicial processes were introduced which again were mixed bag. Muslim countries were dominated at the gunpoint. These challenges thrown up by colonization were quite severe enough but also partially beneficial as they stirred our thinking and caused intellectual ferment.

However, while in non-Islamic countries like India colonial rule brought structural changes both in political as well as economic spheres. No Muslim country experienced such basic structural transformation and as a result of this no Muslim country could usher in either democratic or capitalist revolution. Both feudal politics and feudal economy could not be replaced. Some 'Ulama and Muslim intellectuals who talked of Islamic democracy and Islamic economy also did not succeed in bringing in any fundamental change in political or economic sphere. It was nothing more than empty rhetoric. Thus there is complete stagnation in these countries.

IV

In this section we will deal with the third wave of globalization which we are faced with presently. The challenges thrown up by this phase of globalization are qualitatively very different and response to these challenges are also very different from the ones during colonial phase. There is no political colonization in this phase, only economic colonization. No guns have been used to establish political domination as in colonial period but financial domination has been imposed through various means. Violence has been used in some incalcitrant countries like Iraq and Afghanistan, but not everywhere. Even in these countries direct political control has been avoided. We will shed more light on this little later.

Though globalization always results in connectivity (without which there is no question of globalization as the very term indicates), in this phase connectivity has very significant role to play through computer revolution. Whole world has been connected through the internet. This connectivity is being used by both who are supporters of globalization as well as those who vehemently oppose it.

Ulama too are benefitting from this connectivity. They have set up Islamic websites and websites of their Islamic institutions. Today important Koranic commentaries and entire corpus of ahadith are available on these websites. Not only these facilities have been used for making various arithmetic calculations about the Koranic words, verbs and sentences. Searching Koranic verses and ahadith has also become extremely easy. It has thus immensely benefited Islamic scholars. Thus this connectivity is an important part of present phase of globalization and no one opposes it.

While this is a positive side of globalization in this phase, its negative side is no less problematic. This phase of globalization has bulldozed all native cultures, homogenizing them in one sweep through various media channels. Also, this homogenization is being promoted through gross commercialization of culture. This commercialization has bulldozed all religious, cultural and civilizational values too.

It is this bulldozing of cultural and civilizational values which has created strong reaction from the traditional religious elite and has resulted in what is being termed as 'religious fundamentalism. This is a major challenge which has emerged during the current phase of globalization. As pointed out during before, colonial phase too saw this challenge but not on such massive scale. There was an attempt to impose Western culture as superior culture during the colonial phase but there was no such challenge at marketplace and means of communications were extremely limited and such homogenization could not have been possible as it is today during the current globalization and fast connectivity.

All T.V. channels and print media are at the service of those attempting the bulldozing. Also, unlike earlier colonial days, there is no coercive imposition which could be strongly resisted. In this phase, it is an attempt at popularization through commercial channels. The economic elite consider it their privilege to accept Western culture. During colonial phase, different colonial powers dominated various colonized countries though Britain was largest among them. In this phase, one single country, USA, has established its domination in all spheres political, economic and cultural. American values have emerged as universal values.

Thus, conservative religious elite are strongly resisting this attempt, though not very successfully as people of all communities want to have 'good things' of life. Islamic countries themselves like Dubai and Kuwait have emerged as huge markets for these goods and special festivals are often organized by governments of these countries to promote sale of these goods.

Women's bodies have also been commercialized and one sees photographs of semi-naked women in every commercial advertisements evoking strong reaction from traditional elements. Thus Muslim women are subjected to more controls to protect their chastity. Men continue to enjoy all the freedom but women come under greater male control.

This globalization has also resulted in Huntingtonian theories like 'clash of civilizations', which are in the interest of American domination of Islamic world. And Islamic world is sought to be dominated on account of its reserves of oil and oil is needed to meet the requirements of energy for automobiles as well as industries. Without the oil, wheels of Western economy would grind to a halt. Today, American foreign policy in Middle East, is totally governed by oil politics.

America lends blind support to Israel and keeps on arming it to teeth as Israel is the only reliable ally in Middle East. It was in fact created with an eye on Arab oil. Many Arab rulers are also allies of America, but not the people of these countries. People continue to be anti-America. US lent total support to the Shah of Iran but people of Iran overthrew Shah's rule.

However, in case of Israel, both rulers as well as the people can be totally relied upon and hence its valuable as a most reliable ally in that oil rich region. Thus, when Saddam Husain proved to be recalcitrant, theory of weapons of mass destruction was invented and Iraq was bulldozed. However Iraqi people too have proved to be more recalcitrant. Earlier, Taliban regime, was dethroned as it did not permit USA to lay down pipe lines to ferry Central Asian oil through its region.

The response to American violence has been equally violent by forces like Al-Qaida. Thus, this reactive violence, is resulting in loss of innocent lives and what is worse Islamic notions like Jihad are being invoked by Al-Qaida and other 'terrorist groups'. Such groups are multiplying in regions of South Asia too which has also emerged as volatile region.

However, this reactive violence is not desirable and is against Islamic values of compassion and wisdom. Wisdom is strongly emphasized by Koran, and other measures which could be more effective in correcting American policies without loss of innocent human lives should be adopted. Because of this reactive violence, powerful Western media is reviling Islam though it is none of Islam's fault whose central value is peace. Peaceful, non-violent means would be much more effective and Muslims Ulama and intellectuals should join hands to evolve peaceful, non-violent means to respond to American violence in Islamic countries.

20
Maulana Azad and His Concept of Wahdat-E-Deen

Maulana Abul Kalam Azad's *Tarjuman-al-Koran* is considered an important milestone in modern commentaries on Koran. Maulana's approach to Koran was quite unique-though modern yet not devoid of traditionalism. It is so difficult to balance the two and this is Maulana's achievement. Even most traditionalist would find it difficult to find fault with Maulana's *tasfir* (commentary) and most will find it difficult to disagree with his approach.

It is a well known fact that the Maulana could not complete the commentary due to his political preoccupations, but the portion he could complete (up to 22nd chapter) covers almost all important and relevant issues like approach of Koran to other religions, question of women's rights, certain references to Biblical issues about which there have been great controversies, story of Ashab al-Kahaf and so on. Maulana's approach to these issues, one can say with full confidence, most modern in as much as latest research on these issues is concerned. Maulana's writing on Dhu'l Qarnain is really a model of modern research on the subject and on this question Maulana has left nothing which modern scholars had not written until his time. In fact, his research on Dhu'l Qarnain, is a model to be followed by the commentators of the Koran.

However, we are not concerned here with these aspects of Maulana's work on *tasfir*, but his approach to other religions as per Koran's verses. Based on Koranic injunctions, Maulana comes to form the concept of Wahdat-e-din, i.e. unity of religion. It was not unknown before as Shah Waliyullah too refers to the concept of unity of religion in his Hujjat-u-Allah al-Balighah. Many sufi saints like Nizamuddin Awliya and Mazhar Jan-i-Janan also refer to truth of other religions like Hinduism, particularly in Indian context.

However, Maulana's work on this is much more significant for number of reasons. His arguments are based not only on the verses of the Koran but also on his extensive knowledge of other religions like Hinduism, Judaism, Christianity, Buddhism, Jainism and even Zoroastrianism. He systematically argues, both from Koranic perspective, as well as on the basis of teachings of these religions and tries to validate the concept of Wahdat-i-din.

Maulana's contribution also becomes more important in view of the modern world and its problems. He was writing in colonial India which was rocked by communal violence and in that background Maulana's concept became much more important. Those talking of two nations, both amongst the Hindus as well as Muslims, were emphasizing irreconcilability of two religions, i.e. Hinduism and Islam. And Maulana refers to basic teachings of Islam and Hinduism and contradicts the approach of those who found two religions non-reconcilable. It was a giant stride towards the cause of unity of Hindus and Muslims and common nationhood.

It is also important to note that the post-modern world is religiously plural, and there is no country in the world which is not multi-cultural and religiously prelist. Earlier during medieval ages and even during modern period, Europe and America were almost, if not entirely, mono-religious, mono-cultural and mono-lingual. But the entire scene changed in the period of post-modernity. Today entire world is multi-religious and multicultural. The Western social scientists began to talk about pluralism and multiculturalism only after migrations began to western countries from former colonies and West became multi-religious and multicultural.

Maulana had foreseen the needs of the post-modern world and emphasized the significance of unity of religion. Maulana's further contribution is that while referring to unity of religion, he does not ignore the differences between practices of various religions. Here Maulana assumes the role of what I call socio-theologian and maintains that though essence of all religions is same there are significant differences in shariah of all religions.

He thus distinguishes between din and shariah. He defines din as belief in doctrine of one God, in angels, in day of judgement, in prophets and in revealed scriptures brought by the messengers of Allah. He quotes from teachings of various religions to prove his point. Thus in the concept of *Wahdat-e-din* his, emphasis is on metaphysical doctrines on one hand, and, on value structures of religions, on the other. He finds similarities in these metaphysical doctrines as well as in value structures.

But these religions were revealed or came into existence with different historical and socio-cultural backgrounds and hence the laws given by these religions could not be the same. Laws (sharia) was based on customs, traditions and cultural practices though the basis was justice. However, justice finds different expressions in different cultures. Laws of marriage, divorce, inheritance, properties and so on is culture-specific, They cannot be universal, like values and certain metaphysical doctrines.

I think Maulana's insight into societies, their cultures and differing laws, is quite unique among commentators of Koran. Not many had this insight and that is why I tend to call him socio-theologian, rather than simply theologian. If one accepts this proposition that din and shariah are different, many differences between followers of different religions can be eliminated.

I would also like to emphasize here that Koran also maintains that Allah has sent His prophets to different nations (qaums) with different shariahs. Thus, while making this formulation, Maulana is certainly not deviating from Koranic approach but is providing to his readers proper explanation based on understanding of different societies. Most of the commentators could not explain the causes of differences of shariah as they had not much understanding of societies. However, I must say, Shah Waliyullah before Azad had remarkable understanding of Indian society of his time.

In today's conflict-torn world many powerful vested interests are misusing religious differences for promoting conflict among followers of different religions. Such vested interests are found among all religious communities. They invoke certain doctrines of religion to emphasize differences and then based on these differences they promote conflict and even religious wars to serve their own political interests. It is therefore, all the more necessary to promote Maulana's understanding of unity of religion and causes of differences of shariah to wean away people from evil influence of such vested interests.

Apart from Maulana's concept of wahdat-i-din, his contribution to the concept of *rububiyyah* (sustenance) is also very important and this concept, like the one of *Wahdat-e-din* is also a great unifying concept. In fact the first volume of Maulana Azad is devoted to these two concepts—rububiyyah and Wahdat-i-din and both these concepts are based on universal aspects of religions.

Maulana finds the concept of rububiyyah in the first chapter of the Koran, i.e. surah Fatihah in which Koran describes Allah as Rabb-al-Alamin, i.e. sustainer of this universe and universe includes everything and everyone. Maulana's tasfir is most suitable for modern times and his concept of rububiyyah is no less. This concept also forges unity between followers of different religions and is most suitable for our post-modern society.

Maulana also maintains that every period has its own thought system (fikri nizam) and this nizam influences the mind of the commentator.[1] No commentator can escape these influences and hence no commentary of the Koran could be treated as final and universal. Maulana's own tafsir has been greatly influenced by the period he lived in and hence his great emphasis on these two seminal concepts.

Maulana was also deeply involved in India's freedom struggle and for freedom movement to succeed and for India to become free Hindu-Muslim unity was very fundamental. He was repeatedly imprisoned by the British imperialists and his tasfir was also once completely destroyed. Thus Maulana knew the importance of freedom for India and necessity for Hindu-Muslim unity.

In his Presidential Address at Ramgarh session of Indian National Congress, 1923, Maulana said that, 'Today, if an angel were to descend from the heaven and declare from the top of the Qutab Minar, that India will get Swaraj within twenty-four hours, provided she relinquishes Hindu-Muslim unity, I will relinquish Swaraj rather than give up Hindu-Muslim unity. Delay in the attainment of Swaraj will be a loss to India, but if our unity is lost, it will be a loss for entire mankind'.

Thus for Maulana universal brotherhood was very very fundamental and hence he gives so much importance to concepts of *Wahdat-e-din* and *rububiyyah* (universal sustenance). Maulana rises above sectarian approach and adopts universal one as it was both his political need and also his philosophical outlook. But what is important is that Maulana does not base his arguments on extra-Koranic sources but purely on Koranic sources. He is not emphasizing this as his own outlook but develops his outlook from Koran itself. No one can fault Maulana's approach and call it his own and not Koranic.

For example, this argument that each qaum (nation has its own shariah he quoted the Koranic verse 'For every one of you. We appointed a law and a way' (5:48). This very verse also refers to diversity of religions. Thus it says, 'If Allah had pleased He would have made you a single people, but that he might try you in what he gave you. So vie one with the other in virtuous deeds.' This verse also reflects Koranic position on several religions co-existing.

When Maulana argues about unity of religion, for some theologians there can be one problem, Maulana goes strictly by what Koran says about validity of all religions, and not what theologians of different religions maintain about teachings of their respective religions. The Koranic position is that all religions are one since Allah revealed them but the religious leaders of these religions corrupted original teachings and hence differences arose. Had they followed original teachings, these differences would not have been there. However, religious leaders of other communities would not agree with this view and maintain that their teachings as they are, are original teachings and they have not undergone any change.

Thus we find in the Koran—and Maulana quotes this verse, 'Say: O People of the Book, you follow no good till you observe the Torah and the Gospel and that which is revealed to you from your Lord. And surely that which has been revealed to thee from thy Lord will make many of them increase in inordinacy (tughyanan) and disbelief: so grieve not for the disbelieving people'.

Thus Maulana discusses this in his Tarjuman al-Koran under the title '*Qur'an ka perwan-e- mazahib se mutalibah* (Koran's demand from followers of religions) and goes on to say that Koran did not demand from followers of any religion to accept this new religion (i.e. Islam) but demands from every group (following any other religion) that they follow their respective religion in its original shape which has been distorted by them. If you did that (i.e. followed your religion in its original shape) you will find that it is Islam to which I am calling you.[2]

But the Koran also maintains that there are few in every religious group who follow their religion in its original spirit and thus are closer to teachings of the Koran. Thus Koran says in the next verse 'Surely those who believe and those who are Jews and Sabeans and the Christians—whoever believes in Allah and the Last Day and does good—they shall have no fear nor shall they grieve.' (5:69)

Commenting on this verse (5:69) Maulana says that for this reason Koran has heartily welcomed the faith and actions of these virtuous people who were present in different faith traditions and who had not wasted the real spirit of their respective faiths. However, such people are indeed very few and most of them belong to overwhelming majority who have distorted the original spirit of their faiths.[3]

Some religious scholars like Douglas have objected to Maulana's approach that existing religions have distorted original teachings. But we can say in defence of Maulana that what he is saying is what Koran' says and it is not his own. He is writing commentary and explaining Koran's position. But what Maulana is emphasizing by way of his concept of unity of religion is highly helpful to the cause of human unity.

Also, one should fully comprehend Maulana's as well as Koranic position fully. Koran treats an issue at different levels and does not simply accept or reject something as things are highly complex. Thus Koran treats this matter yet at a different level when it states, 'They (People of the Book) are not all alike. Of the people of the Book there is an upright party who recite Allah's messages in the night-time and they adore (Him). They believe in Allah and the Last Day, and they enjoin good and forbid evil and vie one with another in good deeds. And those are among the righteous,' 'And whatever good they do, they will not be denied it. And Allah knows those who keep their duty' (3:112-114).

Thus essentially Koran is concerned with good deeds (enjoining good and forbidding evil) and Koran praises those who adhere to this course of goodness and maintaining ethical conduct without developing any vested interests. Since world is today multi-religious everywhere our main concern should be moral and ethical conduct and maintaining original spirit of our respective faiths.

Maulana emphasizes precisely this aspect in the first volume of his *Tarjuman al-Koran*. He takes the Koranic words ma'ruf and munkar and explains their meaning. He says ma'ruf means what is known and acceptable and hence it represents good and munkar means what is denied by the society, i.e. evil and Koran, according to Maulana maintains that there may be so many differences in matters of beliefs and doctrines (aoq'id) but there are certain things on which there is complete unanimity of their being good and there are certain things about which there is compete unanimity for their being evil.[4]

Then giving example he says all agree that one should speak truth and that one should not resort to lies. There is also agreement that honesty and integrity is good and dishonesty is bad. All of us also agree that we should serve our parents, be helpful to our neighbors, that we should take care of the poor and needy, to be helpful to the oppressed are among the good deeds for all human beings and to oppress and bad behaviour are most undesirable. And all the religions in the world, all the parties and groups, whatever their differences on matters of faith and doctrines, are unanimous on this.[5]

Thus Azad ultimately advises his readers to avoid doctrinal differences and insist on ethical and moral behaviour. Our world would be very different if we did not fight on differences about our doctrines and instead concentrate on matters moral and ethical. In fact this is Koranic message also.

Thus Koran says, 'And abuse not those whom they call upon besides Aliah (i.e. worship others besides Allah) lest, exceeding the limits, they abuse Allah through ignorance. Thus to every people have we made their deeds fair-seeming; to their Lord is their return so He will inform them of what they did' (6:109).

This is very clear statement by Koran that do not abuse each other or try to prove each other's beliefs and doctrines wrong as Allah has made for each people their deeds fair-seeming to them, i.e. every people think their doctrines and their deeds are best and hence do not quarrel about them and leave it to Allah who will decide on the Day of Judgment about their beliefs and deeds.

Thus Koran prefers coexistence to disputes about beliefs and rituals according to those beliefs and invites people to live in coexistence and leave their disputes to Allah. If human beings try to settle these doctrinal disputes their ego, their interests will come in their way and they will not be able to decide as every people would maintain only their doctrines are best.

Thus we see that at one level Koran says that Allah had sent only one truth through His messengers to different people but they distorted the truth and differences arose and hence if they follow original message there will exist no differences and by following their own original faith all differences will be resolved as truth is one and that is Islam (surrendering to the will of Allah).

Though this is the truth, it can be contentious since all people would maintain we are following true religion and not distorted one and naturally would lead to serious differences and disputes. So at another level the Koran says that do not indulge in such disputations as it will result only in reviling each other and nothing else. So it says We have made each people their own deeds fair-seeming or luring so best thing is to live in peace and harmony and leave it to Allah to decide about their deeds on the Day of Judgement.

This is what Maulana Azad also pleads for as in multi-religious societies this is the best solution. Let us cooperate with each other on what is good and jointly fight against what is evil. Maulana emphasized this approach in early twentieth century when Hindus and Muslims were fighting and communal violence was breaking out everywhere. No one was ready to let people believe what they thought to be true doctrine and emphasized their religion's superiority.

Maulana Azad understood the real message of Koran during very difficult period and tried to explain it to Muslims, this message of the Koran is in simple Urdu. It is also Maulana's great contribution that he tried to translate in very simple Urdu so that common Muslims and even others (as Urdu was widely spoken and understood in entire north India during his time) so that mutual hatred could be reduced, if not completely eliminated.

Even today Muslim can greatly benefit from this message if they care to read it and take it to non-Muslim sisters and brothers.

NOTES

1. Maulana Abul Kalam Azad, *Tarjuman al-Qur'an*, Delhi: Sahitya Academi, 1980, vol. I, p. 42.
2. See *Tarjuman al-Qur'an*, *ibid*., pp. 416-17.
3. *Op. cit*., p. 418.
4. *Tarjuman al-Qur'an*, *ibid*., pp. 420-1.

21
On Kufr, Jihad, Cow-Slaughter and Dar Al-Harb

Whenever I lecture on Islam or even on communalism and secularism participants usually ask me about kufr, jihad, *Dar al-Islam* and *Dar al-Harb* and position of cow slaughter. There is widespread misunderstanding about these terms not only among non-Muslims but also among Muslims themselves. It is therefore necessary to throw light on these terms in Islam. It is highly necessary to remove misunderstandings about these terms in the interest of peace and harmonious co-existence with Non-Muslims both in Islamic and non-Islamic countries.

It is important to note that every new ideology, religion or movement gives birth to its own terminology. The French revolution gave birth to terms like fraternity, equality and justice. The communist revolution gave birth to terms like bourgeoisie, petit bourgeois, proletariat, class struggle, revisionism, etc. These movements were political in nature. Religious movements too gave birth to new terms. Buddhism, for example gave the term dhamma, dukkha, Jainism anuvrata and siyadwad or anekantwad. Christians used terms like heretics, pagans and heathens for non-Christians.

Some terms are used by the text material of the religious or ideological texts and some are coined later by followers of these religions and ideologies. The terms used by religious texts tend to be more precise and rigorous and also have well defined context, But these terms when used by the followers, tend to be used rather loosely and develop personal motives and agendas.

These terms are used not only for non-believers but also for believers themselves when differences among the followers arise. Sometimes these terms are freely used to denounce those who differ in interpretation of the text or try to apply the text in changing circumstances and absorb new developments. Such free use of these terms for denunciation of opponents can and does create serious misunderstandings among others who lack proper knowledge of these terms and their context.

The communists, for example, used terms like running dog of imperialism, petit bourgeois and revisionists and so on against those who differed from official line as prevalent or those who formed another party as against official party. Similarly, when religions split into different sects such negative terms were used against those who split from the mainstream. Thus Catholics will denounce Protestants and Protestants Catholics and so on.

Islam too split into several sects and each sect usually denounces the other as kafirs, zindiqs and so on. Each sect considered the other as either heretic or kafir deviating from the 'truth' of religion. Each sect thought it has the monopoly of truth and the other sect is deviant or committing kufr. These terms are also often used for personal animosity as well. Thus such terms create great misunderstanding.

Also, certain terms though not in original religious or ideological text, are coined later to suit new circumstances. But due to frequent use, these terms acquire originality and are thought to be part of original texts. The non-experts, due to lack of knowledge, think it to be part of original text. Terms like *Dar al-Islam* and *Dar al-Harb* came into existence much later due to spread of Islam in other parts of the world. Their context has to be properly understood.

Islamic Terms and Their Meaning and Origin

Islam arose in a tribal society, which functioned on oral customs and traditions and had no written laws or had no prophet or scripture. Muhammad (PBUH) was first prophet among Arabs and he brought the first scripture—Koran—in the history of Arabia. There were several problems in the Arab society of the Prophet's time, which Islam tried to address. Mecca was fast turning into an international financial and commercial hub and yet lacked any written laws.

Because of commercialisation of Meccan society tribal traditions were being ignored and gross injustices were taking place causing social tensions. The institutions of private property, usually absent in tribal societies had come into existence and conspicuous pattern of consumption was developing. The weaker sections of society like the poor, orphans, widows and slaves were being neglected and women were treated as chattels.

On the other pole of the society there were powerful vested interests who had enriched themselves through international trade between China through India and Yemen to borders of Roman Empire to the North. Thus Meccan society was on the threshold of transformation into a developed commercial society and yet lacked any written law or higher religious and social institutions.

Islam tries to fulfil this vacuum through Prophet Muhammad (PBUH). The Prophet gave higher values to the Arab society most fundamental of which were equity and justice along with the concepts of universal humanity. Meccan society badly needed these higher values and the concept of universal humanity. For that the Koran, revealed to the Prophet, attacked local, divisive, superstitious practices of tribal gods and goddesses and gave the concept of unifying and universal concept of one God—Allah. This could transform the Meccan tribal society into a higher form of universal society.

However, this was not acceptable to tribal chiefs who had formed inter-tribal commercial corporations and were highly proud of their achievements of wealth and prestige. They were highly status conscious and were not prepared to accept claim of prophet hood and revelation by a poor orphan boy though he came from a clan of Hashim highly regarded in Meccan tribal order.

The Koran, revealed to Muhammad (PBUH) brought new truth to Arab society, which did not possess any higher truth so far. Thus those who accepted this higher truth were called either Muslim or Mu'min. It is important to note here that there is definite difference between these two terms—Muslim and Mu'min. Koran itself differentiate between the two. Those who simply accepted Islam without deeper understanding as it was a rising religion and surrendered to prophet's message were termed as 'Muslims (i.e. those who surrender). But those who believed from depth of their heart and developed higher conviction in the prophet's message, were termed as 'Mu'min' (i.e. those who sincerely believed and committed themselves).

Thus we find in the Koran, 'The dwellers of the desert say; We believe. Say; You believe not, but say, We submit; and faith has yet not entered into your hearts, And if you obey Allah and His Messenger, He will not diminish aught of your deeds. Surely Allah is Forgiving, Merciful' (49:14).

Thus there were two stages—submitting and believing. Those who understood higher mission of Islam and its universalising mission and developed deep faith into it were called 'Mu'min', It is these Mu'mins who were ever ready to sacrifice everything including their own life for the success of the mission. Others, Muslims, just joined in for one or the other reason.

It is also to be born in mind that Koran gave Arabs concepts of higher values, which did not exist in their society. The best values among Arabs were chivalry and generosity summed up in the word muru'ah (literally 'manlike'). However, the Koran gave values like truth, justice, equality, benevolence, compassion, peace, forgiveness, humility which were not known to Arabs.

Thus those wealthy Arabs who accumulated wealth were too arrogant to believe in these universal values and higher morality. Thus because they rejected truth of these universal values and continued to believe in tribal gods and goddesses with accompanying superstitions and denial of human reason and higher morality, they were termed as kafir, i.e. unbeliever.

The word kafir literally means one who hides. According to Imam Raghib al-Asfahani, who compiled the dictionary of Koran, the word kafara means to hide. Night is also called kafir as it hides everything. A cultivator is also called kafir as he hides seeds below soil for it to grow (see Imam Raghib Asfahani Mufradat al-Koran, Lahore, 1971, pp. 916-17).

Thus anyone who hides is called kafir and since those Arabs of Mecca who refused to accept higher truth revealed from Allah and hid it were called kafirs. It is important to note that only those who hide higher truth and morality based on this truth are called kafirs (plural kuffar). However, it does not mean all those who are not Muslims are kafirs as they can also possess truth, though in different form or through other prophets.

The Koran makes it quite clear that Allah has sent several prophets and all are not mentioned in the Koran. Only few have been who came with the message from Allah in and around Arab region like Abraham, Moses and Christ. Only Adam and Noah were not from that region. The Koran says Allah has sent His messengers to all the nations (13:7). Thus Allah has sent His messengers, guides to all the people and they possess truth. Thus all non-Muslims cannot be dubbed as kafirs, only those who hide truth in any form. The Koran also creates a category of ahl al-kitab (people of the book). All those to whom Allah sent His messenger and a book were called people of the Book. The Koran mentions Christians, Jews and Sabaens in this category.

But does not exclude those who have not been mentioned in this category by the Koran. Many others like Zoroastrians were included in this category. The Sufi saints like Mazhar Jan-I-Janan also included the Hindus in this category arguing that how Allah can forget to send His Messengers to India as He has promised to send His Messengers to all the nations. He accepts Vedas as revealed scriptures. He also feels Hindus are monotheists as they believe in God who is nirgun and nirakar (i.e. without attributes and shape), which is highest form of *tawhid* (monotheism), (see Mazhar Jan-I-Janan's Letters tr. in Urdu by Khaliq Anjum, Delhi.)

It is also important to note that Koran also emphasises freedom of conscience and rejects any compulsion in matters of religion (2:256) and even accepts right of kafirs to believe in what they believe (see chapter 109) and pronounces the doctrine for you is your religion and for me is mine. Those kafirs who do not fight with Muslims and live and let live can be befriended. Koran permits fighting only with those kafirs who fight Muslims and attack them. See verses 2:190-191.

Thus kafirs have been divided into two categories harbi and non-harbi kafirs, i.e. those who fight Muslims and those who do not. One can enter into pact with non-harbi kafirs. All those verses in the Koran, which refer to fighting or killing kafirs do not apply to all the kafirs but to those who broke friendship treaty or attacked Muslims. Koran does not even permit abusing other gods lest they abuse Allah (6:109), let alone killing those believing in other gods.

Thus one should not read Koranic verses about kafirs piecemeal but in conjunction with all other verses in so that one can understand overall approach of the Koran. The word kafir has been used very loosely in the history of Islam and not in keeping with the text of the Koran. There are several reasons for such misuse of the word.

Of course it is not only particularly so in the history of Islam but as pointed out above, it happens with all ideological and religious movements.

Any disagreement on theological doctrines also results in dubbing the other as kafir. Thus one sect of Muslims denounced the other sect as kafir. It was more out of intolerance than theological error. Even individuals who fell out of grace of powerful 'ulama were denounced as kafirs. Persons like Sir Syed Ahmad Khan who advocated modern secular education was described as kafir and fatwas were issued against him and fatwa obtained from 'ulama in Medina to that effect.

In dubbing someone as kafir various motives are at work including ones disagreement and personal ego or even vested interest. Thus a true Muslim who follows the spirit of the Koran would refrain from using such terms. It should be left to Allah to decide. A human being should only express his/her disagreement. Koran exhorts believers to accept disagreements and leave rest to Allah and excel each other in good deeds (see verses like 5:48, 2:148).

Some people out of ignorance describe Hindus as kafirs. They neither know Koran properly nor Hindu religion. Many Sufi saints who knew Hindu religion even accepted them as people of the book, as pointed out above. And Koran also exhorts Muslims not to denounce others loosely but to argue with them in best possible manner so as to persuade them rather than alienate them (see verses 16:125 and 3:63). It is great lie perpetrated by some hostile or ignorant people that Koran requires Muslims to convert people at the point of sword. There is not a single verse in the Koran to this effect. Koran emphatically rejects coercion and promotes persuasion. It believes in excluding other not on theological but only on moral rounds. On moral grounds it includes all.

Thus kafir is one who denies all morality and moral truth and denies freedom of conscience and human dignity and believes in exploiting others, indulges in wrong doings and injustice, lies to serve his own interests and persecutes others to pursue his own interests and is arrogant of his wealth and power and denies existence of higher power. One who is humble, just, truthful, compassionate and benevolent to others cannot be called kafir whatever his/her theological belief. Koran is very universal in approach and emphasises what it puts as 'vie one with another in virtuous deeds.'

Dar Al-Islam and Dar Al-Harb

The concept of *Dar al-Islam* (abode of Islam or Islamic country) and *Dar al-Harb*, i.e., abode of war or non-Islamic country is not found in the Koran as Islam had not spread to other countries when the Koran was being revealed. Islam spread to other areas after the death of the Prophet (PBUH). This concept was thus developed by later jurists who were confronted with the reality of Muslims living in minority in some countries.

Where Muslims were in overwhelming majority were thus described by jurists as *Dar al-Islam* and where Muslims were living as persecuted minority were called *Dar al-Harb* or abodes of war. But also there were countries where Muslims lived as minority but were free to pursue their religion in peace like India. The jurists distinguished such areas as *Dar al-aman*, i.e. abode of peace.

Whichever country where Muslims can live in peace and pursue their religion freely should be described as abode of peace. In fact in modern times freedom of conscience (which Koran accepted fourteen hundred years ago) is universally recognised in contemporary world, at least theoretically, and so there is no question of any part of the world being *Dar al-Harb* today. Still many people hostile to Islam or totally ignorant of development of such concepts keep on repeating these concepts to defame Islam. No serious scholar or jurist describes India as *Dar al-Harb*.

Thus it should be clearly understood that these concepts were developed by the jurists in keeping with the past realities and have nothing to do with any Koranic doctrine. India and most other countries where Muslims live in minority today accept the right to freedom of religion and hence they cannot be described as *Dar al-Harb* but as *Dar al-aman*. However, there may be practical problems and even a degree of persecution of Muslims but that would not be a good enough reason to declare it as *Dar al-Harb*. Any region can be described as *Dar al-Harb*, if at all, only if Muslims are not allowed to practice their religion constitutionally or by law. There is no such country in the world today. India is a secular democratic country and all are free to profess, practice and propagate their religion. How can it then be described as *Dar al-Harb*. Anyone who invokes such doctrine does so either out of ignorance or out of deliberate mischief.

Jihad

Much has been written on this since the events of 9/11. Jihad is utmost effort to achieve something using ones utmost efforts (see Raghib Asfahani op. cit., 199-200). It may include fighting with weapons as a last resort but also includes fighting against oneself and ones desires which one hadith describes as *jihad-i-akbar*, i.e. greatest jihad. Jihad, if one goes to the literal meaning of the word, does not mean war but only utmost efforts and its other derivative juhud means according to ones capacity.

Many Muslims out of ignorance use it only in the sense of war, which is not correct. Koran uses other words like harb and qital for war but uses word jihad for moral struggle. It is every Muslims duty to continue struggle for moral excellence, of his own and also of society he lives in. To fight against corruption, against environmental pollution, for human rights, for justice for weaker sections of society and such other noble causes is part of jihad. Anything, which brings relief to suffering humanity is part of jihad in the way of Allah.

The Prophet (PBUH) basically devoted himself to fight for justice for weaker sections of society in Mecca and hence Koran's repeated emphasis on helping orphans, widows, poor, women and slaves. The prophet (PBUH) had declared jihad against all forms of injustices in Meccan society and was opposed in his efforts by powerful vested interests as pointed out above. It is this passion for social justice, which needs to be emulated today by Muslims and become precursors of social justice. There is so much injustice all around and vested interests in our times are much more powerful than in Prophet's time. That will be real jihad. There is so much poverty and exploitation in the world.

Cow Slaughter

Koran no where makes it obligatory on Muslims to slaughter cow. It is totally a wrong notion that Muslims should slaughter cow particularly on *Eid al-àdha*, i.e. Baqar Eid. There is absolutely no such injunction in the Koran. Babar had written in his will to Humayun not to permit slaughter of cow to win over hearts and minds of Hindus. Some Nawabs of Bengal used to give death sentence for slaughtering cows. Recently Darul 'Ulum, Deoband, the premier seminary of Islam in Asia advised Muslims not to slaughter cows on Eid al-adha to avoid communal trouble. To respect others religious sentiments is part of higher morality. Islam teaches to respect others' religious sentiments and live in peace and harmony.

22
Islam, Women and Gender Justice

It is generally thought that Islam treats women unfairly and gender justice is not possible within Islamic law known as the sharia law. This assertion is partly true and partly untrue. True as far as the existing sharia laws are concerned. Untrue, as the existing laws were codified during second and third centuries of Islam when general perspective of women's rights was very different from today's perspective. The Koranic verses which are quite fundamental to the Islamic law, were interpreted so as to be in conformity with the views about gender rights prevailing then.

It is important to note that scriptural injunctions are always mediated through prevailing social ethos. Also, and it is more fundamental to framing of laws based on scriptures, scriptures both reflect the given situation and also transcend it. There cannot be any scripture—revealed or otherwise—which is uni-dimensional, i.e. it reflects only given situation. Every scripture tries to go beyond what is given and it faces stiff opposition from those who loose out if the transcendental perspectives are spelled out and enforced. The scriptures condemn prevailing social malaise and provide a new vision. Those who benefit from the new vision embrace the new faith. Those who loose oppose it tooth and nail. But, the vested interests and those who want to perpetuate the old order have their own strategies. Soon they find ways and means to hijack new religion to their own benefit. This is done in number of ways: (1) They capture political power and religion becomes part of political establishment and looses its initial revolutionary thrust as it is appropriated by the ruling classes; (2) they convert religion itself into an establishment and a power-structure develops around it. Religion is then used more for distribution of favours than for spiritual enrichment; (3) intellectual resources are used to restore status quo ante and this is done chiefly by interpreting the scriptures in a way which will rob it of its transcendental thrust. Thus a theology is developed which is supportive of status quo. One must distinguish between what scriptural pronouncements are and what theology is woven around it. Scriptural pronouncements are divinely inspired and hence transcendental and theological formulations are human and hence often contradict divine intentions. Scriptural pronouncements are an option for the weaker sections whereas theological formulations are weapons in the hands of powerful interests. It is therefore necessary that theological formulations be continuously challenged by scriptural pronouncements. One must strive to build up creative tension between theological and scriptural. While scripture remains immutable with its transcendental spirit, theology must change facing new challenges and newly emergent situations.

Those who oppose any change in theological formulations and sharia laws are those who loose their dominant position and the priesthood who monopolise theology and religion for them is instrumental in promoting their interests rather than spiritual source of inner enrichment. The priesthood, monopolising theology, project it as divine and immutable. The run of the mill faithfuls' understanding of religion is mediated through the priesthood and hence they are made to believe that theology as formulated by them or their predecessors is divine and hence immutable. Any change will amount to changing the divine will.

In Islam, it is common belief that the sharia is divine and hence immutable. Whenever any measures for gender justice are proposed one meets with this stock argument. It is important to note that sharia, though undoubtedly based on the Holy Koran, is a human endeavour to understand the divine will. It is an approach to, rather than divine will itself. The priesthood, i.e. the community of 'ulama projects it as a divine end itself and hence refuse to admit any change. 'The sharia is divine' has become a commonly accepted position. Thus what was thought of women's rights during the early period of Islamic history has come to be the final and immutable. Even to think of, much less changing it, is, interfering with the divine, and hence an unpardonable sin.

As pointed out above, there is big gap between the scriptural, i.e. the Koranic pronouncements, and, sharia formulations. While the Koranic pronouncements are purely transcendental in spirit, the sharia formulations have been influenced by human situation as well as human thinking on all related issues. Women were in subordinate position in the patriarchal societies and this subordinate relationship came to be reflected in the sharia laws relating to her rights. The transcendental divine spirit was conveniently ignored and the prevailing situation was rationalised through contextual Koranic pronouncements. As pointed out above, there is always a creative tension between what is and what ought to be in scriptures. However, this tension is often resolved in favour of the prevalent rather than the emergent and prevalent is eternalised by rationalising certain divine pronouncements.

On the Methodology of Creating Islamic Legal Structure

If we want to effect necessary changes in the sharia laws, it is important to understand the methodology of creating of Islamic legal structure. The Islamic legal corpus is known as sharia. As sharia is, after all, a human approach to divine will as reflected through the scripture, i.e. the holy Koran, it is not uniform but has several variants. In the Sunni Islam itself there are four different schools of jurisprudence, i.e. Hanafi, Shafi'i, Hanbali and Maliki. Besides these schools there is what is known as the Zahiri school. Also, there are several schools in the Shi'ah Islam as well. The Ja'fari or the Ithna 'Ashari School, the Isma'ili school and the Zaidi School. The Sunni Islam bases sharia—besides the Koran—on Sunna (i.e. the sayings and doings of the Holy Prophet), *qiyas* (analogy) and finally *ijma'* (consensus). However, except the Koran. the remaining three sources, i.e. Sunna, *qiyas* and *ijma'* are controversial. Some Ahadith (sayings of the Prophet) are acceptable by some while they are rejected by others. Some Ahadith are considered weak (da'if) and some of doubtful origin and some outright forgeries. Also, *qiyas*, analogical reasoning varies from jurist to jurist. There is controversy about *ijma'* as well. The crucial question is whose ijma'? Of the jurists and the 'Ulama or of the entire community? Also, has ijma' ever been possible? Have all 'Ulama, let alone the entire community, ever developed consensus on any issue? There are hardly any instances of this nature in the history of Islamic jurisprudence. Thus it will be seen that except the Koran which is divine and there are no textual differences about it, the three other fundamental sources, i.e. Sunna, *qiyas* and *ijma'* are human and hence controversial. It is also important to point out here that about the Prophet's pronouncements, i.e. Ahadith there is controversy whether they be considered as divine or human. The Ahl-e-Hadith (i.e. the followers of Hadith) consider Hadith as divine like the Koran while many others do not give it that status and consider it as human and hence not eternal.

The Shi'i jurisprudence (sharia) is based on the Koran and the pronouncements of the Prophet as reported by Imams, i.e. the male descendants of the Prophet's daughter Hazrat Fatima and her husband 'Ali. The Koran as interpreted by these Imams is considered as the only right interpretation, every other interpretation is considered as mere conjecture or opinion (ra'i). And tasfir bi'r ra'i (i.e. Koranic interpretation or exegesis through human opinion) is rejected outright in the Shi'a

Islam. But there is controversy in the Shi'ah Islam as to who is rightfully appointed Imam. The Ithna 'Asharis (twelvers), the Isma'ilis (also referred to as seveners), Zaidis, the Qaramitas and the Alavids, all mutually differ on this issue. All these sects have Imams of their own and consider others as not rightfully appointed and hence have no legitimacy. Also, the juridical pronouncements of these Imams differ from each other even on matters of principles, at limes.

Thus had it been immutable the sharia would not have differed from one school to the other and from sect to sect. The Koran, being divine, does not differ and is immutable. It admits of no change. However, its interpretation differs from sect to sect and from one school to the other. Thus the Koran is divine and its interpretations are human and what is human admits of change. The sharia, being based on human interpretations of divine word, can, and does admit change. What was thought to be just in respect of women's rights in medieval ages, is no longer so. The idea of justice also changes with changing consciousness and what is just in one age may not necessarily be just in the other. We will throw more light on this aspect little later. It is in fact very important aspect as far as the Koranic concept of law is concerned.

One of the important sources of the sharia law is Hadith or Sunna. As pointed out above, this too is not above controversy. There are two types of controversies about this seminal source of Islamic law: (1) whether Hadith is divine or human and (2) whether it is authentic, weak or forged. The Koran is unanimously accepted as divine and there is no controversy about it. Also, its contents are accepted with unanimity and without any controversy. No one maintains that this or that verse of the Koran is unauthentic, or added later, or of doubtful origin. But it is not so as far as Hadith literature is concerned. There are several Ahadith which are controversial. Either they are considered of doubtful origin or weak or outright forgery. It is said that Imam Abu Hanifa. the founder of the Hanafi School of law, accepted only 17 Ahadith as true and authentic and yet he used many more while giving his juridical opinions.

There are Muslims who maintain that Ahadith are divine like the Koran. They believe that the Koranic verse 'Nor does he speak out of desire, it is naught but revelation that is revealed' (53:3-4) applies to the Prophet's all pronouncements including his Ahadith. These Muslims believe that Ahadith too, are divine and hence above any human controversy. Thus this source of sharia also becomes equally divine for them. However, there is no unanimity about it. Not only that Hadith is not believed to be divine by large sections of Muslims, it is not above controversy as to its origin. Imam Bukhari, one of the greatest collectors of Ahadith, is said to have collected more than six hundred thousand

Ahadith of which he accepted only four thousand and rejected others as of doubtful origin or outright forgeries. This clearly shows how some interested people were producing Hadith literature to serve their own ends. Unfortunately, many of these Ahadith went into juridical formulations in general, and about women, in particular. These formulations reflect the prejudices and dominant thinking of the time rather than the Koranic principles. These formulations, therefore, cannot be treated above change.

Also, there is yet another problem about Hadith literature. And this problem remains, even if Hadith literature is treated as divine and immutable. The Koran which is unanimously held to be divine by all Muslims contain many pronouncements which are directly related to the then prevailing Arab social structure. These pronouncements also reflect the social norms or social problems as they existed then. These pronouncements cannot be of universal application in other societies and cultures. We would like to cite examples. There was a practice called zihar among Arabs. It is mentioned in 33:4 and 58:2-3. It was a practice to declare their wives like their mothers and abandon them. Thus in verse 33:4 the Koran says, 'Allah has not made for any man two hearts within him; nor has He made your wives whom you desert by Zihar, your mothers.' Edward William Lane defines Zihar in his Arabic-English Lexicon as husband telling his wife thou art to me as the back of my mother. In verse 2 of Chapter 58 the Koran says. 'Those of you who put away their wives by calling them their mothers— they are not their mothers. None are their mothers, save those who give them birth, and they utter indeed a hateful word and a lie.' And in verse 3 of the same chapter it is said, 'And those who put away their wives by calling them their mothers, then go back on that which they said, must free a captive before they touch one another. To this you are exhorted.'.

From above two verses we come to know that Arabs used to desert their wives calling them like the back of their mothers and some used to go back on that vow and would like to touch their wives again. The Koran prescribed that they free a captive (i.e. a slave) before breaking their vow. Now this practice was unique to the Arab society of that time. We do not find such practices in other societies. Also, today there is no institution of slavery, it has already been abolished. If an Arab today pronounces Zihar on his wife and wants to take back his vow there are no slaves available to free. Thus such verses in the Koran should be treated as contextual, i.e. revealed in the context of that society and are no more valid as social practices have changed. Similarly, the institution of slavery is no more. There are several pronouncements about slaves and slavery in the holy Koran but they are no longer applicable as the institution itself does not exist any more. But in sharia as formulated in the second and third century Hijrah (Islamic Calendar) these practices prevailed and hence elaborate laws were made by the jurists based on Koran or Hadith. But they are totally irrelevant today. Thus the proposition that sharia laws are immutable is not maintainable.

The Koranic verses thus should be divided into two categories namely (1) contextual and (2) normative. The normative pronouncements of the Koran are eternal and while re thinking issues in Islamic sharia, particularly pertaining to women's rights the normative pronouncements will have precedence over the contextual. But during the early centuries contextual often had precedence over normative and it was quite 'normal' then. And hence these formulations became widely acceptable in that society. These laws were thought to be normative then and hence struck deeper roots in society as well as in hearts and minds of the people as well and came to acquire status of immutability with the passage of time.

Thus even if Hadith is accepted as divine its contextuality will have, to be kept in mind. It is also said, and rightly so, that the Prophet explained the Koranic verses through his words and deeds and who knew the meaning and import of the Koranic verses better than the Prophet. Quite true. But the question of contextuality remains. The holy Prophet, while dealing with the given society, could not have gone beyond its context in explaining and practising the Koranic pronouncements. Again it can best be illustrated with an example of women's status in that society. While explaining the cause of revelation of the Koranic verse 4:34, all classical commentators like Tabari. Fakhruddin Razi and others maintain that the Prophet allowed a woman (daughter of his companion) right to retaliate against her husband who had unjustly slapped her but, in view of the prevailing social ethos it laid to unrest among the men and Koran reversed the Prophet's decision. This once again shows that the question of contextuality is very important and highly relevant in all judicial pronouncements be they those of the Prophet or other Islamic jurists.

Another example is this respect is that of *milk-e-yamin*, i.e. legitimising sexual relations with a slave girl. There is near unanimity among the Islamic jurists that it is permissible to have sexual relations with slave girls and that the Prophet himself had such relations with a Coptic Christian slave girl. The modernists and some other commentators of course challenge this formulation and maintain that the Prophet had married her. But Maulana Maududi, one of the contemporary Islamic thinkers and founder of the *Jam'at-e-Islami*, maintains in his commentary on the Koran (Tafhim al Koran) that the Prophet had relations with the slave-girl without marrying her. Most of the eminent medieval jurists concur with this. But if this view that sexual relations with a slave-girl is permissible is accepted the contemporary society would not approve of it. Thus the Prophet's Sunna cannot be seen out of its social context.

There were four great jurists in Sunni Islam who founded four different schools of jurisprudence. All four differ from each other on many issues. Much has been written on causes of these differences. But the modern scholars maintain that one important reason was their differing social situations. Imam Hanbal and Imam Malik lived in Medina and thus were quite close to social ethos of that society in which the Prophet himself lived.

They were closer in their juridical formulations to what the Prophet said and did in that society. Imam Shafi'i and Imam Abu Hanifa, on the other, lived in Egypt and Iraq respectively which were confluences of many cultures and thus were unorthodox in their methodology in arriving at juridical opinions. While Imam Malik and Hanbal mainly relied on Hadith, Imam Sahfi'i and Abu Hanifa used qiyas and ijma' more liberally, apart from Hadith. Thus while the former two Imam's formulations were closer to Arab practices in Mecca and Medina, the latter two Imam's formulations had been largely influenced by other practices as well. This clearly shows that sharia is influenced by human situations and can incorporate situational changes. The Arab 'adat (the Arab customary law) also became integral part of the sharia law. Thus the then prevailing opinions about women in the Arab society greatly influenced the sharia laws pertaining to women. The Arab 'adat cannot certainly be considered divine injunctions and hence immutable. In fact the Arab 'adat had great relevance as long as Islam was confined to the Arab society. But once it spread out to far-off areas, the need, to incorporate other practices also became equally important. And now the changed consciousness about women's rights can also not be ignored.

There is yet another problem about the Hadith literature which is, as pointed out above, an important ingredient of sharia. The Ahadith were generally reported by the Prophet's companions. In this respect even the most authentically reported Ahadith present different kinds of problems. Firstly, most of the Ahadith reported by the companions were not the exact words of the Prophet but the overall meaning of what he said. There are hardly few Ahadith which can be said to be the exact words of the Prophet. Secondly, the Hadith literature also incorporates the reports about what the companions saw the Prophet doing. Thus the Prophetic Sunna includes both what the Prophet said as well as reports about what he did in different situations.

Now among the Prophet's companions there were all kinds of people. There were companions who had sharp memory and good understanding and comprehension of the problems. There were companions who had very poor understanding of the complex issues and also there were companions who had poor memory. And there were companions who spent several years with the Prophet and there were companions who spent only a few hours with him, and even those who saw and heard him from a distance. All that these companions reported having heard from the Prophet became part of Hadith corpus which then was used for formulating sharia laws.

Not only that. There is yet another problem. The Ahadith have been reported by people who heard it from the companions of the companions (tab'i tabi'in) and companions of the companions of the companions of the Prophet. Thus there is whole chain of narrators known as rijal (the narrating men or women). The collectors of Ahadith did try to develop the science of rijal (i.e. 'ilm al-rijal) criteria to judge the honesty and integrity of the narrators. But this criterion judged the honesty and integrity of the narrators rather than his or her understanding, comprehension or intelligence. Moreover, there were often missing links. And also the cases wherein much was not known about one or more of the narrators in the chain. Many narrators were of totally different cultural backgrounds—some narrators being Arabs and others non-Arabs not properly acquainted with the Arab affairs. Also, many narrators had their own biases for or against women (also about other matters) and these biases definitely affected their narrative or reports.

It was for this reason that the Prophet had strictly prohibited his followers from compiling his sayings. He knew very well that his sayings may not be reported faithfully to future generations for various reasons. Also, he was fully aware of the fact that the future generations will insist on strictly following what reaches them as the sayings of Allah's Messenger though they may be facing different circumstances. Even the first Caliph Hazrat Abu Bakr did not permit compilation of Ahadith for similar reasons. Still people did compile these Ahadith though much later. And by the time they were compiled spurious ones had mixed up with authentic ones.

Thus it will be seen that Hadith literature, even if entirely authentic, presents several problems. Thus it cannot be considered as highly reliable source of Islamic legislation. But the Islamic juris corpus is as much based on the problematic Hadith literature as on the holy Koran. Still the 'Ulama project it as unquestionable divine and hence immutable. They refuse to admit any change even though sweeping changes are taking place in the social, cultural, economic and political circumstances.

The doctrine of taqlid (mechanical imitation) is emphasised by the contemporary jurists in the world of Islam. They maintain that rethinking about the formulations of the great Imams is not permissible. In fact, these formulations are treated as divine. Also, most of the 'Ulama do not even permit taking more favourable provisions for women from other schools of law. They insist that any one school should be followed in its entirety. Some 'Ulama of course permit such an approach. But they are fewer in numbers. Now more and more 'Ulama are coming around to permitting this approach which has given some relief to women. The Ottoman rulers had adopted this approach in nineteenth century itself. But still it is not widely accepted. Taqlid is the generally established rule. It is causing great deal of hardships to Muslim women everywhere.

The holy Prophet had anticipated the problems which will arise in future. He took care to leave some guidance in this respect. Firstly, he encouraged what is known as *ijtihad* (i.e. exerting oneself to solve newly arising problems if no precise guidance was available in the Koran and Prophet's Sunnah). The Hadith regarding *Ma'adh bin Jabal* is well-known about this. When the Prophet appointed Ma'adh as governor of the Yemen, he asked him how will he govern. According to the Koran, Ma'adh replied. And if it is not in the Koran? The Prophet asked him. According to the Prophet's Sunna, replied Ma'adh. And if he does not find anything of the sort in the Sunna also?, the Prophet inquired. Then I will exert myself to solve the problem (Ana ajtahedo). The Prophet patted his back in approval. Also, the Prophet is reported to have said that even if one makes mistake in doing *ijtihad* he/she will earn one merit and if one does not err he/she will earn two merits. The Prophet did this to encourage Muslims to solve problems which were likely to arise in future.

From this many modernists argue that one must resort to *ijtihad* to solve new problems and issues including women's issues. However, the orthodox 'Ulama argue that the gates of *ijtihad* were closed long ago and also that now there are no qualified persons to do *ijtihad*.

They feel the great Imams and some of their followers had the requisite qualification and none today has such impressive merits. Some 'Ulama do feel the need for *ijtihad* but they too stop short of resorting to it for fear of consequences. Some who did faced the wrath of the fellow jurists and even ostracised. The debate is raging in the Islamic world for and against *ijtihad*. And when it comes to women's issues and rights, the resistance to change and rethink is much greater in the male-dominated Islamic world.

Dr. Muhammad Iqbal, a noted Urdu poet and thinker from India (d. 1938) was greatly in favour of *ijtihad*. He wrote in his Reconstruction of Religious Thought in Islam 'The ultimate spiritual basis of all life, as conceived by Islam, is eternal and reveals itself in variety and change. A society based on such a conception of Reality must reconcile, in its life, the categories of permanence and change. But eternal principles when they are understood to exclude all possibilities of change which, according to the Koran, is one of the greatest "signs" of God, tend to immobilise what is essentially mobile in its nature' (pp. 147–8).

Iqbal states in the above book very boldly. 'The only alternative open to us, then, is to tear off from Islam the hard crust which has immobilised an essentially dynamic outlook on life, and to rediscover the original verities of freedom, equality, and solidarity with a view to rebuild our moral, social and political ideas out of their original simplicity and universality' (p. 156). Iqbal thus maintains that *ijtihad* is necessary to rebuild the law of sharia in the light of modern thought and experience.

Ijtihad, I would like to emphasize here, is even more necessary today in respect of sharia laws pertaining to women. It is highly regrettable that the sharia law is almost inoperative in many other respects (like property and contract laws, criminal laws, financial transactions, etc.) but when it comes to women's issues, the sharia laws are sought to be strictly applied. In several Muslim majority and minority countries modern secular laws are applied in respect of all other things except laws pertaining to marriage, divorce, maintenance, inheritance, etc., i.e. in the sphere of what is called personal laws. The greatest resistance, in the name of sharia, is manifested by men when it comes to according better status to women. In this respect the sharia becomes sacred and immutable and arouses great passions. The Islamic world, if it has to understand the dynamic spirit of Koran, and enact it in real life, will have to enact changes in the sharia laws and accord women an equal status. In fact time has to come put the Koranic vision of sexual equality in practice.

As pointed out earlier there are verses in the Koran which have contextual significance. These verses formed the legal foundations of Islamic law in that age. But these were not the verses having impress of permanence and principles. There are certainly the verses which lay down norms and principles. Today, the Islamic legislation should be based on these verses. Before we examine these verses, we would like to set out certain values which are fundamental to the Islamic teachings. Any legislation which ignores these fundamental values could be anything but Islamic. It is necessary to understand that the classical jurists though did not ignore these fundamental values but the application of these values was constrained by the social ethos of the age. The Prophet's traditions also had to take these constraints into account.

The most fundamental values in Islam, as expounded by the Koran are justice, benevolence and compassion. The Koranic terminology for these values is 'adl, ihsan and rahmah. The Koran talks of these values in imperative category. The Koranic verse 16:90 testifies to this: And surely Allah enjoins justice and benevolence (to others). Thus it will be seen that justice is very central to the Islamic value system—as central as love to the Christian ethics. No legislation in Islam which ignores this value can be valid.

It is this concern for justice which makes the Koran show deep concern for the weaker sections of society. Thus the verse 28:5 expresses this concern for them and says: 'And We desire to bestow a favour upon those, who were deemed weak in the land, and to make them the leaders, and to make them the heirs.' The Koran desires to bestow the mantle of leadership of this earth upon the weak. The Islamic jurisprudence has to imbibe this spirit towards the weaker sections of society. And, women certainly belong to this category as far as the patriarchal society is concerned.

It is important to note that the values like justice and compassion cannot be applied independent of the age. In the medieval period the understanding of the concept of justice was very different from what it is today. Our era is a democratic era and justice in our era cannot be deemed to have been done if equality of all humans irrespective of sex, race and creed, is not ensured. Discrimination between one and other human being on any ground, including the sexual one, will be taken as injustice. But in medieval ages these discriminations were thought to be quite natural and non-violative of the concept of justice. Even slavery was thought to be natural and in keeping with the principles of justice. In fact, if a slave ran away from the master it was thought to be an unjust act. Today, let alone slavery, even bonded labour or child labour is considered as grossly violative of justice. Thus the concept of justice greatly varies in a democratic era from that of feudal one. And yet justice as a value remains important in both the ages. The expression of the concept of justice in a particular era is not fundamental but justice per se is. However, in religious traditions, including in those of Islam, give more importance to the expression of justice in a particular age then to the notion of justice itself. It is because of this that the expression of justice in the Hadith literature is more important than the notion of justice as fundamental value in the Koran. What was thought to be just during the classical period of Islam is thought to be just even today. And not only that the orthodox think the expression of the notion of justice today is violative of divine will. It is this attitude which impedes change in Islamic legislation so as to accord women equality with men.

However, one finds in the Koran full support for sexual equality in several verses. The Koran was certainly mindful of what was just in that era when it was revealed and what ought to be just in the transcendental sense. When the Prophet permitted a Muslim wife retaliation against her husband as a measure of justice, the Koran overruled him and permitted a measure of conditional male domination, though conditionality of justice was stipulated (see the verse 4:34). It would have been thought to be unjust if the Koran had permitted wife to retaliate against her husband and it would not have found acceptability in that society.

However, the Koran also did not intend to eternalise the then acceptable notion of justice. The dynamics of 'is' and 'ought' or interaction between history and eternity informs the whole spirit of Koran. Unfortunately the orthodox miss this very spirit while reading the Koran form their own perspective. The verse 33:35 is much more fundamental in this respect as it clearly accords women equality with men in all respects. While 4:34 is informed by the spirit of that era, the verse 33:34 deals with the eternal dimension. The orthodox, however, do not wish to go beyond the divine injunction expressed in 4:34. They have frozen their minds in the classical age of Islam. What was temporal has become permanent for them and what is permanent is just brushed aside as of no consequence.

The Koran must be re-read and re-interpreted in today's context as the classical jurists read and interpreted it in their own context. No reformation is possible without such re reading and re-interpreting the Koranic verses. The real intention of the Koran—that of sexual equality—comes through several verses. Those verses need to be re-emphasised. The verse 2:228 ('And women have rights similar to those against them in a just manner') is quite definitive in this respect. It hardly needs any comment. Maulana Muhammad Ali, a noted Pakistani commentator says, 'The rights of women against their husbands are here stated to be similar to those which the husbands have against their wives. The statement must, no doubt, have caused a stir in a society which never recognised any rights for the woman. The change in this respect was really was a revolutionising one, for the Arabs hitherto regarded women as mere chattels. Women were given a position equal in all respects to that of men, for they were declared to have rights similar to those which were exercised against them. This declaration brought about a revolution not only in Arabia but in the whole world, for the equality of rights of women with those of men was never previously recognized by any nation or any reformer. The woman could no longer be discarded at the will of her "lord", but she could either claim equality as a wife or demand a divorce' (Maulana Muhammad Ali, 1973, p. 97).

However, much of this spirit of justice and equality was lost when the Islamic doctors legislated under the influence of their own social ethos. The Koranic categorical imperatives were ignored, as pointed out before, in favour of those verses which were of the nature of concession to the age. There are many instances of this. The polygamy, for example. Firstly, it was a permissive measure in some circumstances (large number of war widows and orphans to be taken care of as many men perished fighting in the battle of Uhud) with great emphasis on justice to all the wives (their number not exceeding four). It was great advance over the pre-Islamic practice of marrying unlimited number and without any obligation towards the wives.

Secondly, the verse on polygamy (4:3) is followed by the verse 4:1 which emphasises sexual equality in the words that.'Lord Who created you from a single being (min nafsin wahidatin) and created its mate of the same (kind) and spread from these two many men and women.' and the verse 4:2 which talks of justice for orphans and widows. Then polygamy is permitted provided one marries with widows and orphans (and not any women) and there also justice with all wives is a must failing which one must marry only one. No one before had insisted on such conditionalities for plurality of wives. Thirdly, the verse 4:129 states that even if you desire you cannot do justice between wives and ends by saying that do not leave the one with total disinclination and incline towards the other leaving the first in suspense. If the verses 4:3 and 4:129 are read together polygamy is as good as not permissible. But the jurists, in order to avoid implications of reading the two verses together invented various explanations and took resort of Hadith to keep possibility of polygamy open, and much worse, in practising it, conditionality for justice was hardly enforced. In today's conditions polygamy should be done away with in order to implement the Koranic conditionality. Abolition of polygamy will serve the end of justice far better than its practice today. The arguments that men are more sexual or that in case there are more women than men, it will be better to permit polygamous marriages to avoid immoral relations, etc., are all attempts at human rationalisation than divine intention. These arguments do not hold much water as there may be excess of women over men in one country and excess of men over women in another. And prostitution and immoral sex thrived even when men could marry any number of wives and also keep slave girls without limit.

Also, normatively speaking the Koran has conceded all rights to women which were available earlier only to men. She could exercise her right to divorce her husband as men could divorce her at will. The Prophet permitted a woman called Jamila to divorce her husband—against his will and without consulting him—just because she did not approve of his looks. While the verse 2:229 permits her to liberate herself from an unsatisfactory marriage by suitable compensation to husband (i.e. returning the dower amount) the verse 4:35 gives her right to appoint an arbiter of her own to settle the marital dispute or agree to divorce. Also, the Koran requires of men to keep their wives in goodly manner and to leave them, if necessary, in a benevolent manner. And the verse 4:19 lays down that women could not be inherited or taken as wives against their will, men are also exhorted in this verse not to take a portion of what they have given to their wives and to treat them kindly. It was also emphasised in 9:71 that believing men and believing women are each others friends and they (both men and women) enjoin good and forbid evil. Thus both enjoy equal obligations and from this verse jurists like Abu Hanifa have concluded that a woman can become Qadi, i.e. judge as it is her obligation also to enjoin good and forbid evil.

It is argued from the verse 4:11 that a daughter inherits half that of son and hence man is superior. Some modernists also argue on the basis of this verse that it is injustice to a daughter as she has been given half that of son and hence it is bias against female sex. It is simply not true. From one perspective one can say it was a cautious reform in favour of daughters. In pre-Islamic society daughters did not inherit at all and now they were given right to inherit half that of son. From another perspective it could be argued that it was not bias against daughter that they were given half that of son but daughters were duly compensated by *mehr* (dower amount at the time of marriage) whereas sons had to loose out by paying dower to their wives. And the wives do not have to spend anything by way of maintenance as it is enjoined upon the husbands to maintain their wives. Also, a woman inherited as wife and mother too. Moreover she did not contribute to family wealth in those days by way of earning but now she does and her portion could be increased in view of the changed conditions. Thus the Koran has done no injustice to her in matters of inheritance also.

Another question is of hijab (veil). There is no injunction in the Koran that she veil her face. The verse 24:31 only lays down that women should not display their adornment and fineries publicly and that they should cover their breasts (tribal women in those days used to leave their breasts uncovered) and that they should not strike heir feet with anklets in public so as to draw attention to their adornments. In this verse both men and women have been asked to lower their gaze (4:30-31) and to restrain their sexual passions. As for what constitutes adornment and what should be displayed and what should be not, there are sharp differences of opinion. These differences are human and every commentator has his views. But Tabari, the noted classical commentator has summarised the views of many eminent jurists in his Jami' al-Bayan. According to him adornment means: (1) adornment of dress or the clothes that a woman wears; in other words, she is not required to cover the clothes she wears; (2) it means the adornment which the woman is not required to cover, such as collyrium, rings, bracelets and her face; (3) the exception (*illa ma zahara minha*) relates to a woman's clothing and her face.

These were opinions of the theologians of those days. Today the sensibilities in this respect are very different and the scope of the exception can be made much wider subject to—and that is real intention behind it—to restrain sexual passion and protect ones chastity. To prevent extra-marital sex is the responsibility of both men and women and not of women alone, as per the Koran. Also, both should avoid wearing sexually stimulating dress. They should wear dignified dress. Covering of face by women is not required in the Koran at all. It was cultural practice of some post-Islamic societies. The Koran also does not require women to be confined to homes. On the contrary they could earn and what they earned was theirs alone as per 4:32 (And for women is the benefit of what they earn). The cultural practices like confining women to home were sought to be legitimised later by inventing suitable Ahadith or by far fetched interpretations of the Koran.

In conclusion it should be said that if one goes by those verses of the Koran which belong to the normative category or which are of the nature of laying down principles and givers of value, men and women should enjoy equal rights in every respect. It would be necessary to re-read and re-interpret many verses which were used for centuries to subjugate women in Muslim societies. This subjugation was more cultural and patriarchal than Islamic or Koranic. The whole corpus juris of Islam relating to women needs to be seriously re-thought on the basis of Koran.

23
Koran, Hadith and Women

What is the position of women in Koran and Hadith? It is very interesting to compare what is stated in Koran about women and what do we find on women in Hadith literature? And here I am not referring to Ahadith from another source but from what is known as Sihah Sitta (i.e. six most authentic sources of Hadith). I wish our Ulama reflect on the contrast between how Koran treats women and how Ahadith treat them. Much of woes of Muslim women will be over if we follow Koran rather than these Ahadith.

Women lost in Ahadith what they had gained through Koran. Today if world thinks Islam treats women in a very unfair way it is because we follow hadiths rather than Koran as far as women are concerned. In pre-Islamic period women had lowest of low social status and Koran lifted them far above and our 'Ulama never tire of saying this. But within few decades of the revelation of the Koran women came down to their pre-Islamic status in a fiercely male dominated society. And this was accomplished through Ahadith as a legitimizing factor.

Those who narrated these Ahadith never thought for a moment how they contradict Koran as these Ahadith served the social purpose very well. Koran provided ideals and values but society could not rise to that level and instead dragged Islam to its own level and Ahadith served that interest best.

When Islam was confined to the Arabian peninsula it was different but when it spread to far-off places, parts of Roman empire, Sasanid Empire (Iran), Central Asia, etc. These regions were very different in their culture, religious values and social ethos and it was quite natural for Islam to adapt to what these societies needed. Even sharia, all jurists (fuqaha') agree incorporated much of Arab 'adati (customary law).

It was not easy to avoid these cultural values and customary practices found in non-Arab societies when people of these regions embraced Islam. Position of women in these regions was no different from what it was in pre-Isiamic Arabia and when one embraces a religion which originated outside that region he/she does not automatically caste away his/her own cultural values and social ethos.

Also, it is a well-known fact that Islam spread far and wide much quicker than sharia laws were compiled in different schools. In fact various sharia schools (madahibi) came into existence in different regions where Islam had spread. Even before the Arabs could grasp full significance of Islam and adjust their lives to new values and ideals, it had already spread to various parts of the world, right up to China. In fact Islam spread to these regions with lightening speed.

It is also interesting to note that various companions of the Prophet (PBUH) also had spread to these parts of the world and these companions in many cases married local women and adopted cultural values of the region and being companions of the Prophet (PBUH) they were also source of Islamic knowledge and those converted to Islam would flock to them for guidance and hence number of Ahadith were narrated by these companions relying on their memory and understanding. Thus along with authenticity of Ahadith sociology of Ahadith also becomes equally important.

While Koran was compiled during Prophet's (PBUH) lifetime and when some deviations from standard recitation was noticed (on account mainly of tribal dialects) Hazrat Uthman had wisdom to compile standard copy and destroy all others and thus Koran was saved from differences in the text. All other copies of the Koran were prepared from this copy.

Ahadith, on the other hand, were compiled two to three centuries after the death of the Holy Prophet and underwent much changes due to passage of time. Though there was chain of narrators and despite honesty and integrity of narrators, there was every possibility of change in text with different narrators with even differences in their understanding and cultural background. Unfortunately for Ahadith honesty and integrity of narrators became the only criterion rather than its conformity with the Koranic approach, values and ideals.

Also, there were those who did not hesitate to produce a Hadith to legitimize some action or requirement of someone powerful and influential. Thus, while there never arose any differences about the Koranic text, there have been all sorts of differences about authenticity or otherwise of Ahadith. In fact much problems could have been avoided if Ahadith in such large numbers and in different compatios had not been accepted. For these very reasons the Prophet (PBUH) had discouraged from compiling these Ahadith. But Ahadith became socio-cultural and socio-religious needs in vastly different circumstances.

These needs were such that a doctrine was evolved that even if a Hadith stands in contradiction of the Koran, Hadith will prevail. Many sharia injunctions were developed on this basis. Then various questions arose whether Hadith is da'if (weak), narrated by only one or by several narrators or its different variations or whether its narrators (ravi) were da'if (weak) and so on. The whole Hadith literature is full of these controversies. Also different sects relied on different Ahadith to legitimize their positions. In short many controversies originated due to excessive reliance on Ahadith.

Much more so Ahadith were used to lower women's status as Koranic ideals and values in respect of women could not be accepted by societies which treated women as subordinate to men. Men in any case wanted to retain his superiority. He thought he was ruler over women and many Koranic verses were explained under the ethos of men's superiority. Most of the Koranic verses on women are not explained in the light of other Koranic verses (only reliable methodology to understand real intent of the Koran) but in the light of Ahadith which degrade women.

I would like in this article to compare Ahadith about women with Koranic verses and show how mutually contradictory these Koranic verses and Ahadith are. Koran talks of equal dignity of men and women and even story of Adam and Hawwa is narrated in a way which does not blame Hawwa at all for eating the fruit of a tree which Adam was prohibited to go near to. Koran talks of creation of men and women from one nafs and Hadith says Hawwa was created from rib of Adam. Koran says it is Adam who disobeyed his Lord and acted ignorantly. Thus Koran says 'And Adam disobeyed his Lord, and was disappointed' (20:121).

Also, the entire discourse in Koran on women is rights based but in sharia, thanks to Hadith literature, entire discourse is duty based for women and right based for men, something which one found during period of jahiliyyah. It was too hard for men to accept equal dignity for men and women in the feudal society within which sharia rules were compiled.

Koran gives equal rights and equal dignity to both men and women but Hadith literature is full of Ahadith contradicting this Koranic approach. For example, in Bukhari we find a Hadith which stands in contradiction to the Koranic verse 33:35. The Hadith is narrated thus:

'The Prophet (PBUH) urged the women to be generous with their gifts, for when he had glimpsed into the flames of Hell, he had noted the vast majority of people being tormented there were women. The women were outraged, and one of them instantly stood up and demanded to know why that was so. "Because", he replied, "you women grumble so much, and show ingratitude to your husbands! Even if the poor fellows spent all their lives doing things for you, you have only to be upset at the least of thing and you will say, "I have never received any good from you!", At that the women began vigorously to pull off their rings, and throw them into Bilal's Cloak.' (Bukhari 1,28, Abu Dawud 439).

See the content and tenor of this Hadith. It is full of anti women attitude and women are supposed to be, in this Hadith, ungrateful to their husbands. As against this see the Koranic verse 33:35 which says, 'Surely the men who submit and women who submit, and the believing men and the believing women, and the obeying men and the obeying women, and the truthful men and truthful women, and the patient men and patient women, and the humble men and humble women, and the charitable men and the charitable women, and fasting men and fasting women, and the men who guard their chastity and the women who guard, and the men who remember Allah and women who remember Allah has prepared for them forgiveness and mighty reward.'

See how in this verse Koran treats men and women equally and talks of equal degree of forgiveness and equal reward. In the above Hadith, on the other hand, more women than men are consigned to flames of Hell because they are ungrateful to their husbands. Koran no where requires women to be obedient to their husbands. It is husband who is exhorted to be kind to their wives (see 2:229) 'keep them in good fellowship (bi ma'ruf) and let them go with kindness' (bi ihsanin).

Also men and women are described as each others garment (libas) (2:187). According to Koran men and women are each others zawj (one of the couple) thus indicating equal dignity and love and respect, not obedience or subordination. The Prophet (PBUH) never treated any of his wife as subordinate. He not only treated them with dignity, he often consulted them in various matters and even followed their advice. In fact, Umm Salma's advice to sacrifice animal at Hudaybiya proved very beneficial.

Woman Half a Witness?

Let us examine one more Hadith which apparently appears to be in conformity with Koranic provision but indeed it is not. We find it in Muslim. The Hadith is narrated as under:

Prophet is reported to have said, 'I have seen none lacking in common sense and failing in religion but (at the same time) robbing the wisdom of the wise, besides you.' Upon this a woman remarked: 'What is wrong with or common sense and with religion?' He observed: 'You lack of common sense (in) that the evidence of two women is equal to that of one man, that is the proof of your lack of common sense. And you spend some nights (and days) in which you do not offer prayer and in the month of Ramadan (during the menstrual days) you do not observe fast; that is your failing in religion.' (Muslim 31)

This Hadith has several flaws. Koran nowhere states that she is half witness, much less because of lack of common sense. And messenger of Allah will not say such things which degrade women whom he consulted in difficult times as pointed out above. Koran simply says that when you take loan, write it down and let two male witnesses be summoned as witnesses and if two men are not available let one man and two women bear witness so that if one forgets, other can remind. (2:282)

This verse nowhere says she lacks in common sense. She may have lacked in experience as in those days women did not indulge in financial transaction. Lack of experience cannot be equated with lack of common sense. Also, if women cannot offer prayers or fast during menstruation, how can it be construed as 'failing in religion'? It is state of disability, not lack of belief or commitment. Belief or religion has something to do with ones heart and soul, not physical condition. Our Prophet (PBU) had high respect for women and for his wives. It is unthinkable that he would say such degrading things for women. He loved Khadija, Fatima and Ayesha so much. All these women were highly intelligent and great upholders of Islam. In fact they were more firm in their belief of Islam than many men. Entire Muslim world holds these women in high respect. In fact Islam gave such high status to women and guaranteed their rights when all over the world women had no rights at all. In fact, it was this general demeaning attitude towards women which is reflected in these Ahadith.

Women Rulers Bring Bad Luck to Those Over Whom They Rule

We find another Hadith in Bukhari which is often quoted against women becoming rulers of countries or nations. In fact Bukhari has reported three traditions connected with this episode, two of which were in the chapter on 'Letter of the Prophet to Chosroe and Caesar'. Abu Bakra's Hadith is no. 4425. The preceding Hadith, no. 4424, was reported from Ibn Abbas who said that 'the Prophet of Allah sent Abdullah Ibn Huzaifa with his letter to Chosroe. When Chosroe read it he tore it. I believe said Bin Musayyab said: Then the Prophet prayed to Allah that he tear them up completely.' The third Hadith is no. 6639 reported by Bukhari in the chapter on 'how the oath of Prophet was' and it goes; 'When Ceaser dies there will be no Ceaser after him. When Chosroe dies there will be no Chosroe after him.

Bukhari (4425) reports from Abu Bakra at the following Hadith: 'Allah provided me with considerable benefit during the battle of the Camel with one word (or one statement).' When news reached the

Prophet (S.A.W.) that the Persians had appointed Chosroe's daughter as their ruler, he said: 'A nation which placed its affairs in the hands of a woman shall never prosper!'

Now it is well-known that Abu Bakra narrated this Hadith after battle of Camel in which Hadrat Ayesha participated and the battle was aimed against Hadrat Ali. This Hadith surfaces only with the narration of Abu Bakra who was aspiring for governorship of one of the provinces and wanted to please Hadrat Ali. Abu Bakra obviously had a purpose in narrating such a Hadith.

It is quite contradictory to Koran in as much as Koran upholds leadership of Queen of Sheba (Bilquis) who overrules the advice of her male advisors and makes peace with prophet Salman (Soloman). See verses 32 to 35 of Chapter 27. When Bilquis asks for opinion of all her male advisors whether we should fight or make peace with Sulaiman, they advise her to fight and not to surrender. But she over rules them and decides to make peace arguing 'Surely kings when they enter a town, ruin it and make the noblest of its people to be low; and thus they do.'

Thus we see that Koran upholds wisdom of a woman in not fighting and making peace with stronger ruler and saves the nation from ruin. But the Hadith quoted above says just the opposite that if a woman becomes ruler it would prove ruinous for the nation. The Hadith thus suggests that Prophet contradicts Allah's revelation which is not thinkable. The only conclusion in either the narrator had his own motive in narrating the Hadith or could not at all understand what the Prophet said. I leave conclusion to the readers.

We find even more shocking Ahadith ascribed to the Prophet regarding women. One such Hadith found in Sahih Bukhari and narrated by Sahl ibn Sa'd which says 'Evil omen was mentioned before the Prophet (PBUH)'. The Prophet (PBUH) said, 'if there is evil omen in anything, it is in the house, the woman and the horse.'

This Hadith equates woman with house and horse. There cannot be any comparison between the three. Also both house and horse are extremely useful for human beings which facilitate his/her living and travelling. House is from basic necessity for human beings and horse was needed in those for travel and were valued highly. They were used in wars as well as their movement was quite swift. Such thoughts are product of very low kind of mind unfortunately ascribed to a mind Allah had graced with highest kinds of thought. He had chosen him to be His Prophet, His messenger. One cannot think he would say such things.

There is one interesting Hadith found in Bukhari and narrated by Ayesha. The Hadith is like this: the things which annul the prayers were mentioned before me (Ayesha). They said, 'prayer is annulled by a dog, a donkey and a woman (if they pass in front of the praying people)'.

Ayesha said, 'You have made us (i.e. women) dogs. I saw the Prophet (PBUH) praying while I used to lie in my bed between him and the Qiblah. Whenever I was in need of something, I would slip away, for I disliked to face him.'

We can see how some narrators equated women with dogs and donkeys and Ayesha challenged them. It shows how men held women in low esteem and ascribed their despicable thoughts to the Prophet (PBUH). Always there may not be women like Ayesha to challenge such low thoughts and Hadith may be believed uncritically.

Similarly, we find another Hadith in Sahih Bukhari narrated by Osamah which is again totally contradictory to the Koran. The Hadith says 'And I advise you to take care of the women, for they are created from a rib and the most crooked potion of the rib is its upper part. If you try to straighten it, it will break, and if you leave it, it will remain crooked, so I urge you to take care of the women.'

Very degrading to women, like similar such Ahadith. It completely contradicts the Koran where there is no mention at all of Hawwa's creation from the rib of Adam. This Hadith also has been created to prove inferiority of women. In all the verses on women in Koran there is not a single verse which degrades women like this or proves her inferiority to men in any way.

This was prevailing social attitudes of men towards women which made them create such Ahadith so that they could rule over them and women could not use Koran to claim equality with men. Koran was revealed to the prophet so that he could give equal dignity and status to women but society was not prepared for this in any case and sought to lower the status of women by producing such Ahadith as they could not temper with the Koran they used another weapon to bring down status of women.

It is unfortunate that still our Ulama are not prepared to critically evaluate these anti-women Ahadith. On the contrary they keep on quoting them to keep status of women lower in the society and under the thumb of women. It is precisely for this reason that non-Muslims think very adversely about Islam and how Islam has 'suppressed' dignity and status of women.

Time has come for Muslim women to evaluate these Ahadith critically and refute the fatwas Ulama issued on the basis of such Ahadith. We need great scholars of Islam among the women who could take independent position. Where are such women?

24
Issues in Islamic Feminism

Is there anything like Islamic feminism? Most of the Islamists maintain such a term is contradiction in terms. For them feminism is against teachings of Islam. It is a Western phenomenon and those women who are westernised and want to stick to Islam in name only. They dismiss this phenomenon with contempt. However, this attitude is more because of strong influence on their minds of conservative Islam. The conservative ulama insist on assigning women position subservient to men. Wives, according to them, should accept authority of their husbands.

A deeper examination of Koranic verses makes it clear that it firmly upholds dignity of women as that of men. It does not discriminate between two sexes. In fact, it was social environment in which sharia formulations were made that affected Islamists' viewpoint about women rather than the Koranic teachings. Today's social environment is radically different and women awareness of their rights has increased phenomenally.

There is nothing wrong in revisiting sharia formulations regarding women today and attempt to reformulate issues in the light of contemporary social milieu. After all the great Imams themselves had formulated issues in respect of women's legal and moral status in medieval milieu. Only condition is such reformulation or rethinking should be in the light of the Koran.

One should not be scared of the word 'feminism' as our 'ulama tend to be. After all feminism is all about women's rights. The Koran is so much concerned about women's rights that it will not be wrong to say the Koran preached feminism for the first time in the world and the Prophet was the first feminist. One should not shy away from the new terms. Obviously 'feminism' is not an old Shari 'ah term. But new terms can always be adopted. After all the term human rights does not exist in sharia but today the term like 'Islamic human rights' is freely being used. Why then not 'Islamic feminism'?

What is Feminism?

Feminism is nothing but a discourse on women's rights in modern context. For all these centuries women were treated as subordinate to men. And this was thought to be quite natural. Women were confined to home and hearth and were not allowed any public role in general though there might have been some exceptions. Generally they did not even acquire education. A woman who could perform domestic chores with expertise was considered excellent in marriage market. She could become an ideal wife.

So her maximum achievement was limited to domestic field. She had no independent personality of her own. She was extension either of her father, brother or husband. She could be consulted but could not take decision herself. Decision was ultimately taken by father, brother or husband. Even if she did, she could be overruled. She had no right to earn her own living. It was thought against family pride that wife earns. This was interpreted as husband's inability to maintain his wife. Even if a wife could earn she was prevented from doing so. Even today many husbands to be stipulate condition that their prospective wives will give up the job after marriage.

All this is slowly changing in the modern society. Literacy has become universal. Even most orthodox families now send their daughters to schools and colleges. In fact certain statistics clearly show that more girls are graduating than boys even among backward Muslim communities in India. Recently on my visit to Kolhapur in Maharashtra I discovered that among very poor and backward caste Muslims (mostly baghbans? A backward caste among Muslims in Maharashtra) there are girls who have done post- graduation in science subjects and humanities whereas there is not a single boy who has achieved so much in the field of education.

Earlier primary education was considered more than enough. And coeducation was considered 'sin'. Today Muslim girls are going for coeducation without any hesitation. We have to remember that society is not static. Unfortunately our 'ulama, dyed in the wool orthodox, think society is static and any change is unacceptable. They have frozen society to early Islamic period, i.e. eighth and ninth centuries ad.

Ulama's attitude may be frozen Muslims' attitude is not. Most of them are accepting changes and adjusting themselves keeping their Islamic conscience in tact. All changes are not bad or un-Islamic, those un-Islamic could be surely rejected. Feminist discourse, as we will show, is not unacceptable to one who cares for ones Islamic conscience. Every knowledgeable Muslim has right to decide, there being no priesthood or church in Islam. Even a fatwa by most learned alim could be rejected by a Muslim who does not agree with his opinion. Of course there are less informed Muslims who might consider these fatwas as binding.

However, with increased awareness and sources of knowledge available such less informed Muslims are also decreasing in number. It is also important to note that the 'ulama are accepting modern technology when it suits them. For example, today Internet and e-mail networks are being used by the 'ulama to spread orthodoxy. But it is not going to consolidate orthodox positions in the long run. As Marshal McLuhan, an American sociologist put it in seventies 'media is the message'. The modern media being used by orthodox 'ulama cannot but be influenced by the modernity of the medium which will impact their minds for change in attitudes.

The 'Ulama are also accepting divorce through SMS, which, Islamically speaking, is most unjust and un-Islamic but in keeping with the orthodoxy and medieval ethos. Any modern technology, which can perpetuate orthodoxy, is acceptable but not those values, which uphold the real Koranic spirit of justice.

The modern feminist discourse is based on justice. Suppression of women's rights is gross injustice and hence feminism rejects it. All serious students of Koran very well know that justice forms core value of Koran. Anything unjust is zulm (oppression, wrong doing) in the Koranic terminology. How then the feminist discourse in this respect can be construed as un-Islamic'?

Today, it is considered for women a fundamental right to acquire education. Is not acquisition of Islamic education an Islamic right? The Prophet (PBUH) made it obligatory both for men and women to acquire knowledge (talabul 'Mm faridatun 'ala kulli muslimin wa muslimatin? acquisition of knowledge is obligatory on every Muslim man and Muslim woman). Still the orthodox Muslim society strongly resisted providing education to their womenfolk for several centuries. How 'Islamic' was their stand, which was perpetuated in the name of Islam?

Could not campaign for modern education for Muslim women become an issue of Islamic feminism? Today even in bastion of orthodoxy like Saudi Arabia women graduates are more than fifty per cent. And it is not only in religious education but in modern university education. Saudi society needs female teachers and doctors. But the Saudi women are no more confined to these fields alone. They are going now for aviation training, business management training and so on. Although the Saudi women are still far behind their sisters in other fields in other Muslim countries but change is more than perceptible. It is inevitable.

The Koran also does nowhere restrict knowledge to men alone. In fact 'ilm (knowledge) is most central to Koranic teachings, Allah is also repeatedly described in Koran as knower and urges upon all Muslim men and women to acquire knowledge. It was male dominated Muslim society, which restricted knowledge to men and deprived women of their fundamental right to acquire knowledge.

Islamic and Western Feminism

One must of course make distinction between Western and Islamic feminism. Western feminism today has been heavily influenced by its consumer culture. And in consumer culture instant gratification is central and values quite marginal. Islamic feminism, on the other hand, is based on values and these values are quite central. For example, women are not consumable commodities and their bodies cannot be commercialised.

In Western feminist discourse women are owners of their bodies implying that they are free to let their bodies be used for any purpose, including commercial purpose, if they so decide. Thus they are free to allow their semi-nude bodies for commercial ads, or even for free sex. Thus they have unrestricted rights over their bodies, not circumscribed by any values.

These women can even opt for what is called 'live-in' relationship without any formal marriage. They can also opt for adulterous relationship as owners of their bodies. This is just not acceptable as far as Islamic feminism is concerned. It does not mean they are not owners of their bodies. Of course, they are but subject to certain fundamental values prescribed by the Koran.

These values are prioritised over ownership of the body. Freedom without values and sense of responsibility becomes licentiousness. Hence all human bodies including those of men are subject to fundamental values. One cannot, for example, use ones body freely for sex without marriage. Sex for mere pleasure cannot form part of Islamic feminism. Sex primarily is for perpetuating human species and this can best be done through marriage and family. For perpetuating human species institution of marriage plays very important role. In Western feminism family has lost its relevance and a woman is entitled to sexual pleasure for pleasure's sake. Sexual pleasure is not the tool for raising family but an end in its self.

In Islamic feminism sexual pleasure is a tool, not an end. Islam, it is important to note, does not deny women right to sexual pleasure though it does not reduce it to an end itself. Some Muslims go for female circumcision to deprive her of sexual pleasure. It is more of tribal custom than any religious injunction. Most of the Muslims do not accept female circumcision. It is unjust to deprive her of that. Islamic sharia also clearly lays down that if a man hides his impotency from his bride at the time of marriage and she discovers it after marriage, she is fully entitled to divorce on that ground. This itself clearly shows that she is entitled to sexual pleasure along with raising family.

A woman is owner of her body subject to, as pointed out before, some value-based conditions. She, for example, cannot be compelled for sex, if she is unwilling. She fully controls her body. Sex in marriage also has to be with consent of both the partners. Islamic feminism, however, may not go as far as admitting of 'marital rape', as in Western feminism. But that does not mean husband has absolute rights over his wife's body. Husband's rights are also subject to certain value-based conditions.

A woman, according to the Koran, posses full dignity, as much as a man has and forced sex will be obviously violation of this dignity. But since violation of dignity cannot be equated with marital rape it cannot be punished. A Muslim man has to desist from violation of his wife's dignity.

One can however, quote the Koranic verse 2:223 that women are like tilth and go to your tilth when you like and send (good) beforehand for yourselves. Some feminists might maintain that this verse goes against her dignity as she is like her ploughing field and he can go to his field when he likes. Firstly, this verse should be read along with the preceding one, i.e. verse 222 which prohibits man to go near her when she is undergoing her period and also instructs man to go near her as Allah has commanded and Allah has commanded to respect her dignity.

Secondly, woman being field for man only means she conceives after man's seed is implanted into her womb. It is she who conceives and rears children. In many religious traditions earth is linked to mother as earth grows food to sustain human beings. Similarly, woman has been linked to field as she conceives and produces children to perpetuate human species. It in no way detracts from her dignity. On the other hand, it enhances her respect in our eyes. One has to properly understand the context in which it has been said.

The verse 4:34 is also controversial in this respect as this verse has been grossly misunderstood and implies that woman is subordinate to man and goes against feminist concept. We have discussed this verse and every word in it elsewhere and this is not the place to discuss it here again. This verse also should be read along with 33:35 and if read both together will not create any misunderstanding. The verse 33:35 clearly establishes Islamic feminist point of view that a woman is equal in every respect to man. She is not a wee bit inferior to him. There is no question of her being subordinate to man, much less, his property.

No Koranic verse should be read in isolation and this is precisely what the orthodox 'ulama do. They highlight one verse and suppress the other, in keeping with their prejudices against women. The prejudiced view regarding women? They are inferior, they are created for serving men and it is their Islamic duty to obey their husbands? Are not on account of Islam but on account of the social ethos they are surrounded with.

Need for Islamic Feminism

Why use the term Islamic feminism? What is its need? Before we answer this question let us answer their question why feminist movement arose in the West? When women were educated and their awareness of equality with men found no response in the society and they found themselves subordinated to men, an aggressive feminist movement arose. Women found that they do not have even right to property and they have not been enfranchised in many western countries they reacted strongly. Women in Europe got right to property as late as 1930. Neither they could be elected to high political offices, nor could they become peers to men in higher corporate structures, they began to demand their rights.

Some extremist feminist even began to burn bras as they thought they were being reduced to sexual dolls. But later on feminists developed more balanced viewpoint. However, women continue to be object of lust and in all commercial ads their semi-nude images are used seriously violating their dignity. Though due to pressures of feminist movement, women's position has improved quite a bit, still it is far from being ideal. Still in most of the Western countries women are not elected to high political offices. For the first time in British Political history Mrs. Thatcher became Prime Minister and for the first time in German history a woman has been elected as Chancellor.

In USA still a woman has to become Vice-President, let alone President. Even in France a woman has yet to become President. But their situation is, however, fast improving thanks to the feminist movement. Now more and more women are getting elected as legislators in several European countries. In Sweden more than 40 per cent women are members of parliament.

In Muslim countries situation of women is really despicable. In Saudi Arabia they are not allowed to vote (municipal elections were held in some Saudi Arabian cities) and not allowed to even drive. In Kuwait women won right to vote recently after a prolonged struggle. In several

Muslim countries like Egypt, Jordan, Pakistan, etc. They are killed in the name of family honour if they try to marry a man of their choice or even found talking to some male friend. All major decisions are taken by men even in family matters and they cannot play any public role. In countries like they are even denied right to education and are forced to veil themselves.

There is, therefore an urgent need for Islamic feminist movement. Islam has given them rights like right to marry, right to divorce, right to own property, right to earn their own living, right to education and right to inherit. Unfortunately, all these Islamic rights are being denied to them by the Muslim society. In the West there was no concept of these right until early twentieth century. In Islam these rights existed all along but women were not allowed to avail of them by the conservative male-dominated society.

Unfortunately, Muslim women have to struggle hard to win the rights their religion has given them and denied by their men. Some time ago the leading Islamic seminary in Deoband issued a fatwa that Muslim women cannot contest elections but modified later by saying they have not observe veil while campaigning. It is also to be noted that there is no concept of veil in the Koran, there is only the concept of dignified dressing. However, men everywhere are forcing veil on women. The Koranic verse 24:31 makes it very clear that what should be displayed should be displayed.

The Islamic feminist discourse has to articulate all these rights given to women by the Koran and if there happens to be any grey area it has to be subjected to fresh interpretation in the light of contemporary developments. The Islamic feminist discourse does not deviate from the Koranic rights but does not, at the same time accept male point of view in interpreting the Koran. Women must not only acquire Koranic scholarship but should also display courage in reinterpreting Koranic verses relating to women and develop a Koranic feminist narrative.

Such Islamic feminist discourse is inevitable. But there are formidable obstacles on this way. Modern educated women have no knowledge of Koran and hadith and what is worse, no interest in acquiring such scholarship. Those who have been educated in Islamic madrasas are too conservative to ever attempt such a bold interpretation. They have been brought up in traditional Islamic discourse.

However, it is high time some Muslim women volunteer to acquire deeper Islamic scholarship, mastery over Koranic Arabic and launch Islamic feminist movement. Marriage in Islam is not subordinate relationship between men and women but an equal partnership. Both being party to mutual obligations. She cannot be divorced arbitrarily as is the practice today. Marriage has been described by the Koran as 'strong bond' (4:21) which one cannot break at husband's whim.

Also Islamic feminist discourse should empower women to make their choice whether they want a child or not on grounds of health, family size and economic capability. A man cannot force woman to go on bearing children, as she is much more than a child-bearing machine. An Islamic feminist discourse has to be pro-choice for women.

Thus it will be seen from above that Islamic feminist discourse is not only justified but is essential to empower her to achieve full human dignity accorded her by the Koran.

25
Violence Against Women and Religion

Religion is believed to be divine. It is divine in more than one sense. Firstly it is divine in the sense that its teachings are motivated by purest of intentions; secondly it is divine as its teachings are transcendent as religion exhort us to transcend what is to, what it should be in society as well as in our personal conduct. But soon after birth of religion it gets mixed up with customs and traditions already existing in society on one hand, and, on the other, powerful interests, often very negation of its teachings, begin to control it.

Thus what reaches us is far from religion in its divine form but a mixture of several things. Its divine teachings diluted or even negated and we begin to perpetrate certain dogmas in all their rigidity resulting in several problems and resisting all changes. We even forget that what is divine cannot be against reason and human progress both material and spiritual.

Rigid dogmas and doctrines are not product of religion, as we often believe, but of human mind which itself is product, not of divine teachings but of existing social ethos. Also, theologians and priests acquire, for followers of religion, status of demi-gods. An ordinary follower entirely depends on these scribes and priests for their understanding of religion. Also, psychologically speaking, most human beings feel highly secure by following some 'leader' or 'authority'. To think or act by oneself is quite onerous and avoided by ordinary human beings.

However, true religiosity consists in knowing, thinking and taking responsibility for ones own actions. Taqlid (mechanically following) is not a religious act as responsibility for what one does is not on oneself but on the leader whom one follows. Thus leaders acquire vested interest in their followers and anyone who effuses to follow becomes an heretic and is denounced, even ostracized.

I have said these prefatory words so that we understand real import of religion as against prevailing practices in the name of religion. Unless we discover the real spirit of original teachings we would continue to follow something far away from religion. It cannot be expected of any existing religious establishment to represent true spirit of religion. No establishment can ever represent true sprit of religion. They negate each other. Any establishment represents some form of interests and religion negates all forms of interests. It is an individual spiritual quest.

Today, in all established religions we find women having secondary position. Religious leadership itself has become a male prerogative. Today all established religions represent patriarchal values and hence women cannot enjoy same rights and dignity as men. And this secondary position of women is sanctified through theological doctrines. Now no religion in its divine form can assign secondary position, much less vilify women. All human beings are creation of the Supreme Being. If at all women must have higher position as she partakes of creation through giving birth to human beings. If creation is a divine act, women too perform this divine act.

However, established religions, strayed from divinity, lost this divine dimension and patriarchy overtook divinity and women became subordinate to men and, at best became instrument of production rather than partaking of divine act. Conceiving and giving birth became her weakness rather than divine strength and even means of subjugation. And subjugation, in its extreme form, was enforced trough violence.

And since subjugation was theologized, so was violence against her. Thus violence against her came to be theologically justified in different religious traditions. Here we will discuss violence against her from Islamic theological point of view. When the Government of India passed the domestic violence Act, an Urdu paper from Mumbai Inquilab reported a statement of General Secretary of Muslim Personal Law Board that Government is depriving us of our Islamic right to 'beat our wives'.

It was a shocking statement as there cannot be divine right to beat ones wife. What is the source of this statement? It is a Koranic verse 4:34. Now according to all traditional commentators like Tabari, Zamakhshari, Ibn Kathir and others this verse of 4th chapter was revealed when a woman complained to the Prophet (PBUH) that her husband slapped her unjustly so what should she do? The Prophet (PBUH) who always gave priority to justice over anything else and also always accorded equal dignity to women, asked the woman to go and retaliate.

This created a crisis in the patriarchal society of Arabs and men surrounded the Prophet and said if our women have right to retaliate how will we control our families? It was natural concern in a patriarchal society. The Prophet had to tackle this crisis, according to this story and hence he waited for divine intervention to tackle it as it was of grave proportion. The revelation came in the form of 4:34.

This story also shows that many verses were revealed in response to certain social situation and hence importance of that verse could be understood only in that context. In other words such verses cannot be absolutized, as our jurists and theologians tend to do. This verse today is being debated between modernists and traditionalists and being differently interpreted.

First, let us take traditionalist point of view in understanding this verse. The verse has been translated as under by Maulana Muhammad Ali whom I can describe as semi-modernist, i.e. neither completely traditionalist nor completely modernist: 'Men are the maintainers of women, with what Allah have made some of them to excel others and with what they spend out of their wealth. So the good women are obedient, guarding the unseen as Allah has guarded. And (as to) those on whose part you fear desertion, admonish them, and leave them alone in the beds and chastise them. So if they obey you, seek not a way against them. Surely Allah is ever Exalted, Great.'

I have underlined some words in this translation which are crucial in determining position of women in this divinely revealed book. We have already seen the context in which this verse was revealed. And to a great extent its meaning would also relate to this context. Traditional theologians and jurists read into it clear statement of subordination of women to men. The above translation, as I have said, is by semi-modernist theologian.

If we take traditional translation, it would be even more problematic from feminist viewpoint. The first underlined word in this translation is qawwam which the Maulana has translated as 'maintainer' but traditionalist translate it as 'ruler' or 'authority' and so translated it would mean 'men are authority over women'. However, root meaning of the word is maintainer and protector. So the Maulana is much closer to the root meaning than traditionalists. Maulana Abul Kalam Azad's translation in Urdu also supports this meaning.

The other underlined words are ba'duhum 'ala ba'din. Muhammad Ali has translated it as 'some of them to excel others'. However, Muhammad Asad, in his The Message of the Koran displays greater bias towards men when he translates these words as 'God has bestowed more abundantly on the former (i.e. men) than on the latter (i.e. women). But again Maulana Muhammad Ali is much nearer to root meaning of ba'dahum 'ala ba'din than Muhammad Asad.

Next the words 'good women are obedient' are interpreted as 'obedient' to men. The Arabic word in the Koran is qanitatun which can only mean obedient to Allah, not to men. And to be fair to the Maulana, in the footnote to this word he has explained 'Obedient here signifies obedient to Allah.' Muhammad Asad has translated it as 'devout' which is closer to the root meaning of qanitat.

Another controversial interpretation is of the word what Maulana translates as desertion and Muhammad Asad as 'ill-will'. In Koran the Arabic word for this is nushuz. The root meaning of this word is to rise, to protrude. Thus its more acceptable translation would be to rise up against husband. It can be interpreted as desertion or also, as one Maulana Shoaib points out sexual misconduct. For this meaning of the word, he refers to Prophet's (PBUH) use of this word in this sense in his address after last Hajj known as Hajjat al-wida.

The Koran, in this verse tells men that in case of nushuz (desertion, rising up or sexual misconduct) first they should admonish them failing which they should be isolated in bed and even then if they continue their nushuz then chastise (or beat) them. Now the Arabic word for chastisement used in the Koran is *wadribuhunna*.

The traditionalists argue that Koran clearly permits men to beat women (or their wives) though the Koran does not use the word wife but general word women. And that is why General Secretary of Muslim Personal Law Board gave a statement that this Act against Domestic Violence has deprived us Muslims of our God-given right to beat our wives. However, this translation (i.e. to beat them) is highly controversial and Muslim feminists and modernists are challenging it.

Then how Muslim feminists and modernists understand this word? Before we discuss this it would be better to point out that first major commentator of the Koran Tabari points out to few traditions (ahadith) of the Prophet which say that beating should be mere symbolic, i.e. very light so as not to injure them. Tabari mentions the hadith that when asked how much can we beat? He was brushing his teeth with a brush; he lightly struck the brush on his body and said this much, no more. According to similar hadith also referred to by Tabari Prophet had a kerchief in his hand and he struck with kerchief and said this much and no more.

It is for this reason most of the translators write in the bracket while translating *wadribuhunna* 'so as not to injure them'. In other words do not thrash them. But then if they are to be struck so lightly like with the brush or handkerchief, what is the use? Beating is supposed to be a physical punishment and punishment for rebelling or sexual deviancy (if at all nushuz means that as Maulana Shoaib believes) cannot be as light as that. It should be such as to physically hurt.

Thus one should rethink the meaning of wadribuhunna here. It seems the Prophet's traditions referred to by Tabari may be later inventions. The word daraba translated as to 'beat' has no one meaning in Arabic language. It has several meanings. The meaning chosen should jell with the overall Koranic approach to women and not conflict with it. If word 'daraba' is translated as beating, it certainly conflicts with the overall Koranic approach towards women.

If one carefully studies Koranic verses about women it becomes clear that Koran gives equal status both to men and women and equal dignity to both as human beings. Koran nowhere distinguishs between men and women except in matter of function. Koran even refrains from using word 'husband' and 'wife'. It often uses the word zawj, i.e. couple which is much more equitable expression of marital relationship than husband and wife. Husband and wife indicate dominating and dominated relation.

Also, entire discourse in Koran about women is 'right-based', i.e. talks of their rights only and entire discourse about men is 'duty-based', i.e. talks of their duties only and repeatedly exhorts them how to behave with their wives. This was because in pre-Islamic Arab society women enjoyed no rights and were expected to discharge their duties towards their husbands. The Koran disapproved of this unequal relationship and enhanced her status by insisting on their rights and not on duties.

But patriarchal Arab society was not ready to accept such total transformation and with lapse of time again reversed the relationship and went back to original situation and hence sharia discourse is full of discourse about her duties towards husband rather than rights though in view of clear Koranic verses jurists could not ignore her rights.

Also, Koranic verses talk of qualitatively different relationship between man and women. For example, we find in verse 30:21 'And of His signs are this, that He created mates for you from your own kind that so that you might find quiet of mind in them and He put between you love and compassion. Surely there *are* signs in this for a people who reflect.'

In this verse we find true Koranic approach towards husband-wife relationship which is neither of domination and dominated but of love and compassion towards each other. It is not only of sexual pleasure and procreation either. Men can find peace of mind in them (li taskunu). Thus there is no question of Koran allowing men to beat their wives even in the event of differences between them.

Also, the Prophet (PBUH) never ever beat his wives. Who knew Koran better than the Prophet? If the Koran allowed beating of wife Prophet would have surely known this and in the event of differences with his wives he could have used physical force, even symbolically as hadith ascribed to him shows. But we do not find any such event in his life. Prophet (PBUH) treated his wives most respectfully and with dignity. He knew Koran does not permit wife-beating under any circumstances.

The Koran refers to his differences with his wives when they demanded more material benefit from him which he could not afford. He did not even quarrel with them on the issue and only withdrew himself and sat in a room alone. When Umar whose daughter Hafsa had married Prophet, came to know about this, he came to meet him (and Prophet met him rather reluctantly) and Umar advised the Prophet to beat his daughter Hafsa as she had defied him. One finds reference to this in the Koranic verses 33:28-29.

Umar was known for beating his wife since his pre-Islamic days but the Prophet (PBUH) refused to accept his unsolicited advice. The tension between the Prophet and his wives was soon resolved and normal relationship resumed. Yet in another verse men and women have been described as each others friends. Thus Koran says, 'And the believers, men and women, are friends one of another' (9:71).

Thus we should try to understand one verse of the Koran with another verse or verses of the Koran rather than with the help of Hadith. Koran's authenticity can never be doubted though many Ahadith (plural of Hadith) are of controversial nature. Also, Koran gives norms and values and has transcendental dimension. Ahadith, on the other hand, are often product of patriarchal society and hence are to be treated with extreme caution.

Unfortunately all the commentators on Koran rely more on these ahadith than on the holistic approach to Koran as pointed out above. Even in formulation of sharia laws, more reliance has been put on hadith than even Koran when several problems arose after the demise of the Prophet (PBUH), Most of the Arabs who embraced Islam were not in fact qualitatively transformed and social ethos and cultural values could not be easily caste away.

Thus patriarchy asserted itself again and again and even jurists could not completely disregard patriarchal values. Also, a theory was developed that the sharia could incorporate the aadaat, i.e. customs and traditions of the Arab society in which Islam was borne. This opened the door for much pre-Islamic practices to be incorporated into sharia laws. In this process often Koranic transformative values were compromised.

Thus the word wadribuhunna also came to be understood under prevalent cultural and social ethos of pre-Islamic society. In fact, Meccan society was more patriarchal than Medinese society which had matriarchal traces and hence treated women with more dignity. But many of the prominent companions of the Prophet originally belonged to Mecca who had migrated to Medina either along with or after the Prophet. They wielded great influence in reporting ahadith and interpretation of the Koranic verses.

A careful exegetical literature would show that no scripture can be understood apart from existing social cultural practices. In other words understanding of scripture is culturally mediated. Thus no commentary on Koran can be an exemption. Though Koran is divine, its understanding is surely human and not binding. Human understanding can change in changed circumstances.

A modernist or a contemporary commentator may differ from earlier interpretations. Many modern scholars of Islam maintain that Koranic values can be much better appreciated and understood in today's circumstances when there is much greater awareness about women's rights and dignity. And surely Koran's transcendental approach can find much greater acceptability today.

Thus *wadribuhunna* should not be understood as chastisement but its other meanings must be explored to understand Koran's transcendental dimension. Even in medieval ages some Koranic scholar's like Imam Raghib Asfahani pointed out in his dictionary of Koran mufradat al-Koran that daraba 'ala in Arabic meant male camel going near female camel.

If this meaning is accepted and there is no reason why it should not be expected as it comes from a great lexicographer of Arabic language, the meaning of the expression radically changes. It would instead mean go near them if they are persuaded after isolation in bed and they give up their nushuz through persuasion. Many other modern commentators have also adopted other meanings of the term daraba.

Thus an American Iranian commentator Laleh Bakhtiar who has created a comprehensive data-base on Koran translates it as under: 'But those whose resistance (nushuz) you fear then admonish them and abandon them in their sleeping place then go away from them (wadribuhunna) and if they obey you, surely look not for any way against them; truly Gid is Lofty, Great (4:34)' Laleh Bakhtiar. The Sublime Koran)

Thus the medieval understanding of the Koran in such matters, i.e. in women issues must make way for more modern and contemporary approach so as to give women their due which have been denied them for centuries and should no longer be denied today. The old approach cannot be sustained for long as women today are getting more educated and are active members of human workforce.

I hope Muslim intellectuals and supporters of women's rights within Koranic framework would go for ijtihad (intellectual exertion for fresh approach) as it is long overdue.

26
Internal Struggle for Power—The Sunnis Versus Shi'as

The fight between Shi'as and Sunnis has assumed dangerous proportions in Islamic world in general and in Iraq, in particular. And this despite the rhetoric of ummah wahidah (one community of Muslims). More this rhetoric is used, more cleavages occur between Muslims. Of course this rhetoric is being used to hide reality through the cover of ideality. Ideal is never realized, even not realizable and hence we need soulcomforting rhetoric. More ugly the reality, more attractive the ideal.

Fact is that except during the period of Prophet (PBUH), Muslims never stood united throughout the history of Islam and Muslims. To justify these differences a hadith (saying of the Prophet) was made current that 'Muslims will be divided in 72 sects after me and only one sect among them would be naji (i.e. would achieve salvation)' and each sect of Islam claimed to be naji. Every sect denounced the other as having astrayed from the right path.

Repeated attempts have been made to mitigate these differences in order to stand united against the onslaught of external forces. It meets with temporary success and this unity falls apart again when faced with powerful vested interests. The division was not merely between Shi'ahs and Sunnis but each in term were divided in numerous sects. In the first century of Islam itself number of these sects was running into more than hundred and scholars like Baghdadi wrote books like Farq bayn al-Firaq (difference between sects).

Let alone Sunnis,Shi'ahs themselves were divided into numerous sects like Zaydiyah, Ithna Ashariya, Isma'ilya, Qaramita, Batiniya, Seveners, etc. Zaydiyahs themselves were divided into three subsects: Jarudiya, Sulaimaniya and Salihiya. The Imami Shi'ahs themselves were divided among Baqariya, Ja'fariya, Nawusiya (who believed that Imam Ja'far is still alive and will reappear after some time), Aftahiya and Isma'ilya.

It makes an interesting reading to go through the differences among these various sects. Besides these there are numerous sects both among

Sunnis and Shi'ahs. However, two major sects today are Sunnis (a blanket term for numerous Sunni sects) and the Shi'ahs (refers mainly to Ithna Ashriya sect) and the power struggle is taking place between these two sects.

The American invasion of Iraq in 2003 has suddenly changed the balance of power not only in Iraq but also have had serious impact on balance of power in the Islamic world. The Sunnis though in minority had ruled over Iraq all these years and had held all key posts in administration. However, democratic elections tilted balance in favour of Shi'ahs and internecine fight between Shi'ahs and Sunnis began and we see horrible killing every day—Shi'ahs killing Sunnis and Sunnis Shi'ahs.

Now accusation of rape has also begun. According to Marc Santora's story filed with Baghdad deadline,

> The most wicked acts are spoken of openly and without reserve in Iraq. Torture, stabbings and bodies ripped to pieces in bombings are all part of the daily conversation. Rape is different. Rape is not mentioned by the victims, and rarely by the authorities. And when it is discussed publicly, as in several high profile cases involving American soldiers and Iraqi women, it is usually left to the relatives of the victim to give the explicit details.
>
> Marc continues,
>
> So when a 20-year-old Sunni woman from Baghdad appeared on the satellite television station Al-Jazeerah on Monday night with a horrific account of kidnapping and sexual assault at the hands of three officers in the Shia-dominated Iraqi National Police, people across the country were stunned, some disbelieving, others horrified, but all riveted. Almost immediately, Shia leaders lined up to condemn the woman, calling her charges propaganda aimed at undermining the new security campaign. The Sunni politicians offered the woman their support.
>
> (*The Times of India*, 22 February 2007, Mumbai).

Such killings or rape have nothing to do with religion or religious beliefs. This is thing but struggle for power. In this struggle for power by Sunni and Shi'ah leaders they condemn each other and declare each other as 'heretics'. Shamed by the fact that on one hand, they blame the

West for onslaught against Islam and such fratricidal wars, on the other, they attempt reconciliation and hold conferences to bridge the breach.

A conference was held in the Palace of King Abdullah sometime ago and a declaration was issued that Shi'ahs are also Muslims and unity of Ummah was very much needed in the Islamic world. However, soon after this declaration an influential Saudi cleric issued a fatwa declaring Shi'ahs kafirs and even went to the extent of saying that Christians and Jews are much better than Shi'ahs.

A recent conference of Muslim 'Ulama and intellectuals in Amman, Jordan from 4-6 July 2005 on 'True Islam and its Role in Modern Society' also issued similar declaration. According to this declaration

> Whosoever is an adherent of one of the four Sunni Schools of jurisprudence (Hanafi, Maliki, Shafi'i and Hanbali), the Ja'fari (Shi'I) School of Jurisprudence, the Zaydi School of Jurisprudence, the Ibadi School of Jurisprudence, or the Thahiri (Zahiri?) School of Jurisprudence is a Muslim. Declaring that person an apostate is impossible. Verily his (or her) blood, honour, and property are Sacrosanct. Moreover, in accordance with what appeared in the fatwa of the Honourable and Respectable Shaykh al-Azhar, it is not possible to declare whosoever subscribes to the Ash'ari creed or whoever practices true Sufism an apostate. Likewise, it is not possible to declare whosoever subscribes to true Saafi thought an apostate.
>
> —*Muslim India,* February 2007, p. 32.

These are of course commendable efforts to forge unity among all sects of Islam which pull, theologically speaking in different directions and give rise to powerful establishments and ultimately control over these establishments becomes the preoccupation and power struggle centres around these establishments.

To begin with the differences may be genuine, differences in perspective, differences in theological interpretation but later on when a sect comes into existence on the basis of these theological differences or differences of interpretation, it soon becomes an establishment and struggle for its control begins. Ali Shari'ati, an Iranian intellectual who inspired thousands of Iranian youth to take part in Islamic revolution of Iran and provided inspiring leadership to it, came out with his own theory of Shi'ah-Sunni conflict and coined very creative terms which represent these conflicts.

He said the real conflict is not between Shi'ahs and Sunnis but between what he terms as 'tasunnan-i-Umavi and tashayyu'a-i-Safavid.

Umayyads represent the political establishment of Umayyads who were Sunnis and Safavids represent the ruling Shi'ah dynasty of medieval Iran. Thus according to Ali Shari'ati it is clashes between two political establishments rather than two sects of Islam.

We would like to throw light in this paper on this revolutionary interpretation of Ali Shari'ati as even today these terms represent the reality of power struggle between political establishments. What is happening in Iraq is really fight between tasannun-i-Umavi and tashayyu'a-i-Safavid, i.e. it is a power struggle between the Sunni politicians and Shi'ah politicians.

As against tasannun-i-Umavi we need tasunnan-i-Muhammad and in place of tashayyu'a-i-Safavid we need tashayyu'i' Ali. Ali shari'ati has put his views on this in his book in Persian Tashayyu'i'Alavi wa tashayyu'i-Safavi. In other words when religion becomes part of political establishment it looses its revolutionary message and its core values. It only becomes an instrument of power.

Tashayyu' means partisanship, support and tashayyu'-i-Alavi would thus mean following the cause Ali stood for, not establishing a powerful political or even religious establishment in his name and then fighting or shedding blood to control it. Similarly tasannun-i-Muhammadi would imply following the causes Muhammad (PBUH) stood for, and not establishing political power in his name and then fighting to control it. Then it will represent tasannun-i-Umavi as establishing political power and then fighting to control it in the name of partisanship of Ali as Safavis did. There is always going to be conflict between such tasannun and tashayyu'.

Among all sects of Islam we see huge establishments have come into existence and there is always conflict between various sects, less on account of theologies, beliefs and dogmas but more on account of politics of control of these establishments. Then fatwas declaring each other kafirs fly at each other and some selective Koranic verses or ahadith are conveniently quoted to establish the 'truth' of ones sect.

Ali Shari'ati maintains that Islam came into existence by proclaiming 'no' by Muhammad (PBUH) to what existed in the form of powerful establishment controlled by tribal chiefs of Quraysh. He said no to all that and affirmed oneness of God and oneness of all people created by Him. Islam first proclaims 'la' (no) and then affirms (ilia) what is One God and One people and prophethood of Muhammad who stood for values of truth, justice, compassion and sympathy with weaker sections of society—the poor, the needy, the orphans and widows.

Tashyyu', according to Ali Shari'ati, is saying no to oppression and exploitation, domination and istikbar (arrogance, powerfulness). Ali, who was heir to Muhammad and was manifestation of Islam and justice, and he (Ali) distinguished himself in history of Islam as one who stood for justice and in the council set up for selection of khalifa headed by Abdur Rehman, said no to distinction of birth (nobility) and maslihat (i.e. strategy over principle). This has been the distinguishing feature of Shi'i Islam—love of the family of Prophet (PBUH) and following in the footsteps of Ali and it has been a party of those following Koran and Sunnah, but not the sunnah of families of Umayyad, Abbasid and Ghaznavids and Saljoquis and Changizi wa Taymuri wa Holagu buty the family of Muhammad was its distinguishing feature—before the Safavi period.

Shari'ati says that tashayyu' began by saying no to all that history which adopted traditions of jahiliyyah (period of darkness before Islam) and Qaier wa Kisra (the Roman and Sassanid emperors) in the name of Koran and Sunnah. Shi'ah are not those who follow those who obtained khilafah in the name of being deputies of Messenger and supporters of Islam and cheated people in their glorious names. But Shi'ah are those who stand for justice, who were also oppressed by the rulers and all those who seek justice and fight oppression can join them.

According to Shari'ati, the AI-e-Muhammad, all of them stood for justice of the oppressed and never compromised with the oppressors and rulers, violating all principles of Messenger of Allah—they are real shi'ahs. Thus those who stand by, and become supporters of Messenger of Allah and his family, would always be ready to sacrifice all they have and their lives.

Shari'ati calls, on the other hand, tashayyu' Safavi as tashayyu'-i-Siyah, i.e. black shi'ism. Tashayyu'-i-Siyah is mere symbolic, not substantive. It only uses black as a colour of mourning and is not ready to sacrifice. Safavi Shi'ism is black Shi'ism as while supporting ruling establishment which is oppressive and unjust, it adopts black as a colour of mourning without courting death.

And Shari'ati calls tashayyu'-i-Alavi as tashayyu'-i-surkh, i.e. red shi'ism as red is the colour of martyrdom, of sacrificing and of courting death. Thus real Shi'ah are those who are ever ready to sacrifice in the way of Allah, in the way of justice and for fighting oppression. Black Shi'ism, on the other hand only adopts some rituals mourning the death of Husain, the grand son of the Prophet (PBUH).

Similarly, one must distinguish between tasannun-i-Mohamma-di and tasannun-i-Umavi. Those who follow tasannun-i-Mohammadi always stand for equality on all human beings and justice and never hesitate to sacrifice their lives for the principles of Islam. Their jihad is jihad for justice and uprightness for ma'ruf (what is good) and jihad against what is munkar (evil), what is oppression and exploitation. Those who follow tasannun-i-Muhammadi and tashayyu'-i-Alawi, it would be seen, can never clash. Their paths are same and they have same objectives to fulfil.

It is only those who follow tasannun-i-Umavi and tashayyu'-i-Safavi clash among themselves as they are supporting establishments of respective sects or ruling empires. They are not clashing on the basis of principles but interests. But those who are following tasannun-i-Umavi and tashayyu'-i-Safavi are bound to clash and can hardly accommodate their conflicting interests.

What is happening in places like Iraq is not really clash between Sunnis and Shi'ahs but clash between ruling class interests—and in fact it is not clash between tashayyu' and tasannun but between Shi'i establishment and Sunni establishment. That way the rhetoric of one ummah can be greatly relevant if it is oneness of principles and oneness of values—principles of Islam and values of Islam.

Genuine Sunnis are as much against what can be termed as Yazidiyyat (an ideology of empire-building on the basis of in justice and oppression) as genuine Shi'ahs are. Both can unite to fight Yazidiyyat. It is Yazidiyyat which brought about paradigm shift in history of Islam. This paradigm shift—from khilafat to mulukiyyayt (from deputizing the Prophet to building dynastic empire) changed the very basis of Islamic society. It was this paradigm shift which not only established monarchy in Islam—something one does not find either in Koran or Sunnah—but also made history of Islam bloody and violent.

It was this paradigm shift which brought about gross misuse of concepts like jihad. It was this paradigm shift which made sword central to Islam rather than uswa-e-husnah (model character of the Messenger of Allah), it was this paradigm shift which made Islam a religion of sword rather than religion of peace. It is thus duty of all genuine Muslims to go back to tasannun-i-Mohammadi and tashayyu'-i-Alawi.

Shari'ati also calls the tashayyu 'Safavi as nizamha-i-irtija'i, i.e. a reactionary system. It adopts black colour as colour of mourning in order to ritualize Shi'ism and create an illusion among the Shi'i Muslims that they are followers of Imam Husain. In fact they are not. They are simply followers of a reactionary political system, a system based on injustices and exploitation.

What we need is tashayyu'-i-surkh, i.e. red shi'ism and red is symbol of martyrdom and martyrdom is based on spirit of sacrifice. Genuine martyrdom is not to kill but to get killed for upholding certain principles and values enshrined in Islam. Jihad and martyrdom go together precisely in this sense that one makes maximum possible efforts to uphold uswai-husnah and if necessary to court death for that purpose—to go to gallows, to go to prison for the sake of upholding values of justice, freedom and equality.

To kill is oppression, taking away life of a human being and which Koran equates with the life of entire humanity. But to get killed is martyrdom—gifting humanity values of justice equality and freedom. To kill is yazidiyyat and to get killed is husainiyyat (Husain sacrificed his life and lives of his loved ones for the sake of values of Islam). Those who kill are mustakbirun (powerful and arrogant) and those who get killed are mustad'ifun (i.e. the oppressed and weak).

Tasannun-i-Mohammadi was tashayyu'-i-Alavi are not only ever alive but keep pace with life and changes which keep on occur in life. Thus ijtihad (creative application of principles and values) becomes a living and dynamic application of everlasting teachings and values of Koran. But for tasannun-i-Umavi and tashayyu'-i-Safavi ijtihad looses its importance and it remains only in name and certain rituals acquire lead over values and principles of equality, justice, compassion and wisdom.

Tashayyu'-i-Safavi, according to Shari'ati, is to accept status quo. For the 'Ulama fiqh (jurisprudence) becomes the core of Islam and which jurisprudence? Jurisprudence developed during a period of tribalism of Arabs and feudalism of the period, jurisprudence of the period of agricultural production. Changes ever since, the changes that occurred since then, are ignored. Or do not matter to these jurists.

Living principles and values of Islam do not matter. What matters is what strengthened the ruling establishment. Tashayyu'-i-Safavi be believes in non-interference in politics. Similarly tasannun-i-Umavi wants politics to be left to be the rulers and for others it is their duty to obey the rulers and for which Koranic verse 4:59 is repeatedly quoted. But Koran does not say follow blindly and uncritically those rulers who are unjust and oppressors. Ulil Amr (those in authority) referred to in Koran are those who are just and followers of all the values enshrined in the Koran.

Throughout medieval ages, and even today, unjust and oppressive rulers legitimize their unjust rule by referring to the above verse (4:59) and both tasannun-i-Umavi and tashayyu'-i-Safavi want their followers to remain obedient to the regime. But for a real followers of Sunnat-i-Rasul and tashayyu'-i-Alavi active participation in politics is highly necessary to keep it on the right path. Its continuous criticism is vital for its healthy value-oriented functioning.

Ruling and reactionary establishments have constantly promoted politics of mutual confrontation that has resulted in violence and bloodshed. There is great need today to challenge these ruling establishments which readily compromise with imperialism and grossly exploitative American rule. In fact they come to power with their help or prop up their tottering regimes with their support.

It is therefore, highly necessary to bring Shi'ahs and Sunnis together on the basis of tasannun-i-Mohammadi and tasshayyu'-i-Alavi and end this bloodshed between them. What is happening in Iraq, let us remember, has nothing to do with Shi'i and Sunni religions but with politics of power and playing in the hands of imperialist powers. The common Shi'ahs and Sunnis should come together and end such endless confrontation of interests.

Neither Shi'ahs nor Sunnis should dominate that region but people of that region should be empowered to solve their problems which are any way common. It is only the ruling classes which think Shi'ahs should dominate or the Sunnis, not the people.

27

Identity in a Multi-Religious Society

In a democratic society identities play important role and a democratic society tends to be a competitive society and competitive identity often clash with each other. Also identity could be primordial or acquired. Primordial identity is much more deep-rooted than an acquired identity. Religious, caste, linguistic or cultural identity is examples of primordial identity and professional identities like an engineer, mathematician or banker are examples of acquired identities. Sometimes national identity can also change in this era of rapid transport and globalization though in the past also people migrated from one country to another.

We also have to bear in mind that no person has single identity. All of us have multiple identities primordial as well as acquired ones. One has, for example, a religious, sub-religious, linguistic, cultural identities along with one or the other acquired identity. All these identities are not of course operational simultaneously. One identity can become more important over the other, depending on the context.

Our national identity can become more important when another country attacks us, or our religious identity can become more important, if there are clashes between two religions, or regional identity can become more important if there are regional or linguistic clashes. Thus no one identity can be permanently important identity vis-à-is other identities. It is also unfair to demand, as some ultra-chauvinist forces do, that all should have only one identity like an Indian identity or a Pakistani identity.

In the democratic processes some identities get more politicized than the other identities. It is quite natural that politicians often appeal to primordial identities like religious, caste or linguistic identities. And this results, more often than not, in religious or linguistic clashes. When the Shiv Sena asserts Maharashtrian identity, it comes into clash with Hindi identity and its Hindutva plank suffers. Sometimes it faces dilemma while using both Maharashtrian as well as Hindutva identity.

In all modern nation-states, there are various identity-related dilemmas as no nation-state today is mono-religious or monolingual. All nations today are multi-religious or multilingual. Often majority religious community equates nationalism with the ethos of its own religion and looks upon minority religious groups with suspicion and when some political party courts a minority group for votes, accuses it of 'minorityism'. This often results in religious clashes.

Similarly powerful caste groups or linguistic groups mobilize their primordial identities for retaining their privileges but when weaker groups or minority groups do so they are accused of anti-national activities. Today, no political party in India (except Communist parties) fights elections without using primordial identities. BJP, which claims to be nationalist, is worst offender in this respect. It is now openly using caste identities to fight elections. It spares no stone unturned in this respect.

Identity by itself is not something to be shunned as some rationalists often maintain. Identity is quite natural whether it is primordial or acquired one. It is a psychological force and gives sense of belonging. No human being can live in religious, social or cultural vacuum. But identity can become very problematic when it acts as barrier and excludes other identities. Primordial identity exists by itself, but when politicized, it defines itself vis-à-is other identities.

Thus a Hindu or a Muslim identity can exist by itself but in a competitive political atmosphere one defines itself against the other and becomes totally exclusive, not only exclusive but confrontationist and may result in violence. Acquired identities, on the other hand, though does become exclusivist in certain situations but not confrontationist or violent.

However, in modern times migration has assumed more serious proportions as compared to pre-modern period when means of transport were not so rapid. Migration causes host of problems both to migrant minorities and host countries. It gives rise to friction within host countries. Many Muslims have migrated in recent times to European countries and are facing hostilities with population in the host countries.

It not only creates intense job competition resulting in identity clashes but also in cultural problems. The migration from Asia and Africa has given rise to strong cultural prejudices. France, for example, banned hijab for Muslim women and turbans for Sikhs. The Danish cartoon controversy was also partly result of cultural prejudices. In UK also Indian and Pakistani communities often face great hostility from English people. The 'Paki bashi' term is result of such hostility. It also results in race riots.

The recent riots in France between Muslims of African origin and French police was also manifestation of hostility between French and African identities tending to be most exclusive. Muslims are facing much greater problems due mainly to 9/11 and subsequent bombings in London on 7/7. Generally Muslims of whatever national or ethnic origin are looked with suspicion and arouse hostility.

Now an effort is being made to evolve a new identity for Migrant Muslims in Europe, i.e. Euro-Muslims. Euro-Muslims are evolving their distinct identity vis-à-is the original identity of their fellow Muslims back home. Recently in Vienna a conference of European Imam's on 'Islam's Future in Europe' was held and a declaration was issued in which they talked of European-Muslim identity. It also talked of evolving an 'integration theology', Euro-Muslim identity accepts certain European values like freedom of expression, democracy, etc. However, it also said: Integration is not a one way street, but a mutual process?

'Integration theology' is an interesting concept for conservative Muslims in Europe though it is a familiar term for Indian Muslims who have experience of living in non-Muslim India for a long time, for almost a thousand year. In North America a term like minority theology or minority jurisprudence is being evolved. Thus the migrant Muslims are definitely trying to evolve a new identity and new jurisprudence. This Euro-Muslim or Muslim-American identity is creative combination of primordial and acquired identity. This process of adjustment is necessary for buying peace in a new location.

Also in a democratic society two different trends work simultaneously. One trend represents rigidity and exclusivity and this trend often gets fortified in confrontationist situation or when politicians mobilize respective identities for their opposing goals. The second trend is represented by inclusiveness and openness toward other identities. However, politicians hardly benefit from the second trend and hence always bring about clashes between identities.

Thus it will be seen that identity by itself is not problematic. It is a psychological need as a sense of belonging to some group is necessary for every individual. But it is not correct to assume that identity will always be exclusive and confrontationist. Modern society can hardly ever be homogeneous and hence different identities will have to find ways of coexistence and cooperation.

Blending of identities also can play creative role as our composite culture in India shows. Composite culture in India has played very creative role throughout medieval history of India. It is this blending of identities which created tolerant and creative cultural force. In Western countries too, this process is on and Western social scientists have evolved new terminology like pluralism which west had never known earlier.

Still West is far from evolving a new composite culture. Unlike India Western culture is predominant and minority cultures have not been integrated. It is still one way street as European imams and religious leaders pointed out. The Muslim or Hindu minorities in west are still too insignificant to make a cultural impact. In the UK where Hindu and Muslim minorities are more in numbers compared to other Western countries one sees some impact on eating habits of White British people though not so much so far in other fields. Perhaps it is matter of time.

In fact identity by itself is not a problem but it is rigidity which poses greater problems. For example, the Sufis were much more tolerant and evolved new blend of Muslim and local identity. They evolved even religious rituals which were creative blend of Islamic and local or regional ones. Thus two entirely different (but not hostile) identities merged into one another and a new one came into existence.

In regions like Sindh, Kashmir and Punjab, creative syncretism was even at much higher degree and Kashmiri and Sindhi cultures were entirely different from their pre-Islamic cultures. It was difficult to talk of Hindu Kashmiri or Hindu or Muslim Sindhi cultures. They blended so completely that they were referred to simply as Sindhi, Punjabi or Kashmiri cultures. When one talks of Kashmiriyat, as the Kashmiri people do, they do not define it as exclusively Muslim.

All this happened in medieval ages so smoothly that now one does not even remember pre-Islamic cultures of those regions. In this era of globalization we have to be more accommodative and more tolerant. We need Kabir, Chishti and Nanak, Lal Ded and Nuruddin even more today.

28
The Opening Chapter of Koran: An Ecological Interpretation

Divine scriptures are capable of variety of interpretations specially those verses, which are not specific commandments of dos and don'ts. The first chapter of Koran has seven verses and is in the form of prayer by human beings to Allah. Allah Himself has revealed this prayer to His Prophet (PBUH) so that Muslims could pray to Him. This opening chapter is of utmost significance in Koran and Muslims repeat it in every 'raka' (unit of prayer). This prayer is rich in symbolic language and has been interpreted in various ways by different commentators.

Here I am attempting it yet in a different way to save the world from ecological disaster, which our world is heading to, if no attempts are made to check rising temperature on earth what has been called global warming. It is beauty of the revealed scripture that even if interpreted to tackle contemporary challenges, it does not in any manner, loose its original meaning and significance.

Maulana Azad in early twenties of the last century interpreted this chapter in his multi-volume commentary of Koran to prove unity of whole humanity by emphasizing importance of the words rabb al-'alamin (i.e. nourisher of the whole universe). Maulana's contribution is indeed very important and will remain of great significance for a long time to come. Maulana's learned interpretation is very different from any earlier interpretations. It thus shows that succeeding generations has every right to understand Koran in different ways to seek Divine guidance to solve their problems. This chapter being in the form of prayer, provides greater inspiration.

To seek inspiration from this opening chapter is very very important as world's ecological balance, on which depends survival of humanity, is at stake. According to *The Hindu* of 28 May 2009, which quotes from *Guardian* newspaper,

> Senior doctors in the UK recently published a report warning that climate change is the biggest threat to global health of the twenty-first century. Rising global temperatures would have a catastrophic effect on human health, the doctors said, and patterns of infection would change, with insect-borne diseases such as malaria and dengue fever spreading more easily.

This is just on health side. Other effects like shortage of water, an essential commodity for life, would be equally disastrous. There is complete unanimity among scientists that glaciers, even on North Pole are melting and melting of glaciers will have disastrous effects in more than one ways. It would result even in rise of sea levels submerging many coastal cities causing great disaster. Sea levels along some coastal towns have already risen causing worries to its people.

Faced with such disaster to human survival we have to seek inspiration and succor from Allah's own words, the creator of this universe. The opening chapter of the Koran begins with invocation which Muslims use before beginning of any work, i.e. 'In the name of Allah Who is the Beneficent, the Merciful'. Beneficent and Merciful are translations of Al-Rahman and Al-Rahim. Both are very significant words. Rahim in Arabic signifies tenderness requiring the exercise of beneficence (see Imam Raghib's al-Mufridat). Thus Rahim comprises ideas of love and mercy, Al-Rahman, also a noun, is intensive form and thus indicates greatest preponderance of the quality of mercy.

Thus Allah is greatest benefactor and merciful. The Prophet is reported to have said: Al-Rahman is the Beneficent God Whose love and mercy are manifested in the creation of this world, and Al-Rahim is the Merciful God Whose love and mercy are manifested in the state that comes after. (Bahr al-Muhit, Commentary by Imam Athir al-Din al-Andalusi).

Now the first chapter right in the beginning says, 'Praise be to Allah the Lords of the worlds, i.e. Rabb al-'Alamin. Here both the words Rabb and 'Alamin have to be emphasized. Rabb in Arabic means, according to Arabic-English Lexicon by Edward William Lane, not only fostering, completing and accomplishing. Thus Rabb conveys the idea of evolution of things from the crudest state to that of highest perfection.

And if we praise to that Lord of all the worlds who is Rabbi, i.e. Who evolves things from crudest state to its highest perfection, the praiser's duty is to be of assistance in achieving this stage of perfection. What are we praising the Lord of the worlds for? For his function as Rabb and hence we cannot act contrary to that. Our acts should also reflect the function of evolution towards perfection, not its destruction.

He is not only Rabb al-'Alamin but also Al-Rahman and Al-Rahim, i.e. one Who is Beneficent and Merciful, shows tenderness of love and mercy towards His creation in addition to taking it from various stages of perfection to ultimate perfection. And this not only for our world wherein we humans exist (but also all biological forms of existence, mountains, water streams, oceans, all forms of primitive life, animals and trees. All of us who praise Allah, have to dedicate themselves as agents of beneficence, mercy and perfection.

And, Allah, as this opening chapter says, is Rabb, not only of our world, our earth but of everything in this universe, of planets, stars, moons, black holes and whatever exists in this universe, visible or not visible to us or even of various planets to be discovered and which have not yet been so far discovered.

Adam's story in Koran is also very significant in this respect. According to the Koran Adam lived in paradise along with Eve and was provided with every thing but was prohibited from eating fruit of a tree. Adam would not have lost paradise, if he had not defied his Lord and ate the forbidden fruit. However, Adam was tempted to eat the fruit and was expelled from paradise.

What was that paradise? A perfect balance of needs and supplies and by eating the fruit Adam (representing human race) destroyed that balance through his greed to defy the Lord and violate the ban and that ban was also for human benefit only. It is very close to what human beings are doing with the earth they live on. They are trying to eat that forbidden fruit, i.e. violating the balance of nature.

Allah is highly Beneficent and takes care of all the needs of human beings He has created. Humans were living in the paradise. Paradise, here, is not a fixed place there in heavens but right here on earth. Maulana Muhammad Ali a translator of the Koran, says, 'paradise, according to the Holy Koran, is not a place for simple enjoyment or rest; it is essentially a place of advancement to higher and higher stages: But those who keep their duty to their Lord, shall have high places, above them higher places, built (for them)' (39:20).

'This shows', Maulana says, 'that not only does paradise admit the righteous to high places, but it is, in fact, the starting point for a new advancement, there being higher and higher places still, and it is in accordance with this that they are spoken of as having an increasing desire for attaining to higher and higher excellences, their prayer in paradise being: 'Our Lord, make perfect for us our light' (66:8).

Thus if we have this understanding of paradise (quite in keeping with the verses of the Koran), on earth too, we can create paradise by being obedient to the laws of our Lord, the laws He has made for us.

Had we observed these laws and there is no change in these laws of the Lord. '(Such has been) the course of Allah that has run before, and thou will not find a change in Allah's course.'

Thus Allah has fixed course of His creation. Anyone who defies this course pays for it. Today we are disobeying our Lord and His fixed course and destroying the ecology of our earth, meant to be our paradise, if we faithfully obey the laws of nature, of our Lord. We have eaten the forbidden fruit (over using resources of earth, polluting it and destroying its ecological balance).

It is by these actions that we have been expelled from the paradise and converting it into hell. In the fourth and fifth verses of opening chapter we say 'Thee do we serve and Thee we do beseech for help.' This we say every day in our five times prayers but are we indeed observing it in practice or saying so merely ritually? Obviously we say so only ritually. While we say this in our prayer we continue to violate course fixed by Him, we violate laws of nature on every step.

If we serve Him and saying so again and again, should we pollute His earth, should we overdraw from its resources? Can we still beseech Him for help? Can we deserve that? Certainly not? Are we not sinning against Him and still seeking His help? If we are serving Him we must obey all His laws, the course fixed by Him and then only we can beseech Him for His help.

Allah, in this opening chapter Sura-i-Fatihah is described as 'Master of the Day of Requital', i.e. yawm al-Din. Din, according to Imam Raghib means recompense, requital. And yawm (day) in the Koranic terminology is any period of time from a moment (55:29) to fifty thousand years (70:4) i.e. from indefinitely small to an indefinitely large. So if we violate Lord's laws for a small amount of time to a large amount of time, we will be recompensed accordingly on that Day of Judgement.

We have been violating these laws to fulfil our greed and disturbing the ecological balance. It is true Allah is Ghafur al-Rahim (Forgiver and Merciful) but we can be forgiven only when we repent sincerely and never repeat our mistakes. The earth even today produces in abundance for our survival but if give up our greed and check our consumption and reduce pollution of earth to minimum, rising temperature will come down and our earth will become paradise again.

As we pray to Allah as taught to us through this sura-i-Fatihah we say to Allah 'Guide us on the right path. The path of those upon whom Thou has bestowed favours, Not those upon whom wrath has brought down, not those who go astray.' Allah is our Lord, our Sustainer and if we seek our sustenance from Him we have to follow the right path shown by Him and pray to him to show us the right path. What is this right path (sirat al-mustaquim)?

It is the path devoid of greed and overconsumption and Allah by forbidding Adam to eat the fruit of a tree in the paradise showed us this right path and as long as we follow this path our paradise will remain intact and Allah's bounties will continue to be enjoyed by humankind but we should not do anything to earn His wrath and follow the path of greed and overconsumption that will lead us astray.

This path of Allah's bounties had been available to whole of humankind as long as we followed sirat al-mustaquim (right path) of modest consumption of earth resources and keeping earth pure tayyib and did not over pollute it. Can we now say we are following the same path sirat al-mustaquim? We have to reflect on this serious question. We have violated this law and gone astray in number of ways.

The poor of the earth whom Allah calls mustad'ufin (weaker sections) and favours them have been deprived of their just consumption by those whom Allah calls mustakbirun (the powerful, the rich) who have been unjust and monopolized overconsumption and have overpolluted the earth. As we know the developed and rich nations are consuming more than 70 per cent of earth's resources and polluting it in that proportion.

How correct is Koran's pronouncement when it says, 'And when We wish to destroy a town, we send commandments to its people who lead easy lives, but they transgress therein; thus the word proves true against it, so we destroy it with utter destruction' (17:16). What Allah says in this verse that those habituated to easy life (i.e. the rich) do not hear the words of wisdom and continue to violate it in sheer arrogance (what the Koran calls istikbar) and then Allah destroys them.

The rich of the earth forgetful of final consequences of their lifestyle continue to ignore all the warnings and ultimately face the doom. Are the rich nations of the West, particularly USA, not ignoring all the warning of rising temperature of earth and pushing us all closer to the disaster? They insist the poorer nations and developing countries reduce their consumption and not they. The G8 nations which are all developed nations in their recent conference in Italy once again did not agree to reduction of their consumption of earth resources.

Koran repeats this warning when it says, 'Nay their hearts are in ignorance about it, and they have besides this other deeds which they do. Until, when we seize those who lead easy lives among them with chastisement, lo! They cry for succour' (23:63-4). Do we not find precisely same behaviour on the part of rich nations of the West? Are they not refusing to mend their ways and reduce their consumption of earth resources? Will they not push our earth to the brink of disaster by ignoring the warning?

Technological progress is most welcome but it can be boon or curse depending how this progress is used by the rich and powerful. The weaker sections and poor nations are, after all, totally helpless and their voice is never heard. But warning has to be repeated as Koran says to the Prophet to warn as he has been sent as warner (nazir). If people listen to him they will be rescued, if not, they will face doom.

The technological progress has enabled human beings to consume more and more and also to pollute the earth too more and more. But this ability has to be used with wisdom. It is reason which enables us to discover new horizons and know more about our universe and again it is reason which enables us to discover more and more natural resources below and above ground and use them.

But reason is, let us be clear, a double-edged sword, a mere tool, which could be used or misused. It is because of reason that we have progressed tremendously from primitive to advanced human beings, from caves to skyscrapers but then it is this reason which has given us tools to destroy our planet through overconsumption and overpollution which is leading us to disaster.

What is needed is what Koran calls hikmah (wisdom) and what is wisdom? Wisdom is reason plus values and experience. Without combining with values reason can play very dangerous role also as it did in Europe through weapons of destruction finally resulting in making all destructive nuclear weapons and in Hiroshima and Nagasaki it killed more than two hundred thousand people.

But if reason is used with values like justice, benevolence and compassion, it can prove to be a great boon and that is what Koran advocates. According to Koran there are five key values: haq 'adl, ihsan, rahmah and hikmah, i.e. truth, justice, benevolence, compassion and wisdom. These are Allah's names also. Allah's names are Haq, 'Adil, Muhsin, Rahman and Hakim, i.e. Allah is Truth, Just, Benevolent, Compassionate and Wise. These values are extremely important for balanced progress of human beings.

Koran gives great deal of importance to hikmah (wisdom) and hikmah is most fundamental value in human progress. Koran goes on to say that 'And whoever is granted wisdom, he indeed is given a great good' (2:269). Unfortunately human beings use reason for selfish ends and push us to the brink of destruction. But those who use wisdom behave according to the values of justice, benevolence and compassion and became saviour of humanity.

Thus the path of wisdom is indeed path of bounties and of divine blessings. When we pray to Allah to guide us to that path on which He has showered His bounties, it is the path of wisdom. So if our prayer has to have any meaning we have to follow this path of wisdom and save our earth, created by Rabb al-'Alamin and He has perfected it gradually until all forms of life appeared on it.

It took millions of years for perfect conditions for human life to appear but now because of our irresponsible behaviour we are destroying it and if do not restrain our overdrive for consumption human life may become extinct due to destruction of ecological balance. And this is not exaggerated statement in any way. This is already being predicted by scientists. But mutrifun (those addicted to easy life) refuse to take heed.

As we say we go to hell because of our sins. What is hell? It is not something located out there on high heaven. It is around us, consequence of our own sins of overconsumption and destruction of our earth's ecological balance. Koran describes Muslims as ummatan wasantan (community of middle path) and as believers in divine revelation contained in the Koran it is their duty to lead the world in reducing consumption of oil which results in emission of carbon resulting in climate warming.

The oil wealth is also hidden below deserts in Muslim countries of West Asia and they can certainly ration oil production in such a manner as to reduce carbon consumption. It is they who pray five times every day to Allah to guide them to the right path and thus it is for them to act in a responsible manner so as to compel the Western nations to reduce their carbon consumption.

This will surely save our earth from impending disaster. It is true it is extremely difficult and complex problem. There is every danger that western countries led by USA may invade the countries with oil resources as they did in Iraq. But then they can convene conference of all developing countries and seek their cooperation. Of course it is easier said than done but one has to find solution to what all of us know is sure disaster.

Surely, those who possess rich oil resources can play some responsible as well as creative role in the matter. We posses Koran and Koran shows us path of wisdom. Are Muslims going to use this wisdom specially as they also possess the oil wealth? So far indications are not very encouraging. The Muslim nations hardly have courage to confront USA as they depend so much on it for technology and for weapons of destruction.

If we keep on praying five times every day and this prayer does not reflect in any meaningful way in our conduct, our social responsibilities, what is the use of such mechanical prayers? The quality of our faith (iman) depends in our action which promotes good of whole of humanity. After all believers have been charged with the responsibility of what Koran says amr b'il ma'ruf, i.e. enforcing what is good and nahi 'an'il munkar, i.e. fighting against evil. Is climate warming an evil or not and if it is evil should we not struggle against it?

29
And Now Hindu Terrorists?

Muslims for long had been objecting to the term Islamic terrorists and when the term Hindu terrorists was used by a section of the media the Sangh Parivar members protested how can one use the term 'Hindu Terrorists'? The first to object to this term was Ram Madhav of RSS told *The Asian Age*: 'There is no such thing as Hindu terror at all. It is an orchestrated campaign to protect the real terrorists.' Also when asked about the Sadhvi Pragnya's arrest, he immediately tried to distance RSS from her. The 'involvement of individuals', he said, 'had nothing to do with any Hindu organization.'

Similarly Advani, the opposition leader, also distanced BJP and RSS from the Sadhvi. He claimed he had no knowledge as to who Pragnya was till now. Advani told *The Times of India* that it seemed obvious that she would have parted ways with the pariwar outfits because her thoughts and methods did not match with those propagated by the organizations which she may have belonged to. This was reason enough for her to move out of them.'

Advani went on to cite the example of Nathu Ram Godse who killed Mahatma Gandhi on 30 January 1948. 'Godse was associated with RSS earlier in his life but left the organization way back in 1934 because he did not agree with its ways', he pointed out. Advani at least admitted that Nathu Ram Godse was associated with the RSS which was denied earlier.

Well it is Advani's view that RSS does not believe in violence. Advani himself was in the RSS for long time and who knows better than he that very beginning of RSS was to train Hindus to fight Muslim bullies and all RSS branches give training in wielding lathis. Then it also set up other organizations to give training in arms. Even Durga Wahini gives training to its women members in using firearms.

Advani also must know very well that RSS has great admiration for Hitler and even today in some BJP ruled states like Gujarat and Rajasthan Hitler and Nazism is admired and described as the only solution for the country as the country needs a strong leader to take right decisions in right time. And Hitler was not all about peaceful means. To claim that Hindutva organizations do not believe in violence is to say fire does not burn at all but heals.

Everyone knows what VHP and Bajrang Dal were up to in Gujarat and what kind of violence they indulged in during Gujarat carnage of 2002. It is VHP cadre along with BJP leaders who killed or prompted others to kill 2,000 Muslims most brutally. Was that no violence? Or was it no belief in violence?

Mukhtar Abbas Naqvi, the BJP vice-president tried to argue after arrests of Sadhvi and her associates that 'To protect real terrorists, the artificial terrorists are being shown'. He clearly implies that Sadhvi and her two associates are not real terrorists and the police have arrested them only to protect real terrorists. Naqvi thinks real terrorists could be only Muslims? But he also said, 'There can't be either Muslim or Hindu terror'.

Was this not what all secularists and Muslims maintained all along? Terrorists have no religion but the Sangh Parivar in particular and the media in general always used the terms like Islamic terrorists or Muslim terrorists and the police, whenever arrested some Muslim boys without any proof invariably described them as Muslim terrorists. And even if these boys whom police arrests are in any way involved in those horrific acts of terror it does not mean Islam teaches terrorism or Muslims in any way believe in killing innocent bystanders.

But RSS continued to propagate what has now almost become a proverb 'All Muslims are not terrorists but all terrorists are Muslims'. Now that their own people have been found involved in Malegaon bomb blasts, all Hindutva organizations and their leaders are maintaining that Hindus cannot be terrorists and Hindu culture does not believe in violence. As long as Muslims were being arrested it was quite alright to maintain that it is Islam and Muslim culture which produces terrorists.

The real fact is that neither Hinduism nor Islam nor does any other religion preach terrorism. It is possible that some individuals or even group or organization may employ religious terminology or employ religious rhetoric to justify their condemnable acts but that does not hold that religion or religious community to be responsible for that act of terrorism. The group or concerned organization can alone be held responsible for its acts, not the religion that the group belongs to, much less entire religious community.

Here that Hindutva leaders are cleverly saying that how Hindus or Hindu culture can be responsible for such violence. The Hindus as individuals or as a groups believing in violence can certainly be responsible but not Hinduism. Hinduism is a religion of peace and non-violence as Islam is also religion of peace and non-violence but some Hindus or Muslims or some organization consisting of some individuals form these communities can certainly be responsible for terrorist violence.

The arrests of Sadhvi and her associates has at last brought out in open what was all along known that some Hindutva organizations were making bombs and they should be investigated in terrorist attacks in places like Malegaon (2006), Mecca Masjid blasts in Hyderabad, etc., but the police turned a blind eye to this demand and arrested only Muslims indiscriminately.

Now after arrests of Pragnya and her associates many Muslims feel that the UPA Government arrested these persons only on the eve of election to soothe Muslim frayed nerves, especially after the Batla House 'encounter' which human rights activists and Muslims thought had raised many questions. Thus Muslims and secular forces in the country feel these arrests of some Hindutva activists were done to satisfy them and after elections again the police may continue to harass Muslims.

Also, the Malegaon blasts of 29 September 2008 it was almost impossible for police to arrest some Muslims as all former SIMI activists were under jail already and secondly if Muslims were arrested this time again, Muslims would have protested severely and UPA Government would have suffered another credibility blow on the eve of elections.

I had investigated Malegaon blasts of 2006 and had made all political leaders across party lines and common people and intellectuals and no one was convinced that those arrested after the blasts in 2006 in which more than 50 persons were killed could have been carried out by those arrested by the police. It was important festival and Friday and the bombs went off just when the Friday prayers ended. No Muslim would go for blasting bombs at such a place on such an occasion.

Yet the police was determined to blame it only on some ex-SIMI members and would listen to no arguments. The 2006 blasts should be reinvestigated and I am sure something else would be revealed. I have seen the charge sheets filed by ATS in 2006 Malegaon blasts. It totally depends on confessions obtained in police custody and is bound to fail in any court of law. The real culprits would certainly escape.

The Nanded blasts in which two Bajrang Dal activists were killed had taken place just before Malegaon blasts of 2006 and there was every possibility of involvement of some of those persons in Malegaon blasts. Similarly the Mecca Masjid blasts of Hyderabad should also be thoroughly reinvestigated as it also took place on Friday just at the end of Friday prayers when thousands of Muslims were coming out of the Mosque.

And all those arrested in Mecca Masjid blasts were also mostly innocent persons. I have heard them in a public hearing in Hyderabad and human rights activists and civil rights group worked hard to get them released on bail as there was nothing by way of credible evidence against them. The courts had to give them bail. The Hyderabad police could not, or did not want to lay its hands on real culprits.

The involvement of some army officers even of the rank of major should not be surprising as many RSS sympathizers are regularly employed and after retirement they become active in Hindutva organizations. The army usually claims to be quite secular, and probably it is, but it should be much more careful while recruiting soldiers and officers. No one with communal background should be recruited. This principle is not being rigorously observed at the time of recruitment. Many people who come out of RSS controlled schools and colleges are recruited in army.

I think it will be better if all terror blast cases be investigated by the police of credible conduct under the supervision of retired high court justices. This will reduce possibility of biased investigation though may not all together eliminate it. It is in the interests of the internal security of the country. It appears communal riots are fast being replaced by bomb blasts and some people suspect, it is new strategy of the communal forces. Major communal riots are becoming increasingly difficult to organize.

The civil society should also become vigilant against all terrorists of whatever religion or group. As communal riots were major danger in twentieth century, terrorist attacks are for twenty-first century.

30
Islam and HIV/AIDS

Some people will be somewhat surprised what relation there could be between Islam and this dreaded disease. Yet there is and there was international conference on this subject in Johannesburg, South Africa from 26 to 30 November 2007 in which more than 250 delegates, resource persons, activists and Ulama from all Muslim countries and Muslim minority countries was held. I was also invited there as resource person to speak from Islamic point of view.

I was until then under the impression that Muslim countries in general and Muslims in particular are not victims of HIV/AIDS. But when I participated in this course I realized that quite a few Muslims from different Muslim countries as well as non-Muslim countries were victims of this disease. Africa in particular has the largest number of victims and there are many Muslim majority countries among African countries.

It was this reason that number of agencies including Islamic Relief, UNO and World Vision had supported this conference. I was quite impressed with number of participants, volunteers and number of sessions in which people participated with enthusiasm. What was more appreciable that many Muslim women participated and most of them were in hijab (head covering). Almost half the participants were women. And I was surprised when some Muslim women declared from the conference platform that they were HIV positive.

Every day in the morning first a plenary session took place and discussed various aspects of this disease and then participants will break into different groups, each group consisting of ten persons to discuss things in depth and each group had some expert or experts either from religious or technical point of view. Many groups were headed by women and in general women participated actively in these groups. Also each group was given series of questions to discuss what was presented in plenary session.

Various groups formed were, for example religious leaders and stigma, causes, consequences and approaches, revealing ones status, stigma and violence, mandatory testing, HIV and rights, core values, adoption/fostering, marriage and testing, men and women's rights and roles, property and inheritance, female genital cutting and other traditions, life skills/education, the role of the media, reaching women, the role of faith, constraints and opportunities, vulnerable children, grieving and coping, treatment, etc. I chose to be member of group headed by a women of Indian origin whose family had migrated to South Africa and she currently lives in Canada. Sabra Desai, a woman of very liberal and progressive ideas. The group mainly discussed women's roles. There were five more women of African origin.

Generally Muslims and Ulama in particularly adopt very negative attitude towards those suffering from HIV/AIDS thinking it is result of sinful life. They always attribute it to sex outside marriage be it pre-marital or extra-marital. In other words they think it is result of having multiple partners or result of homosexual relations. It is not always true. In fact HIV/AIDS can be contracted in variety of other ways—husband who is HIV positive infecting his wife who knows nothing about her husband's infection. And if women becomes pregnant and gives birth to a baby, baby is also likely to get infected. Then how can one blame the mother and the child who became victims of man's HIV infection. In fact we were taken to field visit in Johannesburg where we saw large number of innocent children living in special home. These children otherwise looking healthy and playing were not even aware what disease they are carrying. Their parents had died of HIV/AIDS. Thus it is wrong to carry negative attitude towards all HIV positive patients.

Also, even those who have contracted this disease as a result of sinful act like extra-marital relation or drug injection can repent and in Koran Allah describes himself as Ghafur al-Rahim and Tawwab al-Rahim, i.e. One who is Pardoner and Merciful and Accepter of repentance and Merciful. How then we human beings should can reject them with contempt. Such rejection is more cultural than religious. Religious attitude should be more value oriented than contempt oriented.

Social and cultural attitudes are misunderstood as religious even by Ulama. Also Muslims tend to see everything in terms of sharia laws. Sharia laws are for either state to implement or for Muslim organizations to decide. It is very different matter. But ordinary Muslims should not immediately develop negative attitude. Law will take its own course, if anyone has broken it and religion in its sense of fundamental values should take different course.

What are fundamental values of Islam as we find them in Koran? These values are 'adl (justice), ihsan (benevolence), rahmah (compassion) and hikmah (wisdom). These are also Allah's names: Allah is just (adil), benevolent (muhsin), compassionate (rahim) and wise (hakim).

Now let us take HIV positive patients and weigh our attitude towards them in the light of these Koranic values. Is negative attitude towards HIV positive just? Based on justice? Suppose someone contracted this disease due to non-sinful acts then justice will demand that we treat them with dignity due to any other person. But it would be unjust if we reject him/her just because he/she has HIV without knowing the full truth.

Similarly, if we do ihsan (benevolence to someone) to one who has such disease it would have very positive effect on her/him and we will win her/his heart forever. Allah is also Beneficient for all His servants and so his servants should also be benevolent to all His servants whatever status of their health. And if we treat someone with compassion despite being victim of such disease it will greatly help that person. And through acceptance of such person and preventing others from contracting this disease we will be acting as wise. Rejecting them may amount to spreading this disease further. Such person must be persuaded to adopt preventive measures like condoms so that wife/husband is not infected.

When I said this in plenary session many HIV/AIDS patients thanked me for my attitude in the light of Holy Koran which would be so helpful for them. In fact, if one accepts such patient one can not only give him/her longer life but make him/her repentant if this disease has been contacted through sinful act. Rejection will only result in dejection and frustration and may worsen the situation of the patient.

There were quite a few eminent Ulama from different Islamic countries as these Ulama and Imams can play very positive role in spreading awareness among Muslims and hence making them understand real causes of HIV/AIDS would be extremely useful. A fatwa committee of these ulama was constituted to discuss this problem in great details and finalize fatwas in this respect. I was also included in this committee from India.

There were two main issues before the committee of eminent ulama who came from Syria, Egypt, Libya, Qatar, Indonesia some other places. One issue was regarding condoms. Can use of condoms be permitted? The other issue was of use of zakat money, especially for non-Muslim poor patients suffering from HIV/AIDS?

Both the issues were hotly debated. Generally ulama felt use of condoms cannot be permitted as it will encourage sinful acts of adultery or fornication. They gave examples from Western countries that condoms are freely distributed even among school children and condom machines are installed in public places like railway stations and universities. Thus condoms are responsible for spreading sinful life and hence cannot be permitted.

I explained to them no one is advocating that condoms be freely distributed as in the Western countries. There is fundamental difference between our culture and Western culture. Again it should be realized problem is of cultural nature. In Muslim countries social and cultural values are very different. No one would permit free distribution of condoms. Our attitudes towards sexual life are much more rigid and would make fundamental difference.

I also pleaded that condoms are means, not an end. Means can be misused and can also be used properly. If made proper use of, condoms can help prevent spread of HIV and if misused can help spread it. Here we are concerned with prevention of disease rather than its spread. If a husband has contracted HIV in some or the other way and does not use condom while going to his wife, will infect his wife and also probably the child she gives birth to. Our fatwa would never allow condoms to be freely distributed in schools and universities or through vending machines as in the Western countries. But we will advocate its use with strict warning that moral values are primary and it should be used only in marital life, not I otherwise.

The condom packets can also carry the warning as cigarette packets carry certain warnings of health hazard. However, certain people will always misuse it and that is for government or society to take care of in collective way. Condoms per se cannot be held responsible for it.

A question was also raised should doctors who are Muslims should advise people to use condoms or should they advise not to use them. It was pointed out that doctor is concerned with physical health whereas ulama and Muftis are concerned with spiritual and moral health. Doctor's duty is to prevent spread of physical disease and that alone should be his main concern. On the other hand, ulama's main role is prevention of moral disease or moral corruption and they have to play their role effectively. A doctor should not, for sake of guarding morality, let disease spread to other innocent persons. This argument was finally accepted and it was decided that use of condoms could be permitted by ulama subject to certain strict conditions and chemists should be allowed to sale condoms to married couples and a Muslim government could also allow its use in restricted way.

Another important issue was spending zakat money on non-Muslims suffering from HIV/AIDS as non-Muslim agencies often support Muslims suffering from this disease. Again stand was taken by Ulama except two among them that zakat cannot be given to non-Muslims. We maintained this stand is not Koranic nor is it in keeping with the Sunna. The verse on zakat in Koran (9:60) lays down that one portion of zakat be spent on what Koran calls Mu'allafat al-Qulub (for those non-Muslims whose hearts are to be won) and under this Prophet (PBUH) himself gave money to those Arabs who had not accepted Islam but were sympathetic to it.

Thus both Koran and sunnah support the concept of giving to non-Muslims. However, Koran itself does not use the word. 'Muslim poor' but only poor. Also, this verse provides for riqabi, i.e. freeing prisoners, for ibn al-sabil, i.e. travellers and fi'sabil Allah in the way of Allah. All these categories like freeing prisoners or for travellers and in the way of Allah are open to interpretation in favour of non-Muslim poor and needy for support. Thus this verse is so categorical that no one can maintain that non-Muslims cannot be entitled at all.

But still some ulama said it should only be for Muslim poor and none else as there are so many needy among Muslims. Some said that non-Muslims can be provided from general charity (sadaqah) but not from zakkat. I said there is no separate category as sadaqah in Koran and for zakat Koran uses the word sadaqah and the verse (9:60) begins with the word sadaqat. Then one Egyptian 'alim quoted Imam Shafi'l that he is also of the opinion that a portion of zakat could be spent on non-Muslims. That finally clinched the issue and it was then unanimously decided that a portion of zakat could be spent on non-Muslim needy, which could include those suffering from HIV/AIDS.

Thus both fatwas for use of condom and for spending part of zakat money for non-Muslims were finalized and read out in plenary session. It was also decided that these two fatwas will be presented to other ulama of Muslim countries and their opinion sought in their favour so that Muslims could advocate use of condoms for genuine and legitimate purpose (within married couples) and a portion of zakat to be spent on non-Muslim poor, especially HIV/AIDS patients in need of help. It was unanimously approved in plenary session also.

This conference on Islam and HIV/AIDS was also supported partly by non-Muslim fund and that also required that Muslims also spend their funds on non-Muslims be it from zakat or general charity in addition to zakat from rich Muslims. When we visited a home for HIV/AIDS we found many Muslim children in the home run by Christians. So Muslims should also contribute to such homes where non-Muslim victims of HIV/AIDS are given shelter.

Another issue which was discussed in our group 4 was, amongs others, female genital cutting or female circumcision. Generally it is maintained that it is part of sunnah. Since this group consisted of more women and three men (liberally inclined) it was not difficult to agree on maintaining that it is not part of Islamic teachings.

I explained that it is basically a tribal custom which originated in some African countries and since shafi'i school also originated from Egypt (Imam Shafi'l lived in Egypt, he accepted some of local customs and traditions) he also provides for female circumcision. The tribals adopted female genital cutting for depriving women of sexual pleasure arguing that if their genitals are not cut, they may get corrupt before marriage. The Ismaili fiqh also originated in Egypt it also provides for female circumcision and in India only Bohras who are Isma'ilis practice it, not other Muslims.

Another male participant in discussion quoted Prophet's (PBUH) hadith that female genitle should be cut gently. I said this hadith is not unanimously accepted and Prophet of Islam was so much for gender equality that it is quite unlikely that he would require female genital to be circumcised. The hadith might be of later origin when female circumcision was introduced. Any way circumcision, female or male, is not obligatory in Koran but even male circumcision is called sunnah. Of course male circumcision is quite healthy and even reduces chances of HIV/AIDS whereas injury caused due to female circumcision is likely to enhance chances of HIV/AIDS. Thus in any case while male circumcision is useful while female circumcision is against women's right to enjoy sexual pleasure like men.

The Indonesian participant who is of Shafi'i persuasion also supported my viewpoint and it was unanimously decided that female circumcision be opposed as part of anti HIV/AIDS campaign. This measure was recommended by group 4 to be part of conference declaration.

There also was discussion on women, discrimination and violence in our group. One Syrian participant pointed out that Koran permits beating of women in verse 4:34. I said it has been wrongly interpreted by mostly male theologians. The word daraba is used in Arabic language in several different ways and according to Imam Raghib who compiled dictionary of Koran thirteenth century gives several meanings one of which is for male camel to go near female camel.

If we take wadribuhunna in verse 4:34 it would mean after they are persuaded (after their rebellion) go near them. Yet another meaning given by modern feminist interpreters of Koran is to strike away, i.e. send them away. Also beating women is not in keeping with overall approach of Koran towards women's rights. Koran clearly declares equality of women's rights in verse 2:228, and verse 2:229 requires man to retain his wife with kindness.

If we read verse 4:34 in conjunction with verse 2:229 which requires wife to be treated with kindness how beating can be permitted. Beating is opposite of kindness and thus it is wrong to say Koran permits beating of wife. A Muslim women has equal dignity and must be treated by husband with dignity. However, wife beating, even honour killing is quite common in Islamic world.

Also women who contract HIV/AIDS are beaten up by their husbands and often deserted. This is un-Islamic especially when husbands themselves are often responsible for infecting their wives with HIV/AIDS. Thus we must campaign for women's rights and wife beating must not be considered as husbands' right. This aggravates HIV/AIDS infected women. An African woman who declared she is HIV positive also told the audience that she was having three children and her husband deserted her. She married again and man married her with full knowledge that she was HIV positive and yet deserted her after some time.

Thus such heart-rending cases clearly show that men and women from Islamic world should be made aware of rights of women so that they do not maltreat women and do not consider them as their property as they do now. If they have rights on women, women also have rights on their husbands, as declared by the Koran in 2:228.

All the members of group 4 agreed with this viewpoint and the Syrian participant who had earlier pointed out that Koran gives husbands right to beat also changed his view and agreed with this interpretation.

Thus the conference on Islam and HIV/AIDS opened new vistas for delegates who had come from all over the Islamic world and gave them programme to campaign for the rights of victims of HIV/AIDS and also dispelled the illusion that Muslim world is an exempt from this dreaded disease. The Islamic world is also facing this problem. It is different thing that it is difficult in these countries to obtain correct statistics. Due to cultural reasons and fear of ostracism often victims suppress information.

It is also true that incidence of HIV/AIDS is somewhat less in Islamic world for number of reasons. In Islamic world cases of sexual profligacy is rather limited and male circumcision also helps reduce chances of HIV/AIDS. But it should not be taken as cause for celebration as this disease is spreading in Islamic world too otherwise there would have been no need to organize this conference.

I am sure the conference served its purpose and would go a long way to increase awareness among Muslims and caution them to take protective measures and create appropriate funds for the help of HIV/AIDS patients. I must say William, a convert to Islam some 14 years ago in Netherlands, was the moving spirit of this conference and he took great pains to make it successful.

Index